Praise for
When Drug Addicts Have Children:
Reorienting Child Welfare's Response

When Drug Addicts Have Children doesn't flinch from discussing the hard realities of drug addiction. It includes rigorous analyses of the current child welfare system, and wisely calls for its radical reorientation.

—William J. Bennett
Co-director, Empower America
Former Director, Office of National Drug Control Policy
Former U.S. Secretary of Education

This collection of papers tells the thought-provoking and too-often poignant story about what is happening to the children of drug-addicted parents. To keep the cycle of child abuse from perpetuating itself, dramatic changes in our child welfare programs as described in this book are needed.

—Anne Cohn Donnelly
Executive Director
National Committee to Prevent Child Abuse

Unlike many other edited volumes, this one holds together quite nicely; the papers form a narrative that carries the reader from a discussion of the nature of the problem, through a summary of current treatment efforts and then, to a series of recommendations. The result is an agenda for much-needed reform.

—Frederick Green, M.D.
Emeritus Professor of Pediatrics
George Washington University School of Medicine
Former Associate Chief, U.S. Children's Bureau

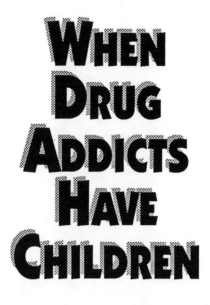

WHEN DRUG ADDICTS HAVE CHILDREN

Reorienting Child Welfare's Response

edited by
Douglas J. Besharov

assisted by
Kristina W. Hanson

Child Welfare League of America • American Enterprise Institute
Washington, DC

CHILD WELFARE LEAGUE OF AMERICA, INC.
440 First Street, NW, Suite 310, Washington, DC 20001

AMERICAN ENTERPRISE INSTITUTE
1150 Seventeenth Street, NW, Washington, DC 20036

CURRENT PRINTING (last digit)

10 9 8 7 6 5 4 3 2

Cover photo by Lloyd Wolf
Cover design by Jennifer Riggs-Geanakos
Text design by Eve Malakoff-Klein

Printed in the United States of America

ISBN # 0-87868-561-8

CONTENTS

ACKNOWLEDGMENTS

This book is the culmination of a collegial effort by a group of program administrators, direct service providers, senior government officials, and scholars. The effort included a series of small-group consultations, a 66-person, four-day conference, and the preparation of this volume. In a fundamental sense, everyone who participated in the process contributed to the final product. Their comments and suggestions identified and sharpened the issues considered herein and helped to refine the thinking of the authors. To all these individuals, too numerous to mention here, go my sincere appreciation and thanks.

The contributions of some organizations and individuals, however, deserve special acknowledgment. First thanks go to the cosponsoring organizations that lent their names, expertise, and staff to the effort: the American Bar Association, the American Public Welfare Association, the U.S. Department of Health and Human Services, the U.S. Department of Justice, and the U.S. Office of National Drug Control Policy. Four people from these organizations served as an informal steering committee: Mark Barnes of HHS, Scott Hamilton of ONDCP, Robert Horowitz of the ABA, and Betsy Rosenbaum of the APWA. Their sound advice during the planning process and the energetic support they gave to the project helped make it a success.

At AEI, Elizabeth Fish organized the project, cochaired the meetings, and performed the initial research that guided its planning. After Elizabeth left the project to have her second child, Karen Baehler assumed the responsibility for organizing and synthesizing these papers.

During the four-day meeting, held in Williamsburg, Virginia, three people toiled selflessly and tirelessly through session breaks and into the night to prepare a summary of conference highlights and recommendations. Jean Bower, David Lloyd, and Norman Sherman, the coordinators of the effort, were exceedingly good sports as they worked to bring together the group's disparate comments. Glenn Shoup ensured that the word processors, printers, and photocopiers kept operating. And Kelly Swanson kept the rest of the conference running smoothly.

Final preparation of the papers was in the capable hands of Kristina Hanson, who probably had no idea what she was getting into when she agreed to take on the job. She performed the first stage of editing on the papers, held the authors to a strict time schedule for corrections and additions, and filled in the remaining gaps in the data and references.

A book like this one passes through many hands before emerging, but I would be remiss if I did not express my appreciation for the efficient professionalism of the Child Welfare League of America publications staff, especially Susan Brite, who guided the book's preparation from start to finish; Carl Schoenberg, who performed the final substantive edit; and Eve Malakoff-Klein, who supervised the volume's final stages of production.

Finally, this project was possible only because of generous support from the Smith Richardson Foundation. Before many others in our society, the foundation recognized that the children of drug addicts need to be better protected. I particularly want to thank our project officer, Cheryl Keller, who was a continuing source of critical feedback and sage counsel.

No single book can solve a problem with such deep roots in our society. Nevertheless, I know I speak for all the contributors when I say that we hope our efforts will help improve the plight of children and parents caught up in the current drug epidemic.

D.J.B.
July 1994

INTRODUCTION

Douglas J. Besharov
Karen Baehler

Since 1986, when crack cocaine first hit inner-city streets, drug use has become a fixture in the lives of many low-income families and in the neighborhoods in which they live. Each night brings new stories of crime and senseless violence. Less visible, but just as serious, is the abuse and neglect of children caused by parental drug addiction. More than alcohol, and more than heroin, crack cocaine threatens the well-being of hundreds of thousands of children, especially African American children.

It is time to abandon the medical model of drug treatment, which posits that crack addiction can be "cured." The plain fact is that—even with the best treatment services available—most crack addicts cannot be totally freed of their addiction. Instead, drug addiction must be seen as a "chronic, relapsing disorder" (to use a phrase often repeated by treatment professionals) and current child welfare programs must be radically reoriented. This book describes what needs to be done.

The papers collected here were originally presented at an American Enterprise Institute (AEI) conference, "Protecting the Children of Heavy Drug Users," which brought together 66 senior government officials, social service providers, and academic experts. Although these materials do not begin to settle all of the complex issues surrounding the dilemma of parental drug abuse, they establish a base of shared knowledge and point to certain principles upon which service providers and policymakers can build. Following are the key points that emerged from the exchange.

Drugs and Children

Drug use is not a victimless crime. The authors of the four chapters in section one of this book draw upon national data, social mapping techniques, clinical experience, and stories from the streets to describe the use of illegal substances and what it means for families, children, and neighborhoods—the hidden victims of drug abuse.

Patterns of Drug Use

Rand Corporation Senior Researcher Peter Reuter and his colleagues have found that, while drug abuse is diminishing among the middle class, it is growing worse among the most vulnerable members of our population—low-income, inner-city dwellers. Casual users have been turning away from drugs, while frequent users and addicts have been increasing their consumption.

Particularly in relation to cocaine, the authors find that this shift in demand toward the lower rungs of the socioeconomic ladder and toward deviant populations means stronger associations between drug use and health problems. The tenfold increase in cocaine-related deaths and emergency room admissions during the 1980s provides evidence of this link. The authors also point out strong correlations between drug use and crime: Over half of the males arrested in most large cities test positive for illicit drugs and drug use rates for arrested persons remain near their all-time peak levels, despite declines in use among other groups.

Thus, even if the general population continues to reduce its drug consumption, the problems that lead to drug-related child maltreatment—frequent, heavy use or addiction, coupled with the stresses of deep poverty—will be with us for the foreseeable future. Inner-city social service agencies can expect their caseloads to continue growing.

Neighborhood Ecology

Sheila Ards and Ronald B. Mincy, senior research associates at the Urban Institute, use special social science techniques to show—at the neighborhood level—the connections identified by the Rand researchers' national data. They confirm what many have long suspected: drug abuse and child maltreatment are tied to a larger ecology of deviance and hopelessness that concentrates geographically in the most depressed inner-city communities.

By mapping geographic distributions of social problems in the borough of Manhattan, Ards and Mincy show that a disproportionate share of infant foster care placements occur in what they call *underclass neighborhoods*, where poverty runs especially deep and families are under constant psychological, social, and financial bombardment. These are also the neighborhoods with the highest drug use rates in the city.

Ards and Mincy's findings paint a dismal picture of the environments surrounding children of heavy drug users. Not only do these children face physical and psychological hurdles at home but they also find themselves living in neighborhoods saturated by drugs, crime, and deep poverty, where families tend to be isolated and supports are minimal. The authors call for specific targeting of child welfare and drug treatment services to these neighborhoods.

Effects on Parents and Children

Dr. Barry Zuckerman, chief of Developmental and Behavioral Pediatrics at Boston City Hospital, asserts that the children of drug addicts are in double jeopardy. In utero, the children—exposed to drugs through their mothers' use—are saddled with a host of biological vulnerabilities that researchers are only just coming to understand; at home with drug-addicted parents, these children suffer the numbing effects of neglect.

The effects of prenatal exposure to drugs are hopelessly intertwined with the effects of poverty and the life-styles of the women who use drugs. Nonetheless, some evidence of physiological impact exists, most notably smaller head circumference, which indicates a potential structural effect on the brain.

Those who use drugs heavily tend to have poor parenting skills. Zuckerman reports that this poor parenting can exacerbate the damage done to children by drug exposure in utero. He describes addiction as a chronic, progressive disease characterized by loss of control and compulsive preoccupation. Thus, research has shown a clear association between addiction to alcohol or narcotics and higher rates of child maltreatment. "With addicted women," he observes, "their primary relationship is with their drug of choice, not with their child."

Zuckerman believes, however, that a stable, nurturing home environment and good social services can help overcome prenatal harms. Preliminary results from the Women and Infants' Clinic, a small pilot project started in 1989, suggest that delivery of key services—pediatric care, child development, and drug treatment—in one "nonstigmatizing" location can have a significant, positive impact on parents and children, at least in the short term. The key, according to him, is to use the mother's interest in her child as the motivation to change.

Victims to Victimizers

Edwin Delattre of Boston University takes Zuckerman's description of drug-addicted parents one step further to show how entire families and neighborhoods—a child's total environment—can be poisoned by drugs.

Delattre paints a chilling portrait of the children who grow up in the most depraved inner-city neighborhoods. As he accompanied police officers on patrol in cities across the nation, he saw children as young as 10 and 11 years old turned from victims into victimizers. He speaks of children abandoned in crack houses and tenement hallways, addicted mothers who trade sex for drugs, and urban gangs that draw young people into the narcotics trade.

With these scenes as backdrop, Delattre reminds us that children learn primarily by example and imitation. No one should be surprised, therefore, when the children reared in these settings come to resemble wild creatures, bereft of the capacity for sorrow, remorse, or tenderness. They learn from the drug culture that surrounds them to live purely on impulse and to employ violence to get what they want.

Delattre establishes the moral grounds for action in behalf of children raised amid drugs, arguing that present conditions cannot be tolerated and help must not be delayed until it is too late and the habits of violence and cruelty are too deeply ingrained. We should begin by doing what we can to improve life in the worst neighborhoods. When we fall short (which we will), we have, in the author's words, "an unconditional obligation to provide alternatives" outside the neighborhood—including educationally sound residential facilities modeled on the best of existing boarding schools, group homes, child care centers, kibbutzim, summer camps, and outdoor programs.

Treating Drug-Addicted Mothers

Everyone's first hope, of course, is to help the children by freeing their parents from addiction. Unfortunately, as the papers in section two reveal, the success rate of existing treatment programs is disappointing. Cures are elusive. Relapse is the rule, not the exception.

A Comprehensive Public Health Approach

Like Dr. Richard Schottenfeld of Yale University School of Medicine, many experts believe that richly funded, comprehensive public health programs with specific services tailored to the needs of women can help mothers manage their drug use and ensure the protection of children.

Schottenfeld contends that not all drug users—even frequent users—are addicts and not all addicts are exactly alike. Even those who use drugs heavily can lead relatively functional lives as workers and parents. Drug use is not prima facie evidence of incompetence.

Drug addiction, argues Schottenfeld, must be considered a chronic, relapsing disorder. For many clients, success means increasing periods of remission and controlling the damage done during relapses rather than achieving permanent abstinence. To meet the special needs of clients who are parents, and who are likely to experience relapse, treatment programs must expand their focus to include services that strengthen parenting and family functioning.

A comprehensive, public health approach to meeting the needs of drug-affected families should include efforts at education, prevention, early intervention in primary health care settings, and family-centered drug treatment. Even in cases where parents continue to use drugs, Schottenfeld is hopeful that such programs will help parents to achieve greater control over their drug habits while protecting their children from abuse and neglect.

Barriers to Successful Intervention

Dr. Judy Howard of the UCLA School of Medicine is less optimistic about treating parents who use drugs heavily. In her paper, Howard reports on two disappointing findings from Project Pride, an early intervention project for drug-abusing mothers and their children funded by the National Institute on Drug Abuse:

- Most of the mothers in the program continued to use drugs despite efforts by the program staff to help their clients identify, enter, and stick with drug treatment. Only 15 percent of the mothers remained abstinent for one year.

- Among mothers who did not abstain from drugs, even high-quality, intensive early intervention services "were not able, over time, to raise parenting skills to a level where the care provided was both stimulating and nurturing." Fully 100 percent of the children of heavy drug users exhibited insecure attachments to their mothers, compared to one-third of the children whose mothers did not use drugs.

The experience with Project Pride sheds light on the enormous obstacles to helping drug-abusing parents overcome their drug habits and bond with their children. These include chaotic neighborhoods and families, the parents' own childhood experiences with family drug use and maltreatment, sabotage by boyfriends and others interested in keeping the mothers dependent, and the drug user's generally chaotic life-style and lack of follow-through.

The Need for Better Research

As Schottenfeld and Howard make clear, far more work is needed to understand which treatment approaches work, which do not, and how social services can help drug users be better parents. The final chapter in this section, by Robert Apsler of the Heller School at Brandeis University, discusses the poor state of evaluation in the field of drug treatment and why we do not know more about effective interventions.

Apsler reports that research in this field has been undermined by competing definitions of the goals of treatment and by the wide variety of different treatment approaches in use. Few studies use randomized trials and control groups. Therefore, they cannot conclusively attribute the effects produced to the treatment provided—particularly given that a large number of users quit on their own, without the help of treatment programs.

Research to date indicates that methadone maintenance for highly motivated heroin addicts is the most effective program available. Very little is known about other treatment modalities. In addition, most evaluations have dealt with adult males, leaving us with scant information about the treatment needs of women in general, and mothers in particular. More and better research—in the form of randomized clinical trials, long-term follow-up studies, and studies of untreated drug users—is sorely needed.

Child Welfare's New Burden

The consequences of our collective failure to recognize the reality of drug addiction and its resistance to treatment are sadly evidenced in the third set of papers. The drug crisis is changing the face of the child welfare caseload and stretching agencies to the breaking point.

The Clients and Their Problems

Beverly Jones, who is long experienced as a frontline child welfare worker and supervisor in Maryland, describes how today's child welfare cases are more complex, more expensive to treat, and harder to resolve than those she saw just five years ago. Substance abuse, family and neighborhood violence, deepening material and spiritual poverty, and weakened links to extended family are just some of the sources of growing trouble.

Even the best-endowed agencies, with a full array of services, are finding it harder to achieve success under these circumstances. Given these realities, Jones argues that the "concept of minimal services should no longer be the standard if, in fact, we are serious about serving this population of children and families." In short, today's cases defy any "quick fix."

Jones wants to focus greater attention on the provision of ongoing services for children and families who are not placed in foster care (the majority of drug-involved cases, according to Jones) but who continue to need supervision and help. She would like to see ongoing services that include more child care options, transitional housing for recovering drug abusers and their children, expanded in-home interventions, better access to pregnancy testing and family planning services, family-focused rather than individually focused treatment, and specialized substance abuse treatment for pregnant adolescents.

Recovering addicts should have quick and easy access to child welfare services when they relapse, asserts Jones. They should be trained to anticipate their own drug-using episodes and seek protection for their children before the crisis hits.

The Drain on Agency Resources

Public agencies are being overwhelmed by the rising numbers of ever more distressed children and families. Barbara Sabol, commissioner of Human Resources for New York City, catalogues the enormous drain on limited agency resources caused by the combination of drugs, AIDS, and homelessness.

The numbers tell part of the story. Almost 5,000 infants were born in New York City with positive drug toxicologies in 1988, an increase of more than two-and-a-half times over 1986. The number of child abuse and neglect allegations related to substance abuse more than tripled between 1985 and 1989. During the same period, New York City's foster care population doubled.

These trends have shown a small but welcome reversal in the last two years, but other dark clouds are on the horizon. In particular, AIDS is spreading more rapidly among women and children than among the rest of the population. Agencies are expecting increases in the number of children in foster care infected with HIV—and also in the number of AIDS orphans.

Sabol describes how the city is responding with a variety of programs. One is "Front End Prevention," which includes Head Start, day care, case management for pregnant and parenting teens, housing subsidies and employment and training for AFDC mothers, as well as family rehabilitation, family preservation, integrated services, and other special initiatives.

But more is necessary. In particular, Sabol calls for greater flexibility in the use of the federal Title IV-E Foster Care and Title IV-B Child Welfare Services. These funds should be available to states and localities interested in testing new and innovative approaches to serving the new child welfare clientele.

African American Children in Foster Care

African American children seem to be suffering most from the problems described by Jones and Sabol. Clarice Dibble Walker of Howard University, reporting on a 1991 national survey conducted by the National Black Child Development Institute, concludes that the child welfare system fails to provide stability or permanency for tens of thousands of African American children removed from drug-abusing households. And the impact of this unhappy foster care experience on these children as well as on the broader African American community could be devastating.

Walker's study illustrates three ways in which African American children removed from drug-abusing households get mired in the child welfare system. First, they miss out on reunification with their parents: Children from drug-abusing households were returned home at only half the rate of children from non-drug-abusing households. Second, they miss out on adoption: The adoption rate for African American children of drug abusers in the study sample was a disappointing 9 percent (measured at 26 months from placement). Third, as a result of the other two factors, they stay in care longer: After 26 months, almost three-quarters of the children of substance abusers in the study sample were still in foster care, compared to less than half of the children whose parents did not abuse drugs.

The study also found that children of African American addicts were placed with relatives more often than were other children. Kinship care is a promising resource for these children, says Walker, but agencies should provide more support services to the relative caregivers.

The Insufficiency of Statutory Protections

The protections in current law designed to prevent children from being lost in the foster care system, such as statutorily mandated periodic reviews of placements, are simply irrelevant to drug-abusing families, concludes Ramona Foley, director of Substitute Care for the South Carolina Department of Social Services. These reforms hastened adoptions for the "fetching, blue-eyed, blonde preschoolers" who had drifted in foster care during the 1970s and they helped reunify children from less dysfunctional families. They did not, however, deal with the problems presented by children like Lucy, a sexually promiscuous, delinquent, drug-addicted eight-year-old whose sad life Foley traces.

According to Foley, the philosophy of foster care has to recognize the new realities. We must not be compulsive about permanency and case closing, she warns, because repeated failures to reunify children with their families or achieve adoption take a toll on the child and drain agency resources that might be spent on improving the quality of the child's care. Likewise, we must not be compulsive about making foster care a short-term experience because some children need long-term care.

Monitoring and reviews remain important, but their targets have to be redrawn. For children in long-term arrangements, for example, success should be measured not by the type of placement, but by the child's physical, mental, and emotional health and development within the placement. States should not be penalized for having a long average length of stay in foster care so long as the children in long-term placements are getting the help they need.

Reorienting Child Welfare

Meeting the special needs of the children of drug addicts will require making hard choices about when agencies should intervene, in what way, and for how long. The authors in section four set forth an agenda for reform of the child welfare system.

Implications for Policy-Making

Wade Horn, formerly the commissioner for Children, Youth, and Families in the U.S. Department of Health and Human Services, discusses strategies for achieving a real marriage between the drug treatment and child welfare systems. A truly integrated and realistic system would acknowledge that drug addiction is a chronic, relapsing disorder and recognize that the children of addicts will be repeatedly in and out of placement.

Horn focuses on the needs of three special populations. For the first group—addicts who abandon their children in the hospital—he recommends expedited termination of parental rights and adoption. These adults have clearly demonstrated their unfitness as parents. Experience suggests that the chances of successfully reunifying them with their children (assuming the parents could even be located) are very small.

A second group of chronic drug-using parents may have a greater probability of successful rehabilitation if appropriate interventions are available. In particular, Horn emphasizes the importance of developing residential drug treatment programs that incorporate on-site child care services, early childhood development opportunities such as Head Start, and training in parenting skills.

Once parents have been discharged from treatment, occasional drug binges are likely. Thus, Horn calls for more comprehensive follow-up services, including home visitors who can provide long-term support to the family and monitor the parents' condition. In these cases, he also argues for the use of kinship care whenever possible so that children fated to suffer multiple spells of foster care may be placed in the same familiar, comforting home each time their parents relapse. A restructuring of kinship care payments and services would facilitate the proper use of this important family resource.

Long-Term In-Home Services

Today, the majority of the children of drug-abusing parents who come to the attention of the child welfare system will not enter foster care. Richard Barth of the University of California at Berkeley recommends that, for those children left at home with their parents, child welfare agencies develop the capacity to provide long-term supervision of the home and long-term supportive services for all members of the family.

Barth reports that in California, in-home services last, on average, less than 90 days. Return home usually means the end of services (including supervision). In the case of drug-abusing parents, this commitment to brevity results in estimated reabuse rates of 30 percent to 40 percent (including just the reported cases) and repeat drug-exposed births in the absence of family planning services. It results in a perverse cycle of opening, closing, and reopening cases, with all of the attendant administrative and investigatory headaches and costs. In effect, Barth argues, we already provide long-term services to the children of drug addicts, but in the most inefficient way imaginable.

The author argues that extended services—particularly services to the children—could improve the prospects for these families. Without follow-up, Barth explains, "The majority of drug-exposed children—even if they begin life under the protection of child welfare services—will fall in the developmental chasm between the neonatal intensive care unit and Head Start." Ideally, initial in-home services would include a year or more of follow-up by child welfare or public health personnel, then give way to community-based developmental services until age three, at which time the Head Start package would kick in. The building blocks for such a seamless system can be found in various model programs around the country. They deserve greater support.

Termination of Parental Rights

Michael Wald—formerly with Stanford University Law School and now Deputy General Counsel at the Department of Health and Human Services—calls for expedited procedures to terminate parental rights in cases where drug-addicted parents have left newborns in the hospital, where they refuse treatment, and where children have been in foster care for 18 months or more. In other cases, though, he cautions against severing ties between parents and children without making real efforts at reunification.

Wald emphasizes that decisions about termination policy must be made based on a realistic appraisal of the entire child welfare system. At present, the system offers little to families on the verge of collapse. Far more could be done to treat drug-abusing parents and reunify families. Developing a decent system, however, will not be easy. It will require significant improvements in services and social work practices.

Until these elements are made the standard, Wald argues, early termination of parental rights should be authorized only where there is substantial evidence that reunification will not work even when quality services are offered— as in the case of addicts who simply refuse help. When the day comes that a broad array of quality child welfare services is available and removal from the home is used truly as a last resort, early terminations may make sense in more situations.

Long-Term Foster Care

For older children who can neither be adopted nor returned home, Ruth Massinga, director of the Casey Family Program, describes the importance of programs that provide high-quality, long-term foster care placement—programs like those of her agency, which operate in more than a dozen western states. She advocates greater acceptance of more permanent living arrangements for foster children and calls for the development of stable, emotionally supportive environments.

Central to Massinga's model would be each child's individual, goal-based service plan, developed jointly between social workers and the foster parents, who should be viewed as agency employees and professionals rather than as substitute parents. The agencies should have a broad array of services available so that treatment plans can be tailored to the needs of each child. Moreover, the delivery of services should be recognized as a dynamic process, with case plans being reviewed and modified to meet the child's changing needs.

Implementing the new model will depend, in part, on changes in public policy. In particular, the author recommends financial support for a fuller range of medical and mental health services to sustain long-term foster care placements, equalized payments for relative and nonrelative care providers, ongoing professional training for foster parents and social workers, smaller case loads, and specialized services such as respite care and marital and family therapy to help strengthen foster families.

Kinship Care

Massinga's vision of long-term foster care is based in part on her agency's favorable experiences with kinship care. Tens of thousands of grandparents, aunts, uncles, cousins, and older siblings over the years have opened their homes to children who need a safe and supportive place to live.

Ivory Johnson, deputy director of San Diego County's Children's Services Bureau, points out that African American and other racial, ethnic, and cultural communities long have embraced the concept of relatives or kin participating in the raising of children. Building on this tradition, she urges agencies to view kinship care as a variant of family preservation rather than a form of substitute care. She recommends that kinship caregivers be provided with the same array of services and supports available to biological parents.

Johnson also suggests a reformulation of the nature of kinship care. The debate about which category of payment to use for related caregivers (AFDC or foster care maintenance) should give way to the larger question of whether AFDC grant levels are adequate for anyone trying to raise children—be they biological parents or extended family. The question of permanency for children in long-term relative care should be reexamined in light of the possibility that placement with kin is equivalent to a return home.

According to Johnson, agencies must establish clear policies about the roles and expectations of kinship caregivers: Are they parents, professionals, both, or neither? Staff members of child welfare agencies need training to increase their cultural sensitivity and their understanding of the special needs of kinship families.

Legal Guardianship

Carol Williams, formerly of the Center for the Study of Social Policy and now the associate commissioner of the Children's Bureau, at the Administration for Children, Youth, and Families, reminds us that many foster parents (relatives and nonrelatives alike) might be willing to accept permanent custody of a child, even though they would not adopt the child. She calls for the much wider use of what state laws call either "legal guardianship" or "permanent guardianship."

Although rarely used, guardianship has multiple benefits. When the court appoints a caregiver as guardian, it sanctions the relationship legally and socially, and protects it from inappropriate disruption. Moreover, guardianship proceedings offer an opportunity to examine the relationship between the child and the foster parent and assess the suitability of the proposed guardian as a long-term caregiver.

After a limited period of court supervision, guardianships should be able to continue without judicial oversight. Williams notes, however, that in some cases, social supports may be necessary to sustain the arrangement. Guardians and wards should have access to social services, such as counseling and mental health care, as well as financial supports—similar to subsidized adoptions—where necessary to preserve permanence.

As kinship placements become more common, the importance of placing them on a sounder legal foundation increases. Guardianship may be particularly appropriate for these situations.

The Quality—Not the Category—of Care

Because government is unlikely to provide stable and nurturing family foster homes for all the children who must be in care for long periods of time, Dr. Marilyn Benoit, former director of Outpatient Psychiatry at the D.C. Children's National Medical Center and now medical/executive director of the Devereux Children's Center, emphasizes the need to consider all categories of substitute care, including large congregate institutions (what used to be called "orphanages"), as long as they can provide "good-enough parenting."

A basic understanding of what children need—good physical and medical care, socialization, education, and positive, enduring relationships with reliable and consistent adults (whether parents or even social workers)—can provide guideposts for those who must decide where children will live. When drug-addicted parents fall short of providing these minimum requirements, their children become the victims of "environmental failure." As Benoit states, "In such an environment, children...lack consistency in their lives, they cannot develop a sense of predictability and trust, they feel unprotected and come to realize that dependency, to which they are entitled, is not safe." In such cases, the child must be removed despite our preference for preserving families.

Any substitute caregiving arrangement that provides a child with the basic building blocks of trust, self-esteem, and healthy emotional development should be embraced. Despite our bias against certain institutional arrangements, Benoit argues that they are often best for children. It is the quality, not the category, of care that matters.

No More Wishful Thinking?

This collection of papers tells a thought-provoking and often poignant story about what is happening to the children of drug-addicted parents. Taken together, the papers set a realistic agenda for reforming the nation's child welfare system.

Despite the diversity of disciplines and political orientations represented, the authors speak with a surprisingly harmonious voice about the problem of parental drug addiction and what to do about it. Although summarizing such a large and multifaceted body of scholarship is always dangerous, one theme does seem to run throughout the book: It is time to end our wishful thinking about parental drug addiction and recognize its threat to the welfare of children.

If the children of drug addicts are to have a fair chance in life, we will have to be much more realistic about the problem of addiction and its likely solution. This theme ties the chapters together and, from it, flow seven precepts:

1. *Recognize that widespread parental drug addiction will continue to endanger children.* Although the number of new addicts seems to have declined in recent years, hundreds of thousands of parents continue to be addicted to drugs. On their own, most true addicts (as defined by the DSM-IV, see figure 1) simply cannot take adequate care of their children. Without societal intervention, their children are condemned to lives of severe deprivation and, often, violent assault.

2. *Assume that parental addiction to crack and other drugs will not be cured.* Although there has been some success in treating heroin ad-

Figure I

Criteria for Substance Dependence

A maladaptive pattern of substance use, leading to clinically significant impairment or distress, as manifested by three (or more) of the following, occurring at any time in the same 12-month period:

(1) tolerance, as defined by either of the following:

    (a) a need for markedly increased amounts of the substance to achieve intoxication or desired effect

    (b) markedly diminished effect with continued use of the same amount of the substance

(2) withdrawal, as manifested by either of the following:

    (a) the characteristic withdrawal syndrome for the substance . . .

    (b) the same (or a closely related) substance is taken to relieve or avoid withdrawal symptoms

(3) the substance is often taken in larger amounts or over a longer period than was intended

(4) there is a persistent desire or unsuccessful efforts to cut down or control substance use

(5) a great deal of time is spent in activities necessary to obtain the substance (e.g., visiting multiple doctors or driving long distances), use the substance (e.g., chain-smoking), or recover from its effects

(6) important social, occupational, or recreational activities are given up or reduced because of substance use

(7) the substance use is continued despite knowledge of having a persistent or recurrent physical or psychological problem that is likely to have been caused or exacerbated by the substance (e.g., current cocaine use despite recognition of cocaine-induced depression, or continued drinking despite recognition that an ulcer was made worse by alcohol consumption)

Source: American Psychiatric Association, *Diagnostic and Statistical Manual of Mental Disorders*, 4th ed. (Washington, DC: American Psychiatric Association, 1994), 181.

diction (because of methadone) and alcoholism (because alcohol is less addictive), even the best treatment programs report that, in most cases, they can break patterns of crack usage only temporarily—because of the addictive qualities of the drug and the social factors that encourage addiction. That is why drug treatment professionals consider crack addiction to be "a chronic, relapsing syndrome." So should child welfare professionals.

3. *Provide intensive—and prolonged—child protective supervision.* Many children of addicts remain at home in their parents' custody. At present, child protective agencies provide only short-term services to these families, on the assumption that a referral to a drug treatment program will cure the parents' addiction. Since drug addiction (even if treated) is likely to be a long-term affliction, this short-term orientation is a grave mistake. Case planning should be based on the assumption that, for the foreseeable future, the family will require regular home visits (perhaps from a newly created corps of case aids) and other services that include a continuing cooperative relationship with the drug treatment program.

4. *Formalize kinship care programs.* Members of the extended family can be an invaluable resource in efforts to treat the parents and as providers of substitute care. But, too often, children are placed with relatives without due regard to their need for a stable and nurturing home environment. Although it would be a mistake to apply all the formalities of nonfamilial foster care to these relative placements, a set of minimum standards for licensing, monitoring, and supporting these placements should be developed. Innovative legal mechanisms, such as permanent guardianship, should be employed. In addition, the disparities between kinship foster care payments and AFDC grant payments that exist in many states should be reduced to lessen the incentive to leave children in these temporary situations.

5. *Increase adoptions, especially of abandoned infants.* Child welfare agencies do a poor job of identifying the children who should be freed for adoption (because of negative attitudes toward the termination of

parental rights, administrative and decision-making breakdowns, and, to a lesser extent, current statutory provisions). The test should be the parents' demonstrable inability to care for the child coupled with an unwillingness to accept or respond to a reasonable offer of drug treatment. Since termination should only be pursued when there is a reasonable likelihood of adoption, the focus should be on younger children, especially abandoned infants.

6. *Create new, long-term substitute living arrangements that are stable and nurturing.* Many children who are not appropriate candidates for adoption (because they are older or have behavioral problems) and who cannot be placed with relatives (because they have none or their relatives do not want to take them or have problems of their own) are nevertheless likely to spend many years, if not their entire childhoods, in substitute care. These children are in desperate need of the kind of constancy and support that only secure home environments can provide. Among the possibilities are explicitly designated long-term family foster care homes, group homes, and even larger congregate care facilities (if designed to provide the degree of nurturing children need). Various new legal arrangements, such as permanent guardianship, should be used to obviate the inappropriate application of periodic foster care review requirements.

7. *Make family planning a child welfare service.* Most drug-addicted women would do much better if they had better control over their own fertility. Although some of these mothers want to have more children, many others do not—but their life-styles (and the men in their lives) limit their ability to use contraceptives effectively. Family planning should be one of the services that is automatically offered to clients (just like parenting education). The aim should not be to coerce abstention or contraceptive use, but, rather, to help motivate clients to gain control over their own lives. Technology may also help; both Norplant and Depo-Provera provide protection against pregnancy without a woman's active participation.

The obstacles to adopting the recommendations made in this volume are great, and there can be legitimate debate about their specifics. But the continuing tragedy of drug-addicted parents and their suffering children imposes a moral duty to respond. To ignore their needs diminishes us all.

Section 1:
Drugs and Children

PATTERNS OF DRUG USE

Peter Reuter
Patricia Ebener
*Dan McCaffrey**

For most of the last decade, the available indicators on drug use and abuse have been telling a confusing story. On the one hand, general population surveys find that fewer people report using illicit drugs; on the other hand, measures of problems related to drug use seem to be increasing.

Many people have argued that the surveys are in error and that we should focus only on the indicators that have continued to worsen, such as death rates and emergency room admissions. However, the indicators, all of which are flawed, can in fact be reconciled fairly simply to provide a consistent account. An important change in patterns of drug use and abuse has indeed taken place since about 1987; overall use is down substantially, and even frequent use of drugs seems to have declined. The problems caused by drugs, however, may not have declined, because those who have used drugs most heavily in the past will continue to use, and the longer they use, the more damage they will cause to themselves and others.

* The research reported here was supported by the Ford and Weingart Foundations. The authors wish to acknowledge the help of Carol Edwards, Eva Feldman, and Joel Feinleib.

The basic story is almost a cliche by now but it is worth repeating. Initiation into the use of drugs (as measured by the percentage of 17-year-olds experimenting with drugs) rose through the late 1970s and perhaps into the early 1980s, but began to decline by the middle of the 1980s. The total number of current users (including those who began earlier and continued use for some years) may have continued to rise a little longer but almost certainly was in decline by 1987. Not unexpectedly, the number of drug *abusers*—those persons with serious drug problems—only a modest share of all drug users, continued to rise even as the initiation and use rates declined; the number of abusers may only have begun to decline in 1989. Those that continue to abuse may be, on average, incurring and causing more harm.

Over the last 20 years, the demographic composition of drug users has changed in important ways. First, an increasing percentage of those who use drugs are experiencing problems because a higher percentage of them are in the later years of their career. Second, the decline in drug use, probably driven largely by health concerns, has been sharpest among the educated middle class. Nevertheless, it now appears to be occurring even among less educated populations as well.

The first section of this chapter describes available data about drug use and abuse in the United States, and what those data tell us about changing use patterns over the last five years, with particular attention to data on emergency room episodes involving cocaine. The analysis goes beyond national patterns because there appears to be considerable variability across cities. The second section offers an integration of the different indicators, and the final section speculates briefly about the future of drug use.

Measuring Drug Use and Abuse

Three types of data are available that measure drug use and abuse: federally supported surveys (i.e., the High School Senior Survey and the National Household Survey on Drug Abuse), urinalysis of arrested persons (i.e., the Drug Use Forecasting system), and hospital and coroner reports (i.e., the Drug Abuse Warning Network). Each has its strengths and weaknesses. While data from the three systems can be synthesized in useful ways, such a synthesis is still at a very preliminary stage, as will become apparent later in this chapter.

Surveys

The most widely reported measures of the extent of drug use are provided by two national surveys, both funded by the U.S. Department of Health and Human Services. Since 1975, the National Institute on Drug Abuse (NIDA) has provided funding for the University of Michigan to conduct the High School Senior Survey (HSSS), an annual survey of drug use by high school seniors.[1] Approximately 16,000 high school seniors are asked to provide information on their own use of licit and illicit drugs. The results provide the best measure of changes in the pattern of initiation into drug use in the general population.[2]

A counterpart to the High School Senior Survey as a measure of drug use in the general population is the National Household Survey on Drug Abuse (NHSDA), now conducted under the auspices of the Substance Abuse and Mental Health Services Administration. Every two or three years during the 1980s and annually since 1990, a survey of the household population has been carried out; as of 1991, about 30,000 members of the household population over the age of 12 had been interviewed. (Note that nonhousehold populations—defined as those living in college dormitories, prisons, and so forth, and the homeless—constitute only about 2 percent of the adult population.)

The weaknesses of the two surveys are well known but not crippling. The surveys rely on the willingness of individuals to report disapproved or illegal behavior, but not everyone is willing to do so. The universe from which the sample is taken excludes some populations known to be rich in drug abusers—HSSS excludes dropouts from its sampling frame; NHSDA excludes institutional populations (college dormitories, prisons, military barracks) and the homeless. The household survey response rate, about 80 percent through the 1980s, raised concern that the survey was having trouble reaching transient populations (formally in the household population) that might include many drug abusers.

Because of these concerns, the survey data should be used with caution. Specifically, NHSDA should not be used to estimate the total number of persons who use drugs frequently, a temptation hard to resist given the media's appetite for numbers and the lack of any other systematic basis for annual estimates. Heavy use of drugs is a rare behavior and sampling error, sampling frame limits, underreporting, and selection bias all make general survey-based estimates unconvincing.

The surveys are useful, however, in that they provide evidence on trends in general population behavior. The survey data become even more useful when put together with the other data, as we do below.

The household and the high school senior surveys have been consistent with each other in their portrayal of drug use in the nation since the mid-1970s. Figures 1 and 2 present some of the basic data.

Using HSSS data, figure 1 shows the percentage of each successive high school class reporting use within the last 30 days of (a) marijuana, (b) cocaine, and (c) any illicit drug. After a steep rise in the late 1970s, the numbers have generally declined sharply. Marijuana use rose from 27 percent in 1975 to 37 percent in 1978 and then declined steadily to 12 percent in 1992. For cocaine, the pattern is slightly more complicated; prevalence rose from about 2 percent in 1975 to nearly 6 percent in 1979 where it remained until a sharp peak in 1985 (6.7 percent). From 1985 to 1992, it then declined steadily to 1.3 percent. The rate of decline in use, however, slowed between 1990 and 1992.

Figure 2 shows that the pattern for NHSDA young adults (18- to 25-year-olds who have the highest prevalence rates) is similar, although measures are not available for every year. For marijuana, 30-day prevalence rose sharply in the late 1970s and then fell throughout the 1980s. Since 1990, the rate has been stable. For cocaine, prevalence increased in the late 1970s, then leveled off and did not begin to reverse until the mid- to late 1980s. This rate has also been fairly stable since 1990.

In these surveys, females uniformly show substantially lower use rates than do males, although the trends are roughly parallel. For example, the 30-day NHSDA marijuana prevalence rate for 18- to 25-year-old males peaked in 1979 at 45 percent; for females, the peak rate, also in 1979, was only 26 percent. By 1992, prevalence had fallen to 15 percent for males, and 8 percent for females. Table 1 shows 30-day NHSDA prevalence rates for males and females from 1979 to 1992.

The most likely explanation for the observed decline in the prevalence of drug use is a rising awareness of the dangers of drug use and an increasing disapproval of drug use.[3] Certainly, decreased availability is not a factor. The percentage of those reporting that marijuana is available or readily available has been around 85 percent every year; the percentage reporting that cocaine is available or readily available has risen from 46 percent in 1979 to 59 per-

Figure 1

Trends in Drug Use by High School Seniors

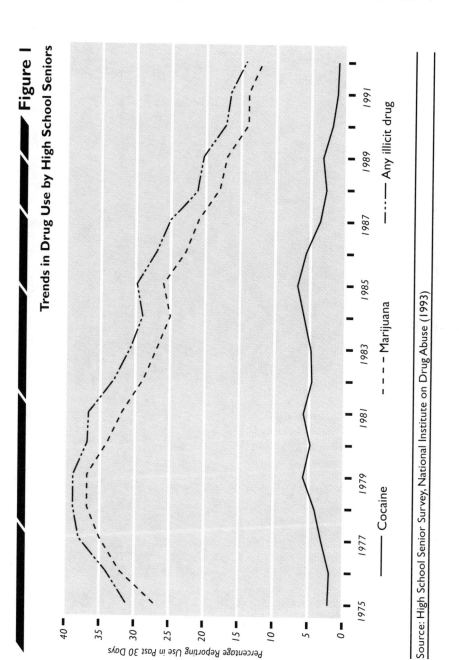

Source: High School Senior Survey, National Institute on Drug Abuse (1993)

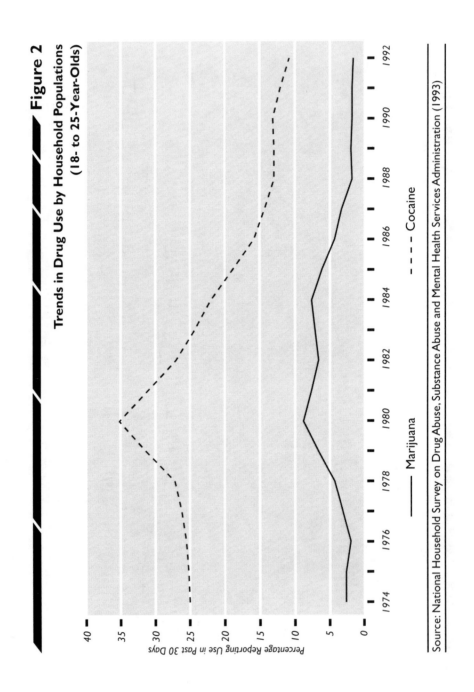

Figure 2

**Trends in Drug Use by Household Populations
(18- to 25-Year-Olds)**

Percentage Reporting Use in Past 30 Days

—— Marijuana   - - - - Cocaine

Source: National Household Survey on Drug Abuse, Substance Abuse and Mental Health Services Administration (1993)

━━━━━━━━━━━━━━━━━━━ **Table I**

NHSDA 30-Day Prevalence Rates for 18- to 25-Year-Olds
(Percentages)

	1979	1982	1985	1988	1990	1991	1992
Marijuana							
Males	45	36	27	20	17	16	15
Females	26	19	17	11	9	11	8
Cocaine							
Males	N/A	9.0	9.0	6.0	2.8	2.8	2.9
Females	N/A	5.0	6.2	3.0	1.6	1.3	0.8

Source: National Household Survey on Drug Abuse, Substance Abuse and Mental Health Services Administration (1993)

cent in 1992. The cocaine availability figure did decrease in 1990, probably because of the reduction in prevalence; with fewer users in school, marketing was less aggressive, but availability was still higher than it was in the early 1980s.

In light of these explanations, it is interesting to examine how educational attainment correlates with changes in prevalence, as shown in table 2. Among a birth cohort of males born between 1959 and 1964, with more than 12 years of education, regular use of cocaine (i.e., use in the past 30 days) decreased between 1985 and 1990 only slightly more than it did for those with 12 years or less of education. During this same period, use of cocaine during the past month by females with more than 12 years of education actually fell less than did use by their less-educated counterparts (although the proportionate decrease was larger for the more-educated group). For both males and females, however, annual prevalence rates for the more educated decreased far more sharply between 1985 and 1990 than they did for the less educated. The proportionate decrease by males was greater than for females for both education levels. Education apparently plays a much more distinct role for occasional users of cocaine (use in the past year) than for more regular users (use in the past month).

A final note of caution is needed about the trends found in these surveys. As society becomes more disapproving of drug use, the willingness of individuals to report it is likely to go down. That does not mean the trends are in the wrong direction; given the role of peer pressure in the initiation of drug

■■■■ ■■■■ ■■■■ ■■■■ ■■■ ■■ **Table 2**

Cocaine Prevalence by Level of Education
1959–1964 Age Cohort (Percentages)

Years of Education	Monthly Use 1985	Monthly Use 1990	Change 1985–90	Annual Use 1985	Annual Use 1990	Change 1985–90
Males						
≤12 years	8.9	2.5	-6.4	20.6	10.8	-9.8
>12 years	9.0	2.1	-6.9	21.8	6.4	-15.4
Females						
≤12 years	5.5	1.9	-3.6	9.1	5.1	-4.0
>12 years	4.1	0.8	-3.3	12.6	5.2	-7.4

Source: National Household Survey on Drug Abuse (unpublished data)

use, rising disapproval will also lower use. But the trends are likely to be less sharp than they appear in the surveys.

Urinalysis

Given concern about the willingness of individuals to report drug use and about the coverage of the primary national surveys, increased attention has been given to urinalysis of arrested persons. Although arrestees represent a population thought to be highly involved with illegal drugs and to be poorly represented in the household and high school senior surveys, urinalysis is a more objective, yet imperfect, measure of recent drug use.

These data provide a different picture of drug-use patterns (or, at least a different part of the drug-use picture). Drug use among arrestees (an uncomfortably high percentage of young males are arrested at some stage of their lives) is very much higher than the self-report rates found in the surveys of the general population, particularly for cocaine.[4] Moreover, these usage rates do not show the same time pattern found in the surveys. Although rates are no longer rising, the decline has been quite modest.

The District of Columbia is the only jurisdiction that has a universal urinalysis program to test for drugs in persons who are arrested.[5] Since 1984, each person arrested has been tested for the presence of five drugs (opiates, cocaine, PCP, amphetamines, and methadone). Half of those arrested had not finished high school.[6] Adults have been tested since March 1984 and juveniles since January 1987. Figure 3 plots the percentage of adults testing positive for cocaine, PCP, heroin, or any drug, from March 1984 to September 1992. The percentage testing positive for PCP and heroin did not drop until late 1987, when crack first became widely available in the District. Apparently, cocaine was not a substitute for other drugs until it was available in the more accessible and potent form of crack. The percentage testing positive for cocaine (including crack) rose from 15 percent in March 1984 to over 60 percent four years later. The third quarter of 1988 saw a plateauing of the rate for cocaine use. Then, in the third quarter of 1989, the figure began a steady decline. Even so, three years into the decline, close to 50 percent of arrestees were testing positive for cocaine.

The Drug Use Forecasting (DUF) system, created by the National Institute of Justice and building on the work of the D.C. Pretrial Services Agency, shows that this extraordinary rate of drug involvement is not restricted to the District of Columbia.[7] DUF currently collects urinalysis data from a sample of arrestees in 24 cities throughout the nation, mostly from persons arrested for nondrug-related felony offenses. In the first quarter of 1992, over 50 percent of male arrestees in 21 of 24 cities tested positive for at least one illicit drug, including marijuana; in seven of the 24 cities, 50 percent or more of the males tested positive just for cocaine. For female arrestees, over 50 percent tested positive for at least one illicit drug in 21 of 21 cities; in 12 of 21 cities, over 50 percent tested positive just for cocaine. Moreover, prevalence rates for female arrestees tend to be noticeably higher than for males. Table 3 presents DUF figures for five cities for the first quarter of 1988 and for the first and second quarters of 1992.

The arrested population is now, and always has been, predominantly male; the figure is about 82%. That the females who were arrested show higher drug prevalence rates is scarcely surprising; they represent a far more deviant segment of their sex. What is striking about the DUF data, however, is that the drug-positive rates in most cities continue to be near their peak, at least through 1992. For only one of the 24 DUF cities was the most recent figure the highest, but for few was it much below that peak.

The DUF data also show some interesting variation among cities. Although cocaine use is widespread in every DUF city, with a range of positives from 25 percent to 64 percent in 1992, there is much more variation among cities in

Figure 3

Washington, DC Pretrial Services Urinalysis Results.
Percentage of Adult Arrestees Testing Positive for Drugs

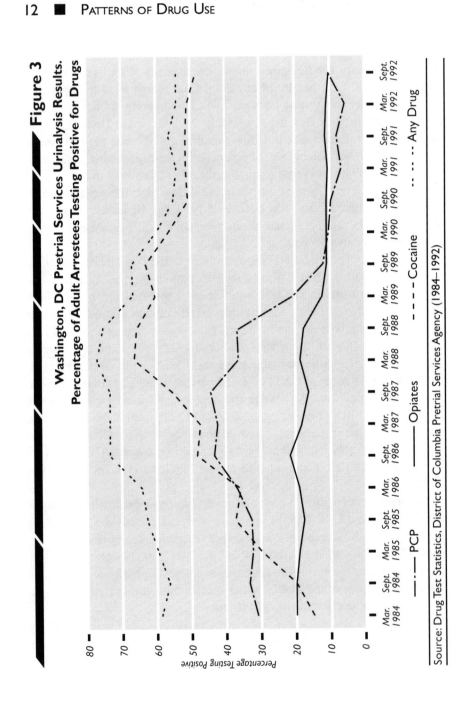

Source: Drug Test Statistics, District of Columbia Pretrial Services Agency (1984–1992)

Table 3

Arrestees Testing Positive for Illicit Drugs (Percentage)

City	Any Illicit Drug		Cocaine	
	1988 (Q1)	*1992 (Q1–Q2)*	*1988 (Q1)*	*1992 (Q1–Q2)*
Los Angeles				
Males	74	69	58	53
Females	79	73	66	59
New Orleans				
Males	58	60	32	48
Females	60	56	37	52
New York				
Males	82	77	73	62
Females	83	85	78	69
Portland				
Males	75	57	38	32
Females	79	68	47	48
Washington, DC				
Males	67	56	59	43
Females	76	74	73	65

Source: National Institute of Justice, Drug Use Forecasting (1988 and 1992)

the use by their populations of other drugs. In San Diego, amphetamines are detected in 25 percent of adult males arrested, but in most cities, the figure is less than 5 percent. Heroin is detected in 19 percent of those arrested in Chicago but in less than 2 percent of those arrested in Miami. Until crack supplanted PCP in Washington, that city had PCP prevalence rates that were five times as high as those in most other cities. These local variations may be important for policy purposes; they certainly point to the ability of local indicators like DUF to supplement the national indicators.

What can we learn from these results? Obviously, they suggest a strong relation between drug use and crime, a suggestion that has been part of folk wisdom for centuries and the research literature for decades. For policy purposes, the results focus attention on the desirability of controlling drug use among those on probation, parole, or pretrial release in order to reduce their recidivism rate. For our purposes, however, the question is what the DUF results tell us about the extent and pattern of drug abuse.

First, the results show that there is considerable variation among different segments of the population. In particular, the criminally active show much higher drug-use rates than their peers in the general household population. Moreover, it does not appear that drug use in those high-rate groups is going down nearly as rapidly as it is in the general population. With almost 50 percent of those arrested showing signs of recent cocaine use generally in 1992, it is unlikely that the prevalence of cocaine in the population has fallen by half. Indeed, for females arrested, there is little evidence of any decline between 1988 and 1992.

Integrating the DUF data with that from the broader surveys is difficult. Most of those who are arrested are at least eligible to be in the household population sampled by the NHSDA, but we do not know whether their response rate is lower than that of other parts of the young male population. Estimates of the overlap between the two populations are largely guesswork.[8] We cannot simply add the estimated numbers of drug-positive persons arrested to the household estimates.

Hospital and Coroner Reports

The Drug Abuse Warning Network (DAWN), sponsored by the Substance Abuse and Mental Health Services Administration, collects information from a sample of emergency rooms and medical examiner offices in 22 major metropolitan areas. Prior to 1989, the sample was an opportunistic one and did not permit estimation of the absolute number of emergency room cases either nationally or for individual cities; changes made in 1989 to DAWN are detailed later in this paper.

Because DAWN is dependent on information registered in medical records, not on direct patient reports, the system is vulnerable to changes in record-keeping procedures and in the extent to which doctors ask their patients about specific drugs or order tests. How these factors have changed in recent years is difficult to assess.

What does DAWN add to our knowledge of the prevalence of drug use and abuse? The implicit interpretation has been that it provides data about the numbers of those most heavily involved with illicit drugs. That is, an increase in the number of emergency room admissions or medical examiner cases involving cocaine is taken to indicate an increase in the number of persons who are heavy users of cocaine. That is clearly a simplistic view. It is common to think of an emergency room episode involving a drug as reflecting an overdose of that drug. In fact, individuals come to the emergency room for many reasons; since 1987, DAWN has coded six major reasons, such as "seeking detoxification" or experiencing "withdrawal" symptoms. Thus, emergency room episodes might go up if more people were trying to quit heroin and were experiencing trouble with withdrawal; indeed, withdrawal accounts for about 12 percent of those showing up at emergency rooms with heroin-related problems, although this motive accounts for less than 2 percent of cocaine mentions. A first-time user who had an unexpected reaction from a drug could also become a DAWN mention. Or, a steady number of users could make more frequent use of emergency rooms over time.

DAWN data on reasons for going to emergency rooms and motives for using the drug suggest that cocaine episodes involve mostly dependent users suffering chronic effects of drug use or withdrawal. Mortality rates (per use episode) are likely to be higher for people later in their drug-using careers after they have incurred extensive harm from chronic use; the medical examiner data are also probably dominated by the number and behavior of long-term users. For purposes of this analysis, we adopt the conventional view that DAWN provides information about the tail of the distribution of drug use. DAWN may be more likely to capture this portion of emergency room episodes than it is to pick up accident and injury victims and recreational drug users. The latter are less likely to appear with symptoms indicating drug use and therefore are less likely to be registered in DAWN.

Throughout most of the 1980s, the DAWN series showed a dramatic increase in the number of emergency room visits and deaths related to cocaine and heroin, with not much of a decrease for other illicit drugs; in late 1989, the DAWN emergency room figures start to turn down for cocaine, only to increase again in 1991 and 1992, as we discuss below. Figure 4 presents data on cocaine use for the period 1980 to 1989 from an overlapping series of samples of hospitals that reported consistently for three years.[9] Figure 4 also presents data from the medical examiner series. The number of deaths and emergency room admissions went up about tenfold over the decade.[10]

The number of medical examiner cocaine mentions paralleled the emergency room data for most of that time. Only after 1988 did the medical examiner data begin to diverge from the emergency room data, continuing to show increases; we discuss this matter and more recent trends below.

The demographic composition of those dying from cocaine use has also

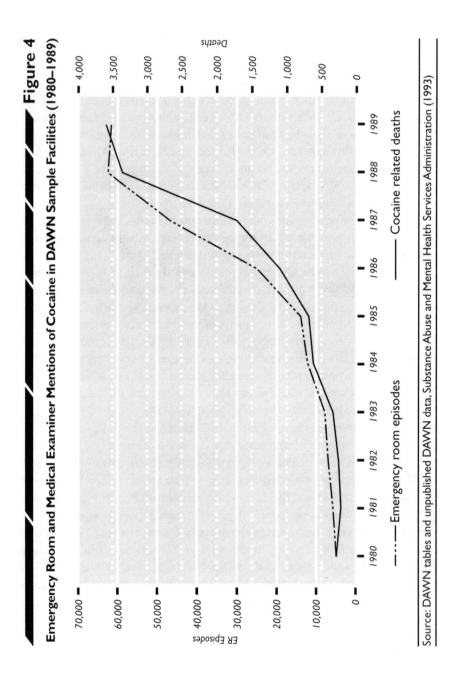

Figure 4

Emergency Room and Medical Examiner Mentions of Cocaine in DAWN Sample Facilities (1980–1989)

------- Emergency room episodes ——— Cocaine related deaths

Source: DAWN tables and unpublished DAWN data, Substance Abuse and Mental Health Services Administration (1993)

changed sharply. In 1982, about 23 percent of those dying were African American; by 1989, that figure had risen to 46 percent. Somewhat more surprisingly, there was also a sharp increase in the age of decedents. In 1982, almost half were over the age of 30; by 1989, that percentage had risen to 76 percent; correspondingly, the percentage of decedents ages 18 to 24 fell from 23 percent to 14 percent.[11] Emergency room data show similar trends in age and race composition.

The DAWN data, like those from the Drug Use Forecasting system, also point to great local variations in the use of particular drugs. For example, in 1989, 35 percent of San Diego arrestees tested positive for amphetamine use; in nine other cities, less than 5 percent tested positive for that drug. In 1988, San Diego accounted for 20 percent of all the DAWN amphetamine emergency room incidents. In the District of Columbia, where PCP dominated urinalysis figures until 1988, there were more emergency room episodes in 1986 involving PCP than cocaine; in Philadelphia, PCP episodes were only one-fifteenth as frequent as cocaine episodes.

The New DAWN

In 1989, NIDA completed implementation of a new sampling scheme that, for the first time, permits estimation of the total number of emergency room episodes related to particular drugs or classes of drugs in individual metropolitan areas. The new sampling procedure also permits more refined analyses of the demographic characteristics of those showing up in emergency rooms. This section analyzes the new DAWN data, viewing both trends and prevalence rates across population groups; the analysis should be regarded as preliminary, being an early product of an ongoing research program on the DAWN data. Our focus will be on cocaine.

Quarterly estimates of the total number of emergency room episodes involving cocaine in the coterminous United States are presented in figure 5. Note the dramatic fall in the fourth quarter of 1989; the total number of episodes decreased 25 percent (from 29,900 to 22,600). That decrease came after three quarters that showed a plateau in the rate and was followed by three quarters of steady and more modest decline. Then, beginning with the first quarter of 1991, the pattern changed. DAWN episodes involving cocaine began to increase and have continued to increase almost each quarter ever since—

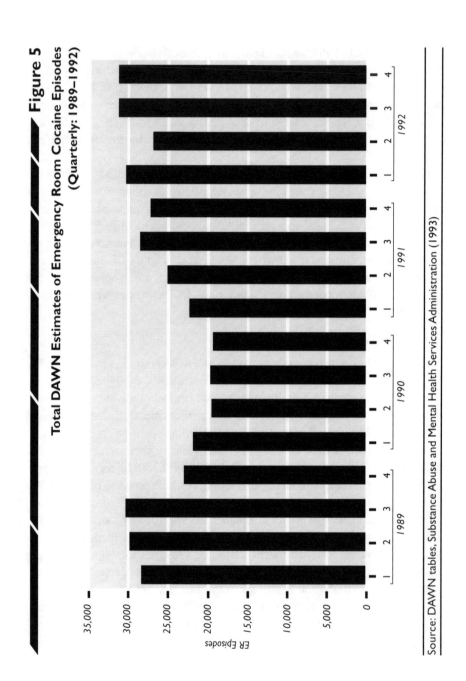

Figure 5

Total DAWN Estimates of Emergency Room Cocaine Episodes
(Quarterly: 1989–1992)

Source: DAWN tables, Substance Abuse and Mental Health Services Administration (1993)

━━━━━ ━━━━ ━━━━ ━━━ ━━ **Table 4**

Characteristics of DAWN Cocaine-Related
Emergency Room Patients (Percentages)

	1989				1990				1991				1992		
	_Q1_	_Q2_	_Q3_	_Q4_	_Q1_	_Q2_	_Q3_	_Q4_	_Q1_	_Q2_	_Q3_	_Q4_	_Q1_	_Q2_	_Q3_
Female	32	34	37	34	36	35	34	32	36	34	32	32	33	31	31
Caucasian	35	37	34	32	32	30	30	28	27	30	31	27	29	26	27
African American	47	46	45	49	50	54	54	56	58	55	54	56	56	58	56
Latino	9	8	8	8	8	8	8	8	8	9	9	9	10	10	10

Source: DAWN tables (1989–1992)

reaching a high (for the new DAWN) in the third quarter of 1992 of 30,924. This represents a 60 percent increase since the end of 1990.

The sharp one-year decline in 1990 is very puzzling, in that most DAWN cocaine incidents involve persons who have been using cocaine heavily for some time. Almost 60 percent of the DAWN cocaine records indicate dependency as the motive for taking the drug. This is a population that is likely to find it difficult to quit in a short period of time. Hence we have been investigating changes in the characteristics of those showing up as DAWN cocaine mentions. Table 4 presents the relevant data.

The population continues to be about one-third female, a figure that has not changed much over time and, surprisingly, is almost identical to that of the population showing up in DAWN as heroin mentions. The racial composition has changed even in the four-year period from 1989 to 1992; the percentage of Caucasians has fallen from about 35 percent to about 27 percent; the percentage of African Americans has risen from mid-40 percent to mid-50 percent. On a per capita basis for these 21 metropolitan areas, the prevalence rates of cocaine-related emergency room episodes for African Americans are an order of magnitude higher than for the non-African American population. That statistic clearly should be interpreted with caution; it may represent primarily differences in access to particular types of medical facilities for different income groups, given the higher poverty rates of African Americans.[12]

The new DAWN shows a sharp aging of the population taking place, an acceleration of a trend observed in the old DAWN data. Table 5 presents the

■■■■■■■■■ ■■■■■■■ ■■■■■ ■■■■ ■■■ ■■ **Table 5**

Age Distribution of Male and Female DAWN Mentions (Percentages)

	1989				*1990*		
	Q1	*Q2*	*Q3*	*Q4*	*Q1*	*Q2*	*Q3*
Males							
<19	4	4	4	6	3	3	5
19–29	50	51	47	47	44	42	40
≥30	46	45	49	47	53	55	55
Females							
<19	7	6	5	5	5	4	4
19–29	48	58	56	54	54	48	54
≥30	35	36	39	41	41	48	42

Source: DAWN tapes (unpublished)

data for males and females. The women are younger than the men; most are in their twenties, the peak fertility years, whereas the men tend to be in their thirties. But even for women, over the seven quarters for which we have raw data, the percentage of women over age 30 rose from the mid-30s to the low 40s. For men, the percentage of men over age 30 increased from the mid-40s to the mid-50s.

There are at least three possible explanations for the lower median age of the women if we assume that DAWN figures reflect patterns of use. First, female addicts may cease drug abuse at an earlier age than do men (i.e., a 25-year-old female addict is more likely to cease or reduce her cocaine use by age 30 than is a 25-year-old male addict). Second, women may have become involved with these drugs more recently than men. Thus, for example, whereas cocaine use became widely prevalent among men from 1980 to 1985, it spread among women from 1985 to 1990. Third, women may start at a younger age.

These alternatives clearly have significant implications. On the one hand, if women cease their drug involvement earlier, then drug use detected during pregnancy may not be a strong indicator of lack of fitness to parent, at least in the long run. On the other hand, if women get involved with cocaine later than men, then we may see, even as the total numbers go down, an increase in the number of female cocaine abusers.

The new DAWN also permits analysis of intercity differences in the composition of the population showing up at emergency rooms, as well as more reliable comparisons in time trends. Figure 6 presents data on five major metropolitan areas (Chicago, Washington, Los Angeles, Newark, and New York), showing how the number of cocaine episodes per 100,000 population changed from 1989 through 1992.[13] Note that all the cities show substantial declines in episodes between 1989 and 1990, although the timing of the drop varies somewhat. Four of the five cities experienced significant increases beginning in late 1990 or early 1991 and continuing through the first half of 1992. By 1992, Chicago, Newark, and New York exceeded their 1989 levels.

The data also permit examination of some variations within metropolitan areas. Figure 7 cumulates the number of cocaine episodes for the above five cities and distinguishes episodes in the central city emergency rooms from those in the surrounding suburban areas. The temporary decline between 1989 and 1990 was sharper and more prolonged in the outlying areas; persistent heavy use of drugs leading to acute incidents seems to be increasingly concentrated within central cities.

In addition to differences in the time patterns, the populations of the five cities differ in important ways. For the same five metropolitan areas, table 6 presents figures on the age, race, reason for using drugs, and motive for presenting at the emergency room. There is modest variation in the sex composition and considerable variation in motive for use and reason for emergency room visit. We offer no explanation for the sex composition variation. The motive variation may represent differences in the timing of the epidemic, but the patterns and explanations are complex. For example, Newark's high percentage reporting dependence may reflect the very high rate of heroin use by cocaine emergency room entrants. Similarly, Newark's high percentage seeking detoxification as a reason for emergency room visit may reflect the fact that this major city hospital emergency room performs medical clearances for those seeking entry to the affiliated detoxification unit, a practice not common to all emergency rooms.

Integrating the Indicators

The data sets described above were not developed through an integrated scheme intended to describe patterns of drug use and abuse in the nation. Each series was generated by a particular institutional interest or need. As one might expect, it is not easy to put the pieces together to describe the whole picture. We

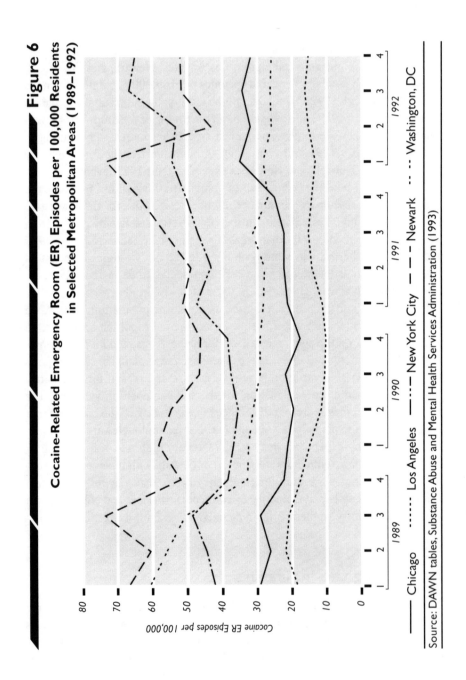

Figure 6

Cocaine-Related Emergency Room (ER) Episodes per 100,000 Residents in Selected Metropolitan Areas (1989–1992)

Cocaine ER Episodes per 100,000

—— Chicago   ⋯⋯ Los Angeles   —— New York City   — — Newark   ⋯⋯ Washington, DC

Source: DAWN tables, Substance Abuse and Mental Health Services Administration (1993)

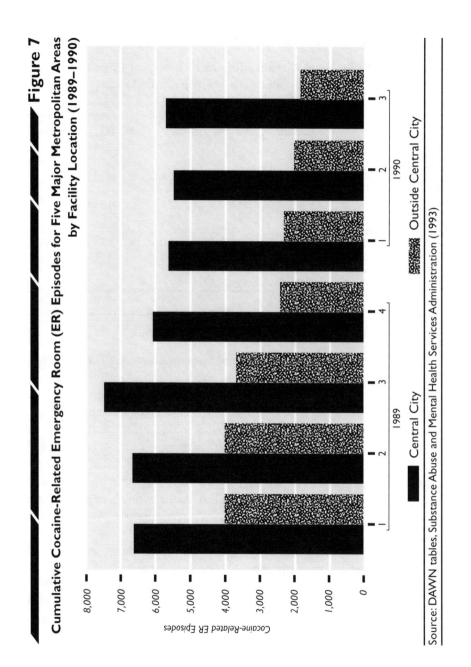

Figure 7

Cumulative Cocaine-Related Emergency Room (ER) Episodes for Five Major Metropolitan Areas by Facility Location (1989–1990)

Source: DAWN tables, Substance Abuse and Mental Health Services Administration (1993)

━━━━ ━━━━ ━━━ ━━ ━ ━ **Table 6**

Characteristics of Cocaine-Related Emergency Room Patients for Five Metropolitan Areas (1989–1990)

	Chicago	Los Angeles	New York City	Newark NJ	Washington DC
Sex					
% Female	30.6	34.6	33.1	29.1	36.7
Age					
% over 30	55.2	47.7	53.9	49.1	40.6
Motive for Use					
% Dependence	62.6	47.1	62.6	81.9	70.5
% Recreation	14.9	24.2	19.9	4.7	6.9
Reason for ER Visit					
% Unexpected reaction	39.6	31.7	12.0	9.8	14.3
% Chronic effects	19.2	34.1	44.8	14.9	11.7
% Seeking detox	15.4	4.6	25.6	60.7	44.7

Source: DAWN tables (1989–1990)

focus here on the long-term changes.

It should already be apparent that the various indicators need careful reconciliation. The stability of the household and high school senior survey figures, showing a slow increase between 1979 and 1985 in the total number of cocaine users, contrasts with the dramatic increase in total numbers of medical-examiner-reported deaths and emergency room admissions that occurred even before crack had become widely available in most cities. The downturn in the survey figures between 1985 and 1992 appears inconsistent with the sharp growth in the DAWN figures. Skeptics have suggested that this invalidates the self-report surveys. Instead, we believe that it points to a need for an understanding of drug use as a career rather than as an event. As we interpret the indicators, we will continue our focus on cocaine.

During the late 1970s and early 1980s, many individuals, mostly young adults, experimented with cocaine. Some became regular but occasional users; a smaller group went on to become regular and frequent users. While the flow of initiates had slowed down substantially by the mid-1980s, the total stock of drug users did not begin to decline because so many of the earlier initiates were still using.

As the dangers (medical rather than legal) of cocaine use became much more prominent, regular users who were not dependent (generally less frequent users) became increasingly likely to quit. The deaths of Len Bias and Don Rogers, young men in excellent physical shape, may have had a pronounced effect; that is certainly one plausible explanation for the sudden drop in the high school senior rate in 1986. The better-educated occasional users were more likely to be influenced by the health messages than their less-educated counterparts.

Thus, beginning in the mid-1980s, a marked change in the composition of the cocaine-using population occurred. As cocaine became cheaper (and more addictive), those who used it became increasingly likely to use it heavily; and low-income persons, whose use has more serious effects both for themselves and for society, may now constitute a larger share of the total user population. As a result, there is now a strong association between cocaine use and health problems (thus the DAWN rise) and a strong association between cocaine use and crime (the high DUF figures as compared to the low cocaine positives in workplace testing programs).[14]

The lack of a downturn in the medical examiner figures in 1989, when the emergency room figures dropped sharply, is consistent with this story. Death from cocaine-related causes comes later in drug-using careers than does appearance at emergency rooms. We mean something more than the tautology that death is the last event; death is more likely later in a drug user's career than earlier. Thus, even as the population of users or abusers declines, the total mortality of the user population may rise with a higher share of them in their fifth or later year of regular use.

The Future

Outside the drug abuse research and treatment professions, projecting the future course of drug abuse seems to be considered foolish; new drugs are constantly being developed and no one predicted the impact that crack has had. Among those who study drug use, however, the consensus is surprisingly strong, as demonstrated at a recent NIDA Technical Review meeting on where we stand in the current drug epidemic.[15]

The consensus arising from that meeting was that the prevalence of drug use will probably continue to decline, even with the introduction of new forms of drugs such as Ecstasy and Ice. The simple fact is that few drugs make it nationally or even, in any lasting fashion, locally. The usual pattern is for a drug to appear in a few cities and disappear after a brief surge of popularity. Moreover, what has led to the decline in drug use since 1985 is probably a change in attitudes toward the use of drugs in general rather than toward a specific drug. Initiation rates are likely to remain low among successive cohorts of adolescents for the next few years, although the recently announced results of the 1993 High School Senior Survey, which show a marked increase in the use of marijuana among eighth, tenth, and twelfth graders, are a useful reminder of the difficulty of making projections.[16]

This is a case in which there may well be a benign trickle-down effect. The declines in initiation are almost certainly greatest among the middle class, but they will help contribute to the decline in the inner city as well. The following argument is a web of speculations but one that seems quite plausible.

We begin by drawing an analogy to the end of the heroin epidemic in American cities in the mid-1970s. Initiation rates among 18-year-old males in areas of high poverty fell dramatically between 1970 and 1975. Clayton and Voss report that the annual prevalence of drug use among young men in Manhattan, after climbing from 3 percent in 1963 to 20 percent in 1970, had already declined to 13 percent by 1974.[17] Although that was undoubtedly influenced by increasing price and declining purity of the drug, the more significant influence may have been the visibility of the low quality of life of heroin addicts in those communities. Whereas what was initially most salient about heroin was the pleasure it gave its users and their enthusiasm for the drug, by 1975, the degradation of physical and social lives may have been most noticeable.

That may also be the pattern for crack in inner cities. Crack users no longer seem to be the self-confident proselytizers of the early days. Many of them have chronic health problems as well as difficulties in social functioning; they are not attractive role models. For these purposes, however, there is an important difference between heroin and cocaine. Selling heroin was never an important source of economic mobility for young, poorly educated, inner-city males; selling cocaine appears to be. It is believed that much of the drug sellers' income comes from middle-class users. Although the youthful sellers are mostly not users, there is reason to expect that over time they are likely to become heavily involved—certainly the pattern that current adult sellers have followed.[18]

Thus, the shrinking of the middle-class cocaine market has important potential consequences for inner-city use patterns as well. With the decline of middle-class demand, selling drugs will become less attractive economically. Committed current adult users may keep out new youthful sellers;[19] that, in turn, will reduce future use in the inner city.

None of this is to say that the drug problem will go away. Indeed, it is possible to paint quite dismal scenarios of the health and crime consequences of a decline in the prevalence of drug use. If selling cocaine has been the primary source of earnings for the poor, who are also the most dependent on cocaine, then they may turn to more dangerous forms of crime to finance their continued consumption. The heroin market has long been dependent on property crime. That may be true of the 1990s cocaine market.

We conclude with two observations. First, for many social service agencies such as child protective services in large cities, the decline in the number of drug-affected clients may be very slow indeed. Although the recent NHSDA declines point to a higher quit rate among those who are frequent users of cocaine than would have been expected, the evidence from studies of treatment point to very high relapse rates. The number of drug-exposed infants may not decline much in the next few years, although the only data available to us (from New York City) do point to a drop since 1989.[20] Equally important, the problems of frequent cocaine abusers are likely to continue to worsen as they suffer accumulated problems related to drug use.

Second, an important factor influencing the urinalysis and DAWN figures may be the increasing population of persons incarcerated. Between the end of 1985 and the end of 1990, that figure increased from about 775,000 (including federal, state, and local correctional facilities) to about 1,225,000.[21] Moreover, there is reason to believe that, over that time, drug users become more numerous in the incarcerated population; in 1990, one-third of those sent to state prison were convicted of drug offenses, compared to only 16 percent in 1986. Thus, if we also take into account high use rates among those charged with offenses unrelated to drugs, perhaps 500,000 additional drug users were removed from the population that might be captured in the DAWN system.

It is also important to note that the populations under supervision of probation and parole agencies have risen substantially in recent years—from 2.9 million in 1985 to 4.3 million in 1990. These programs are giving increasing emphasis to monitoring and punishing drug use in their populations. That may also contribute to measured declines in the extent of frequent drug use.

These declines may thus be something of an artifact. The measured reduction in drug use may be overstated. Many drug users may simply be currently incarcerated or under correctional supervision. This lowers the evidence of damage that drug use does to the rest of the community, while also reducing the harm that the incarcerated drug users do to themselves. But the rising incarceration rate of drug users also changes the interpretation of declines in DUF and DAWN. Enforcement may not so much have changed the behavior of drug users as it has changed their circumstances. If incarceration and supervision do not reduce the propensity to use drugs (and few observers believe that current correctional programs offer much hope in that respect), then, unless the nation is willing to maintain its currently extraordinarily high correctional population, the drug indicators may continue to worsen.

When the cocaine epidemic began, many believed that it would burn itself out because cocaine addiction, unlike heroin addiction, could not be sustained over a long period of time; its strong stimulant qualities would place too much of a strain on the individual. The evidence now suggests that such addiction certainly can last a long time; many cocaine users have now been dependent for close to a decade and the term "chronic lifetime relapsing condition" now seems almost as applicable to cocaine as to heroin and alcohol abuse. As cocaine use becomes more concentrated among the poorer and more dependent users—fewer of whom will be able to finance their consumption either by selling to wealthier non-dependent users or by working—these users are likely to become an increasing burden on society. Drug epidemics create long aftershocks and policy makers need to accept that fact and shape their policies accordingly.

Notes

1. Lloyd D. Johnston, Patrick O'Malley, and Jerald G. Bachman, *Drug Use among High School Seniors, College Students, and Young Adults* (Ann Arbor, MI: Uni-

versity of Michigan, annual). Since 1992, the survey has also included data on drug use by eighth and tenth graders.

2. The data concern drug use by 18-year-olds; few of those who become drug-dependent have yet reached that stage at age 18. See Patrick O'Malley, Jerald G. Bachman, and Lloyd D. Johnston, "Period, Age, and Cohort Effects on Substance Use among Young Americans: A Decade of Change," *American Journal of Public Health* 78, no. 10 (1988): 682–687.

3. Jerald G. Bachman, Lloyd D. Johnston, and Patrick O'Malley, "Explaining the Recent Decline in Cocaine Use among Young Adults: Further Evidence That Perceived Risks and Disapproval Lead to Reduced Drug Use," *Journal of Health and Social Behavior* 31 (June 1990): 173–184.

4. Tillman estimates that 34 percent of Caucasian males born in California in 1956 were arrested between ages 18 and 29; the figure for African American males was 66 percent. See Robert Tillman, "The Size of the 'Criminal Population': The Prevalence and Incidence of Arrests," *Criminology* 25, no. 3 (Fall 1987): 561–579.

5. The program is voluntary but judges request the results of urinalysis for purposes of pretrial detention decisions; thus, over 95 percent of persons arrested provide a specimen. For details of the program, see John A. Carver, "Drugs and Crime: Controlling Use and Reducing Risk through Testing," *National Institute of Justice Reports* (Washington, DC: National Institute of Justice, September/October 1986).

6. Peter Reuter, Robert MacCoun, and Patrick Murphy, *Money from Crime: A Study of the Economics of Drug Dealing in Washington, DC* (Santa Monica, CA: RAND, 1990).

7. Carver, "Drugs and Crime."

8. Wish used DUF data to estimate the total number of current cocaine users at about two million. See Eric Wish, "U.S. Drug Policy in the 1990s: Insights from New Data on Arrestees," *International Journal on Addictions* 25, no. 3A (1990–91): 377–409.

9. DAWN relies on voluntary reporting by a sample of facilities; not all facilities report each month. The series in figure 4 was put together from published data on three-year intervals.

10. The medical examiner cases do not include homicide victims whose deaths may have been related to drug market activities.

11. As already suggested, the rise in the age of decedents may represent the increasing vulnerability of users as their careers lengthen. This certainly seems the most likely explanation for recent increases in heroin-related emergency room and medical examiner figures, given that the user population has apparently not increased in size.

12. No systematic data are available on differences in utilization of the emergency room for drug-related emergencies by socioeconomic status. While it is generally true that poverty populations make much greater use of the emergency room for medical services, if most drug-related episodes are emergencies and occur outside of the usual operating hours of doctors' offices (as might be the case if these episodes occur during evening recreational drug use), then the emergency room may be the first choice of even middle-class drug users.

13. We include data from Newark because we have been involved in a large-scale assessment of that city's drug problems and programs.

14. This mirrors a phenomenon noted by Courtwright in analyzing patterns of change in opiate use in the early twentieth century. Whereas, in 1895, most opiate addicts were middle-class people suffering the consequences of careless prescription, by 1915, the addicted population comprised the poorer, more criminally active, heroin users. Opiate use and crime had a much stronger association by then. See David Courtwright, *Dark Paradise: Opiate Addiction in America before 1940* (Cambridge, MA: Harvard University Press, 1982). For a discussion of workplace testing programs, see Dean R. Gerstein and Henrick J. Harwood, eds., *Treating Drug Problems: Volume I* (Washington, DC: National Academy Press, 1990), 120–125.

15. National Institute on Drug Abuse, *An Assessment of the Incidence and Prevalence of Drug Abuse in the United States: Report on the Technical Review Meeting* (Rockville, MD: U.S. Department of Health and Human Services, 1991).

16. Preliminary results released January 31, 1994, by Donna E. Shalala, Secretary of the U.S. Department of Health and Human Services, press release issued by the U.S. Department of Health and Human Services.

17. Richard Clayton and Harlan Voss, "Young Men and Drugs in Manhattan: A Causal Analysis," *Research Monograph* 39 (Rockville, MD: National Institute on Drug Abuse, 1981).

18. Reuter et al., *Money from Crime.*

19. The frequent user will take some of his reward in the form of discounted drugs, which lowers the enforcement risk associated with a given total earning and thus advantages the user-seller over the abstinent seller.

20. National Institute on Drug Abuse, *Epidemiologic Trends in Drug Abuse—Proceedings, Community Epidemiology Work Group, December 1992* (Rockville, MD: U.S. Department of Health and Human Services, NIH Publication No. 93–3560, 1993), 237.

21. Bureau of Justice Statistics, *Correctional Populations in the United States, 1986* (Washington, DC: U.S. Department of Justice, NCJ–111611, February 1989) 6, 44; Bureau of Justice Statistics, *Correctional Populations in the United States, 1990* (Washington, DC: U.S. Department of Justice, NCJ–134946, July 1992), 8, 83.

 *2*

NEIGHBORHOOD ECOLOGY

Sheila Ards
*Ronald B. Mincy**

Between 1986 and 1989, the number of children in foster care in the United States increased from 280,000 to 360,000.[1] This 29 percent increase in just three years left many policymakers concerned about how best to provide child welfare services. Before options can be explored for meeting the increased demand for child welfare services, however, policymakers must understand why that increase is occurring and how to direct services to families with the greatest need.

Poverty status and social distress—and the spatial concentration of such indicators—can help policymakers identify areas of greatest need. Children from the poorest and most distressed families are at greatest risk of maltreat-

* This paper is a product of the Underclass Research Project. Funding for this paper was provided by the Rockefeller Foundation. The authors thank Fred Wulczyn for the maps on infant placements, Christine McRae for comments on an earlier draft, Susan Wiener and Jennifer Pack for their assistance in developing the map on underclass and drug neighborhoods, and Mary Coombs for her assistance in preparing the manuscript. Opinions expressed are those of the authors and should not be attributed to the Urban Institute or its sponsors.

ment. Furthermore, low-income families usually have fewer familial or other private sources of financial and emotional support upon which they may rely in times of need. Instead, in a crisis, these families must rely on public services. When the issue is child maltreatment within these families, the public service most frequently offered by local departments of social services is foster care.

Our earlier work on the spatial concentration of poverty and social distress within underclass neighborhoods provides important insights for targeting the provision of child welfare and related services.[2] We define *underclass neighborhoods* as census tracts in which certain social problems—drug abuse, teenage pregnancy and parenting, welfare dependency, failure to complete high school, and adult joblessness—reach specified levels. Since several of these social problems are also predictors of child maltreatment, we expect that underclass neighborhoods will contain a disproportionate number of families in need of child welfare services.

The focus of our paper is on one particular child welfare service—foster care—and the correlation between underclass neighborhoods and foster care placements. We want to know whether neighborhoods that are especially plagued by underclass social problems are also neighborhoods with disproportionate numbers of foster care placements. If so, policymakers can reach the families in greatest need of foster care and related services by targeting underclass neighborhoods.

In this paper, we first define underclass neighborhoods and present some of our previous research findings on 880 such neighborhoods, as estimated from 1980 U.S. Census data. Using heuristic and empirical analyses of foster care placements, we explain why we believe many placements originate with families in underclass neighborhoods. We next present an analysis of the correlations between drug abuse, underclass neighborhoods, and foster care populations in New York City, and conclude with the policy implications of our findings.

Underclass Problems and Foster Care

Underclass neighborhoods are census tracts where certain social problems are commonplace. These problems include crime, drug abuse, teenage pregnancy and parenting, welfare dependency, failure to complete high school, and joblessness. While we do not include poverty among the criteria for an underclass neighborhood, as described above, poverty rates are characteristically high in these neighborhoods. Several of these social problems are also risk factors for child maltreatment.

We define an underclass neighborhood as a census tract with a "high proportion" of:

- males over 16 years old not regularly in the labor force,
- households headed by single women with children,
- households dependent on welfare, and
- dropouts among the high school-age population.

By *high proportion*, we mean a value of at least one standard deviation above the mean value for all census tracts in the nation in 1980.

Our definition of underclass neighborhoods is quite restrictive. To be counted as an underclass neighborhood, a census tract must have high values for *all four* indicators. Although we wanted to include measures of crime and drug abuse in the definition, we could not because census files lack such data.

Applying the above definition, we found that, in 1980, there were 880 underclass neighborhoods containing 2.5 million people; 1.1 million of those persons also had poverty-level incomes.[3] (See table 1.) Almost all of the underclass neighborhoods were urban (99 percent), located predominantly in large northeastern or midwestern cities, and comprised disproportionately of African Americans (59 percent). Almost two-thirds of the adults had less than a high school education, more than half of the adult men were not regularly employed, and more than a third of the households received public assistance.

The size of this group may appear small, but one must remember that our definition is very restrictive. By requiring high values on *all four* underclass indicators, we included only the most extremely depressed neighborhoods within our group of underclass neighborhoods. Other studies have used poverty as a criterion for measuring the underclass. Doing so would expand the underclass in 1988 to 1,887 neighborhoods and 5.6 million individuals[4] as there were many neighborhoods not meeting all four criteria in which 40 percent or more of the population was poor.

━━━ ━━━ ━━━ ━━━ ━━ ━━ Table I

Total Underclass Tracts and Tract Populations by State (1980)

State	# of Underclass Tracts	Rank by # of Tracts	Underclass Tract Population	Rank by Underclass Population
New York	165	1	476,750	1
Illinois	69	3	208,005	2
Michigan	75	2	207,096	3
California	57	5	189,385	4
New Jersey	44	6	136,235	5
Pennsylvania	38	7	133,288	6
Ohio	60	4	123,550	7
Georgia	31	8	88,393	8
Maryland	26	9	84,315	9
Texas	23	11	79,813	10
Massachusetts	24	10	71,067	11
Florida	18	15	60,624	12
Louisiana	22	12	58,011	13
Alabama	20	13	56,670	14
Missouri	16	17	50,511	15
Connecticut	19	14	50,254	16
Kentucky	18	16	43,069	17
Virginia	16	18	41,667	18
Tennessee	15	19	40,083	19
Indiana	12	21	32,315	20
Arizona	8	23	31,397	21
Wisconsin	14	20	24,831	22
Colorado	8	25	24,091	23
District of Columbia	7	27	18,775	24
North Carolina	10	22	18,090	25
Oklahoma	8	24	16,242	26
Mississippi	6	29	16,205	27
Washington	6	30	14,983	28
South Carolina	7	26	14,080	29
Rhode Island	4	33	13,627	30
Minnesota	6	28	11,466	31
Delaware	5	31	9,639	32
Arkansas	3	34	9,061	33
Oregon	3	35	5,488	34
New Mexico	2	38	5,442	35
Utah	3	37	5,017	36
West Virginia	2	39	3,950	37
Nebraska	4	32	3,683	38
Maine	3	36	3,293	39
Hawaii	1	41	1,651	40
Iowa	2	40	1,598	41
United States	**880**		**2,483,710**	

Source: Urban Institute Analysis of the 1980 Census

Further, even our restrictive definition results in a rapidly expanding population. Between 1970 and 1980, the population living in underclass neighborhoods increased more than threefold, from 752,000 to 2.5 million.[5]

Our conception of underclass neighborhoods is geographically inclusive, that is, underclass and nonunderclass persons live in such neighborhoods. Underclass persons are those who exhibit the social problems we use to define underclass neighborhoods; nonunderclass persons do not exhibit these social problems but, by living in neighborhoods where such problems prevail, they are potentially affected by them and at risk of developing the same problems.[6]

Children in underclass neighborhoods are probably the most important example of nonunderclass persons placed at risk due to the prevalence of social problems. The greater the proportion of neighborhood families headed by underclass persons—men who rarely work, single teenage mothers, welfare dependents—the larger the number of neighborhood families operating under the stress produced by poverty and isolation. This stress can lead to child maltreatment by family members, and ultimately to foster care placements. If this stress, or other factors, leads to drug or alcohol abuse, the likelihood of child maltreatment and foster care placement increases.

When a significant proportion of adults in a neighborhood exhibits these problems, we hypothesize that there are also indirect effects on the incidence of child maltreatment and foster care placements. First, unstable adults moving about in the neighborhood may assault children who are not closely supervised by their parents. Second, stable families and community institutions tend to flee such neighborhoods, reducing the likelihood that stressed families in the neighborhood will find help from community residents or local social service institutions. Thus, we should not interpret a finding that a disproportionate share of foster care placements originates in underclass neighborhoods as an attempt to stigmatize all residents of such neighborhoods. Instead, such a finding may suggest the need for child welfare and family preservation services that compensate for the effects of living in a social environment lacking in family and community resources.

Having defined and described the underclass neighborhood population in statistical terms, the next step is to explain why we believe that a disproportionate share of foster care placements originates in underclass neighborhoods.

Heuristic and Empirical Models for Foster Care Placements

We hypothesize that the level of foster care within an area depends on three components: 1) the level and severity of child maltreatment within the area, 2) the support systems for families within the area, and 3) the local department of social services' policy toward foster care (see figure 1). These three components are not mutually exclusive, but are interconnected in important ways. For example, high levels of child maltreatment do not necessarily translate into high levels of foster care if resources are available to the maltreated child from family supports and the local department of social services.

Ecological theory posits that the incidence of maltreatment of children is a product of the environment in which the children live. Neighborhood characteristics—a part of that environment—can be used to predict the child's risk of maltreatment. Research suggests a high correlation between the socioeconomic characteristics of a neighborhood, the availability of social support networks, and the prevalence of child maltreatment.[7]

Our earlier work examined the correlation between an area's economic and demographic characteristics and its levels of child maltreatment.[8] The level of stress, the types of social support systems, and the number of sanctions against violent crimes were used to predict the level of child maltreatment in a given area. In those studies, to approximate the level of stress, we used proxies such as per capita personal income and the level of unemployment.

We assumed that areas with low per capita income were those likely to be touched by the behavioral dimensions of poverty. Our work showed that child maltreatment was prevalent in these areas. In addition, as the level of per capita income decreased, the level of child maltreatment within the area increased. This result suggested that poor neighborhoods suffer from higher levels of child maltreatment than do nonpoor neighborhoods. We also found that:

- areas with high levels of unemployment had high levels of child maltreatment;

- areas with stricter sanctions against violent crimes—measured as the number of arrests divided by the number of known assaults—had lower levels of child maltreatment; and

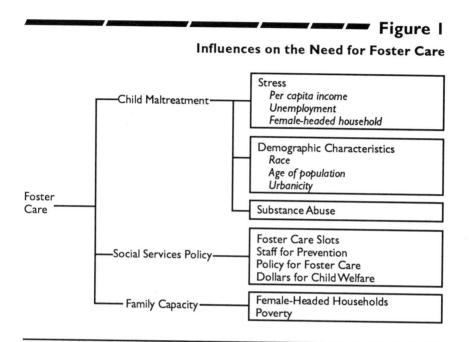

Figure 1

Influences on the Need for Foster Care

- after controlling for economic characteristics, predominantly African American areas had lower rates of child maltreatment.

This research shows that neighborhood characteristics can be good predictors of the level of child maltreatment within an area. In addition, African Americans were shown to have higher child maltreatment rates because they were disproportionately poor, not because of a cultural acceptance of physical violence toward children. As stated earlier, however, the number of child maltreatment cases did not necessarily translate into increased foster care demand.

This research leaves an important question unanswered. One explanation for the growth in foster care placements is that the number of child maltreatment cases grew while the severity of cases remained constant. Alternatively, increases in drug abuse among parents could have lead to an increase in the severity of child maltreatment cases, although the number of such cases remained constant. Finally, there could have been an increase in both the number and severity of child maltreatment cases. To date, no one has tried to sort out the importance of these two factors.

The second component for predicting demand for foster care is the support systems for families within the neighborhood. Garbarino notes the importance of support systems within a neighborhood as a predictor of the prevalence of child maltreatment.[9] He contends that child abuse feeds on privacy. Families who engage in child maltreatment fail to use even the limited social service supports available.

In addition, Garbarino notes that socially impoverished neighborhoods are at a high risk for greater than expected levels of child maltreatment.[10] Socially impoverished neighborhoods are environments in which individuals cannot afford to give to and share with their neighbors because of their own needs and limited resources. Garbarino also shows that these "socially impoverished" families tend to be clustered together.

The degree to which family support will be able to buffer potential problems can be approximated by using the area's poverty rate and the percent of families within the area headed by single parents. Single-parent families have lower levels of support available for their children than do two-parent families. Most single-parent families have female heads. In addition, the poverty rate within an area may serve as a proxy indicator of the economic resources available to maltreated children.

Finally, the role of local public policy has not been fully explored within the foster care literature. The foster care policies of the local social services department can be inferred, however, from the level of expenditures and allocations for foster care relative to total expenditures.

The three components noted above must be considered jointly in order to understand the level of foster care demanded in an area.

Placements and Underclass Neighborhoods in New York City

The vast majority of children in foster care are in a few states, with California, Illinois, New York, Pennsylvania, and Ohio accounting for nearly 50 percent of the foster care population in 1988.[11] These same states also account for 44 percent of the underclass neighborhoods and 45 percent of the underclass neighborhood population. Our research supplements the empirical findings outlined above by mapping the correlations between foster care placements and underclass neighborhoods, evaluating the data for one metropolitan area, New York City.

Before examining our findings, we should point out several caveats. First, these findings are preliminary and reflect foster care placements for a major metropolitan area in a single state. Second, the data from New York City on foster care placements are for infants only; the spatial distribution of foster care placements for *all* children could be different.[12] We show that underclass neighborhoods in New York City are spatially correlated with neighborhoods in which drug abuse is high. Therefore, our estimates of the correlation between infant foster care and underclass neighborhoods should underestimate the correlation between all foster care placements and underclass neighborhoods because of the relationship between infant placements and drug usage. Finally, data on foster care are for 1984 to 1989, data on drug use are for 1989, and data on underclass neighborhoods are for 1980. It is unlikely, however, that the spatial distribution of underclass neighborhoods has changed significantly since 1980.

Wulczyn created a spatial mapping of infants placed in foster care in Manhattan between 1984 and 1989 (see figure 2).[13] That map showed that Central Harlem, East Harlem, and Union Square (the southeast cluster of points) contained the highest proportion of infants entering foster care. The other boroughs contained relatively few foster care entrants. Figure 3 shows the neighborhoods that: 1) meet our definition of underclass, 2) have high levels of drug usage, and 3) both fulfill our underclass definition *and* have high levels of drug usage.

When we overlay the map of foster care entrants (figure 2) with data on drug usage throughout Manhattan and our work on underclass neighborhoods (figure 3), a strong association emerges.[14] Neighborhoods with high levels of drug abuse also have high levels of foster care placements. Similarly, these same areas rate high on all four behavioral characteristics defining underclass neighborhoods. Although preliminary analyses of data for New York strongly support these conclusions, extrapolation to other parts of the country is somewhat risky. This risk is mitigated, however, by our finding that the four states with 50 percent of the foster care placements also had 45 percent of the underclass neighborhood population.

The relationship between drug abuse and foster care placements comes as

**Figure 2**

Distribution of Infants Placed in Foster Care in Manhattan, New York*
(1984–1989)

* Includes infants discharged and still in care.

Source: Fred H. Wulczyn, *The Changing Face of Foster Care in New York State*, New York State Department of Social Services, Division of Family and Children Services (February 1990)

Figure 3

Underclass and Drug Neighborhoods in Manhattan, New York

Source: Fred H. Wulczyn, *The Changing Face of Foster Care in New York State,* New York State Department of Social Services, Division of Family and Children Services (February 1990)

little surprise. The emergence since 1987 of crack cocaine as the drug of choice coexists with the rising demand for foster care that same year. The rising incidence of placements is in part caused by the growing number of female drug abusers. Between 1972 and 1988, the number of women as a proportion of all persons testing positive for drugs jumped from 25 to 40 percent.[15] In addition, the National Household Survey on Drug Abuse estimates that nearly 35 million women in 1988 had used drugs at least once in their lifetime. Of that number, six million had used illicit drugs within the past month.[16]

These women were not teenagers, unaware of the dangers of drugs. Drug-abusing mothers are on average between the ages of 18 and 25 years old, and have an average of two to four children at home.[17] In addition, a large number of pregnant women are using crack cocaine, resulting in tens of thousands of infants born each year who were exposed prenatally to drugs. A study at Harlem Hospital in New York City estimated that 10 percent of all newborns test positive for cocaine in their urine.[18] A large number of these newborns become "boarder babies" and must rely upon public health and social services.[19]

Implications

The recent growth in foster care placements in the United States shows that there is a greater demand for child and family services than policymakers anticipated only a few years ago. Although one can identify the characteristics of families at risk, it is difficult to predict in which *specific* families child maltreatment will occur. This targeting problem discourages efforts to develop preventive services. It also makes it difficult for policymakers to deploy services designed to intervene quickly when reported or confirmed incidents of child maltreatment occur.

Yet policymakers can efficiently provide such services, using knowledge about the spatial correlation between foster care placements and underclass social problems. We have shown that foster care placements occur disproportionately in underclass neighborhoods. This suggests that policymakers can effectively deploy services even though the families that need such services are not specifically identified. These services, which may be preventive or responsive in nature, will allow families lacking private sources of financial and emotional support to obtain that support in a time of crisis.

Although Garbarino's work suggests that families in high-risk neighborhoods are more involved with treatment agencies than with their preventive counterparts, we recommend emphasizing preventive services.[20] For example, centers that teach parenting skills could be provided in such areas. Maryland has a number of preventive programs called Family Support Centers in localities across the state. In addition to classes on parenting skills, these centers offer sports activities for teenagers and other classes for adults. These centers are open to all families within the locality, not just families receiving services through the social services department. Besides preventive services, treatment services can be located in neighborhoods in which child maltreatment is likely to occur, so that the appropriate authorities can respond quickly to suspected and confirmed reports.

The correlation between drug usage and foster care placement within neighborhoods suggests the need for targeting drug treatment facilities within underclass neighborhoods. Residential treatment facilities designed for women—and for women with children—are scarce. Redirecting resources toward these types of facilities may reduce the need for greater resources in foster care in the long run.

Just as the stress-inducing characteristics of neighborhoods seem to contribute to the incidence of child maltreatment, stress-reducing policies should help reduce that incidence. Increased police presence in high-risk neighborhoods is one strategy for reducing stress. Besides the indirect effect of increased police presence—a greater sense of security among neighborhood residents—such a presence would also directly deter child maltreatment. Family members are less likely to abuse and neglect children if such maltreatment is more likely to be discovered by police. Other neighborhood stress-reduction policies could include environmental improvements such as renovation or destruction of dilapidated buildings, effective trash removal, maintenance of drug-free environments so that children can play safely, and assurance of quality housing for all qualified low-income residents. Neighborhood-specific policies such as these would address some of the intangible effects of living in a high-risk neighborhood that are not addressed through either economic-based programs or emotional-support programs.

Our model of the influences on the need for foster care depicts the level of foster care within an area as dependent upon the area's level of child maltreatment, family capacity, and social service policy. Although data limitations inhibited the testing of this model, this paper shows that areas with high levels of foster care placements also have high levels of drug usage and measure high in all indices for being defined as underclass areas. In an attempt to provide preventive health and social services to areas with the greatest potential need for foster care services, indices for defining underclass populations can be used. Those neighborhoods meeting the definition of underclass, then, could be targeted for extensive social services.

Notes

1. U.S. House of Representatives Committee on Ways and Means, *Overview of Entitlement Programs (1990 Green Book)* (Washington, DC: U.S. Government Printing Office, 1990), 793.

2. Ronald B. Mincy, "Metropolitan Areas and the Underclass Neighborhood: Interactions with Race and Poverty." Paper prepared for the American Economics Association meeting, December 1990.

3. Erol R. Ricketts and Isabel V. Sawhill, "Defining and Measuring the Underclass," *Journal of Policy Analysis and Management* 7, no. 2 (Winter 1988): 316–325.

4. Mary Jo Bane and Paul A. Jargowsky, "Urban Poverty Areas: Basic Questions Concerning Prevalence, Growth and Dynamics," prepared for the Committee on National Urban Policy, National Academy of Sciences, February 1988 (earlier version).

5. Erol R. Ricketts and Ronald Mincy, "Growth of the Underclass: 1970–1980," *The Journal of Human Resources* 25, no. 1 (Winter 1990): 137–145.

6. There has been some controversy surrounding our underclass neighborhood concept because it is geographically inclusive. Some observers object to this inclusive concept because it stigmatizes nonunderclass persons based on their address. Such a stigma is regrettable. However, we maintain the inclusive concept in order to allow policy discussions to extend beyond people who exhibit underclass social problems to those who may be placed at risk because of the prevalence of such problems. It is easy to see the value of this kind of discussion when the policies involve children.

7. James Garbarino and Anne Crouter, "Defining the Community Context of

Parent-Child Relations: The Correlates of Child Maltreatment," *Child Development* 49, no. 2 (September 1978): 604–616; Susan J. Zuravin, "The Ecology of Child Abuse and Neglect: Review of the Literature and Presentation of Data," *Violence and Victims* 4, no. 2 (1989): 101–120; Sheila Ards, "Estimating Local Child Abuse," *Evaluation Review* 13, no. 5 (October 1989): 484–515.

8. Ards, 484–515.

9. James Garbarino, "The Human Ecology of Child Maltreatment: A Conceptual Model for Research," *Journal of Marriage and the Family* 39, no. 4 (November 1977): 721–735.

10. James Garbarino and Deborah Sherman, "High-Risk Neighborhoods and High-Risk Families: The Human Ecology of Child Maltreatment," *Child Development* 51 (1980): 188–198.

11. *1990 Green Book*, 793-794.

12. Fred H. Wulczyn, "The Changing Face of Foster Care in New York State," New York State Department of Social Services, Division of Family and Children Services, February 1990.

13. *Ibid.*

14. Data on drug abuse within Manhattan came from the New York State Division of Substance Abuse Services, Bureau of Research and Evaluation, 1989.

15. Philip Elmer-DeWitt, "A Plague Without Boundaries," *Time*, 6 November 1989, 95.

16. National Household Survey on Drug Abuse, 1988 Population Estimates, DHHS Publication No. (ADM) 89–1636.

17. Richard Kusserow, "Crack Babies," *Inspector General* (June 1990): 1.

18. Ira J. Chasnoff, "Perinatal Effects of Cocaine," *Contemporary Ob-Gyn* 29, no. 5 (May 1987): 163–179.

19. U.S. General Accounting Office, "Drug-Exposed Infants: A Generation at Risk" (Washington, DC: U.S. Government Printing Office, June 1990).

20. Garbarino and Sherman, 188–198.

 **3**

EFFECTS ON PARENTS
AND CHILDREN

Barry Zuckerman

Great concern is being expressed about the growing number of children who have been exposed prenatally to drugs and the potential burden that these children are placing on society. Infants exposed prenatally to cocaine are often represented as so severely or permanently brain-damaged that they are uneducable and incapable of normal functioning.[1] Although concern about the outcomes of children exposed prenatally to drugs is legitimate, the predictions of adverse developmental outcomes are being made in the absence of reliable scientific information.[2] These premature conclusions about the severity and universality of the effects of prenatal exposure to cocaine are potentially harmful. If society believes that these children are beyond help and labels them as permanently damaged, caregivers and teachers will have lowered expectations for the children's performance, and the prediction will become self-fulfilling.[3]

Psychoactive substances used by women during pregnancy can potentially affect the developing child's brain and cause future learning and behavior problems. Fetal alcohol syndrome in children—the result of excessive alcohol intake by their mothers during pregnancy—is the best example of this problem. At birth, children exposed prenatally to narcotics and cocaine have on average smaller head circumferences, indicating the possibility of a smaller brain. The developmental consequences for these children, however, are less well known. Nevertheless, poor parenting, a frequent concomitant of addiction, can exacerbate the impact on children's development of prenatal exposure to psychoactive substances.[4]

The development and behavior of infants exposed prenatally to drugs can only be determined by the child's dynamic interaction with the social environment.[5] Consider, for example, a child born to a cocaine-using mother who did not eat well during her pregnancy and received minimal prenatal care. Following a three-day hospitalization, the infant has difficulty remaining alert and is minimally responsive. The child's passivity engenders maternal feelings of inadequacy that may deepen already existing depressive symptoms and promote continued reliance on cocaine to alleviate these painful feelings. During the first year, the mother's attempts to get her infant's attention lead to overstimulation, general irritability, and at times, inconsolable crying. The mother's feeling of inadequacy and depression increases, and she continues to use drugs and alcohol to self-medicate these painful feelings. In the second year of life, as the child strives for independence, struggles develop between the mother and her toddler. The mother sets unusual or inconsistent limits, and most interactions with her child are negative and involve commands, especially on the days following a drug or alcohol binge. At two years of age, the child is hyperactive and impulsive, with delayed language development.

What is the cause of these developmental and behavioral problems? Are they secondary to poor prenatal nutrition, to prenatal cocaine exposure, or to both? Or, are they the result of the mother's depression? The transactional model of child development provides the best explanation as it considers all of these factors and their interactions with each other.[6] Improving parenting skills and providing nutrition and other needed services can interrupt this cycle and improve outcomes for children.

In-Utero Exposure to Psychoactive Drugs

Some drugs affect the fetus indirectly by decreasing maternal nutrition or constricting blood vessels, resulting in decreased oxygen and transfer of nutrients. Psychoactive substances cross the placenta and the blood-brain barrier, potentially affecting the developing brain directly. A consistent, specific insult to the central nervous system (CNS) from prenatal exposure to drugs and alcohol has not been well documented, however. Maternal cocaine use, excessive alcohol consumption, and narcotic use during pregnancy are associated with a smaller head circumference in the newborn, indicating a potential structural effect on the brain.[7] It is important to emphasize that some, but not all, infants are affected. For example, in the largest study to date of prenatal cocaine exposure, 10 percent of the infants of mothers with a positive urine assay for cocaine during pregnancy had microcephaly or small head circumference.[8] Although other specific effects have been described in some, but not all, infants exposed prenatally to drugs, their clinical implications are unknown. Neonatal neurobehavioral disturbances that may reflect direct CNS effects are consistently found only in heroin- and methadone-exposed newborns. Neonatal neurobehavioral abnormalities have been reported in some, but not all, studies of newborns exposed prenatally to cocaine.[9]

Most available outcome data deal with children prenatally exposed to narcotics, specifically methadone. At present, there are five studies of narcotic-exposed newborns with follow-up information obtained when the children were two years or older. These studies do not show differences in developmental scores between children who were exposed prenatally to drugs and those who were not.[10] The developmental outcome of children exposed prenatally to cocaine and not opiates has been published by only one research group. When compared with socially matched controls, the cocaine-exposed children show no mean differences in development at two and three years of age.

However, the combination of cigarettes, alcohol, and marijuana, with or without cocaine, was associated with lower developmental scores at three years of age. The effect of drugs on the home environment contributed, in part, to this finding.[11] Since the children in all these studies were located to be tested, it is likely that they were receiving some form of help or intervention from the system. Infants who do not receive these services may not do as well. Thus, the results of these studies may actually show the beneficial effects of intervention.

Global measures of developmental outcome may not provide critical information on how drugs affect children. In a preliminary study using other measures of development and behavior, 18- to 20-month-old children who were exposed prenatally to drugs were more insecure, more disorganized, and more poorly attached to their primary caregiver than a group of premature infants.[12] Anecdotal reports regarding school-age children exposed prenatally to heroin showed that, while they had cognitive functioning comparable to that of other children, they were likely to be inattentive and impulsive.[13] The extent to which these behaviors are due to a prenatal or biological effect rather than to a postnatal or caregiving effect is not known.

Parenting by Drug-Abusing Mothers

Heavy use of drugs—especially actual addiction—interferes with a mother's ability to provide the consistent nurturing and caregiving that promote children's development, self-esteem, and ability to regulate their affect or impulses. Poor or dysfunctional caregiving has been demonstrated among alcohol- and narcotic-abusing mothers.[14] Heroin-abusing mothers often demonstrate aversive interactions, characterized by commands, disapproval, provocation, and threats.[15] Addiction to both alcohol and narcotics is associated with an increased rate of child abuse and neglect.[16] By 15 months of age, children of cocaine-using mothers are more likely to be placed in foster care primarily for reasons of neglect than are children of mothers who do not use cocaine.

To best understand why heavy use of drugs results in inadequate parenting, it is important to understand the dynamics of addiction. Addiction is a chronic, progressive disease with characteristic signs and symptoms. Central to the understanding of addiction is the idea of loss of control over the use of, and compulsive preoccupation with, a substance, despite the consequences. All aspects of the self are affected—the physical, the psychological, and the spiritual. With addicted women, their primary relationship is with their drug of choice, not with their child.

Among the many theories of addiction, evidence is growing that many addicted women have been sexually or physically abused as children.[17] Thus, it is possible that women use drugs in part to self-medicate the intense, painful feelings and even physiological changes that are associated with these significant traumatic events. Not all women who use alcohol or illegal drugs are addicted. In one study, a third of the pregnant women used cocaine less than once a month and 25 percent used it three or more times per week.[18] Becoming addicted to alcohol, heroin, or intranasal cocaine may take years.

Crack cocaine appears to be the most highly addictive of all agents. In animals, the self-administration of cocaine is so persistent that rats press levers to obtain it until they die of an overdose. In contrast, comparative heroin studies demonstrate that rats can modulate their intake of heroin, with a smaller number dying of an overdose. It is these highly rewarding properties of crack cocaine that result in the progression from recreational use to addiction within weeks or months of first use.

Other problems associated with heavy use of drugs or addiction, such as depression or violence, also impair parenting ability and adversely affect children. Depression may precede or be a consequence of cocaine use. Depression itself, without drug use, has been shown to adversely affect parenting and to result in negative consequences for children.[19] Drug and alcohol use increase the likelihood that a woman will be the victim of violence.[20] Additionally, children of drug users are more likely to witness violence in their homes and to be victims of violence. Concern is mounting that this exposure to violence has serious and long-term implications for children's development, including an inability to pay attention and function in school, impaired emotional stability, and a disoriented perception of the future.[21]

Preschoolers may be especially vulnerable to the effects of traumatic exposure to violence. They are both the most defenseless and the least able to communicate their reactions and fears. Adults tend to deny the impact of violence on young children, assuming either that they will "forget" or that they will not understand.

As part of an ongoing study of young mothers, we evaluated caregiving behaviors in the homes of 35 mothers, two of whom used cocaine.[22] The person conducting the evaluation was unaware of the mothers' drug use.

Case #1

E.J. was the 18-year-old mother of A.J., who was 14 months old at the time of the home visit. They lived in a two-bedroom apartment with E.J.'s three-year-old son, her 19-year-old boyfriend (the father of both children), her mother, and four other maternal family members (three aunts and an eight-year-old cousin). The overwhelming impression upon entering the apartment was one of chaos. E.J. appeared depressed and withdrawn and demonstrated little tolerance for her son's behavior. In general, her involvement and interaction with him was minimal and, at times, she shouted at him or was hostile to him. A.J.'s father and other family members, however, did provide positive stimulation and nurturing for him.

E.J. was asked to teach her son to make a tower of three blocks. Her teaching consisted of saying, "Do this," building a tower of three blocks once, and then returning to her breakfast and cigarette. A.J. played idly with the blocks; after three or four minutes, his three-year-old brother and eight-year-old cousin helped him to build a tower. Finally, A.J.'s father helped as well; it appeared that he wanted his son to succeed.

Two weeks later, A.J. was admitted to the hospital with second- and third-degree burns on his chin and chest. He had pulled a can filled with hot coffee onto himself from the kitchen table. Following an investigation by the state department of social services, A.J. was placed in foster care because of neglect.

Case #2

K.T. is the 17-year-old mother of T.T., a 13-month-old boy at the time of the visit. They live with K.T.'s three-year-old daughter, her mother, and an aunt and uncle. K.T. reported that T.T. rarely saw his father. The active living area of the spacious apartment was a small cramped hallway furnished with a couch and a television. Play materials in the setting were limited.

K.T. was quiet, withdrawn, and appeared depressed during the visit. She reported that, although people were often in the apartment, she generally felt isolated and lonely. She demonstrated limited emotional and verbal responsiveness and little involvement with her child. Many of the positive interactions toward T.T. were provided by his maternal grandmother.

K.T.'s behavior in the teaching interaction (mother teaching her child to build a tower of three blocks) was characterized by a passive and noninteractive style. For example, K.T. allowed her three-year-old daughter to take the blocks from T.T. as she sat by herself looking off into space. Further, K.T. showed minimal positive behaviors such as patting, praising, or smiling in response to the child's performance or even verbally explaining what she wanted T.T. to do.

Similar to his mother, T.T. appeared somewhat withdrawn. Toward the end of the visit, T.T. sought out his grandmother in the next room. It was apparent to the observer that she was an important figure to him. His affect brightened and he appeared more positive with her close by.

Both of these case descriptions show that the mothers' interactions and their ability to nurture their children were limited, but the role of other individuals in the children's lives is important. T.T. received important attention and nurturing from his grandmother. E.J.'s boyfriend, a member of the household, appeared to be an important figure in A.J.'s life. Unfortunately, we do not know whether these individuals used drugs.

Child Protective Agency Responses

Parents who use drugs heavily pose special problems to child protective services. First, child protective service workers—as well as other professionals or individuals—often feel angry with women who use drugs heavily during pregnancy because of the potential damage this may cause the child. Although the feelings of anger are understandable, they can interfere with the practitioner's ability to help these mothers. If a mother senses judgment and criticism, she will not be able to trust the practitioner, and will be less likely to accept help. Even unintentional imposition of moral shame or guilt can be destructive, resulting in denial and increased drug use (to numb the shame). It is important that practitioners or clinicians have a good understanding of their own feelings so that those feelings do not interfere with their professional responsibility to help drug-using mothers and their children.

One way to adjust one's own attitudes is by learning about the disease of addiction and how it affects women and their children. The best method is to speak with women in recovery. Their stories often reveal that they were once children who suffered abuse and that they often grew up with addicted adults. Knowledge of the mother's individual history, and how she got where she is, will foster empathy and understanding and will help the child protective worker or clinician form a therapeutic alliance with the mother. Child protective workers must approach addicted women with empathy and concern, emphasizing the possibility that, with drug treatment, a woman can improve the future for herself and her children.

Because drug-using families tend to experience more chaos and difficulty than others, and may be less able to invest in supportive programs, they often leave child protective workers and other service providers feeling drained, angry, and helpless. Even after recovery is well established, providers often find they may still have to deal with other psychiatric disturbances or comorbidities. This frequently results in feelings of a never-ending struggle— similar to what the mothers feel. If child protective staff are to provide appropriate services, then support strategies must be available. They must have access to good clinical support and supervision so that they can recognize, acknowledge, and look beyond the feelings evoked by their clients.

Second, there are no consistently applicable criteria for measuring the risk of danger to children of drug-using mothers and the necessity of removing the children. The frontline workers making these Solomon-like decisions are usually the least-trained workers in the social welfare or maternal and child health fields. Denial of drug use is a symptom of addiction that further complicates evaluation and decision-making. Child protective workers, pediatricians, public health nurses, and most other professionals do not have the appropriate expertise to determine whether a woman is addicted. Drug-using women should be evaluated and treated by a substance abuse specialist. If the mother is addicted, the child's safety can be assured only if an adult who does not use drugs is in the household and is willing to take care of the child, or if the mother is actively involved in treatment that regularly monitors the child.

Finally, more treatment and family support resources are required to ensure the children's health, safety, and well-being. For infants, such services include adequate nutrition, health care, and early intervention programs; for mothers, they include drug treatment, health care, and family support assistance. While the availability of these services is important, their effectiveness will depend on the way in which they are organized and coordinated. It is difficult for any parent to go to multiple facilities with multiple appointment systems and multiple practitioners; it is especially difficult for someone who is an addict. Treatment and service programs have to be set up for the whole child and the whole family and not to meet the turf needs of the service provider. So-called "linkages" and case management are not enough. Programs need to be integrated, coordinated, and, ideally, located in one place. Our experience with such a program is described below.

Parent/Child-Focused Treatment

Treatment facilities available for substance abusers in general are inadequate, but drug-using women, especially pregnant and parenting women, face additional difficulties in obtaining treatment. Treatment programs were initially designed by and for men, with little attention to the emotional, social, and economic realities of women's lives, especially their interest in, and responsibilities for, their children. Mothers may feel stigmatized by attending drug treatment programs. Many do not come into residential treatment because they do not wish to put their children in foster care, or they are fearful of losing custody of the children. The lack of child day care may even interfere with participation in outpatient treatment. Treatment programs for women and their children must integrate addiction treatment principles with care for the child as well as the mother.

Based on our clinical experience that the best way to help such children is to help their mothers, we developed the Women and Infants' Clinic in 1989. This small pilot project sought to determine if drug treatment could be effectively provided in a pediatric primary care setting. By combining pediatric care, child development services, and drug treatment, the Women and Infants' Clinic is an example of "one-stop shopping," an integration and coordination of services recommended by the National Commission on Infant Mortality. The pediatric primary care clinic was chosen as a setting because it was nonstigmatizing and supported the mothers' interest in their children. In addition to a weekly clinic session, a relapse-prevention group and a mother-child group were implemented on another half-day.

Seventeen consecutive cocaine-using mothers were identified by the hospital staff following the birth of their drug-exposed infants. (Opiate-using mothers were excluded.) The mothers were asked if they wanted to participate in the program. Three were receiving care for their other children in another setting and were therefore not eligible to participate. One woman who abstained from drugs for three months moved back to her country of origin and is not included in the data. Of the remaining 13 mothers, all used crack cocaine three or more times a week during their pregnancy. Eight reported alcohol consumption and three used marijuana. Twelve had a history of physical or sexual abuse or of witnessing a shooting. Four were homeless and three were HIV positive.

The drug therapist played an important role in these women's lives, emphasizing care for their babies as well as for themselves. Key aspects of drug therapy were breaking through denial and helping mothers to identify the triggers to their drug use. Alternative responses to these triggers were discussed. For example, if a mother said she took drugs when she experienced a certain feeling, heard a certain song, or received money, other responses such as calling a friend, a sponsor, or a drug therapist; speaking to a relative; going to church; and so on, were suggested. The drug therapist also provided case management by acting as a liaison with DSS and welfare services, making and reminding the mother of other medical appointments, identifying food pantries, helping the mother obtain Women, Infants, and Children (WIC) benefits and identifying family members who did not use drugs to help the mother and her child. Community resources such as Narcotics Anonymous and Alcoholics Anonymous were recommended. A weekly relapse-prevention group was an important part of the treatment program.

The pediatrician provided preventive health services and monitored the child's health and growth. In addition, the pediatrician helped the mother better understand her infant's behavior and development while supporting the mother's maternal self-image and competency. This was done by asking questions and making observations about the child's behavior, and by emphasizing the infant's competencies and responses to the mother. The pediatrician modeled interactive behavior with the infant and identified and acknowledged the mother's positive caregiving responses.

The weekly mother-child group focused on mother-infant interaction with the goal of strengthening parental attachment and awareness of the infant's needs. By modeling developmentally appropriate interactive behaviors and play, commenting on the infants' play with toys and each other, and modeling language expansion and limit setting, the early childhood educators who ran the group helped the mothers understand the developmental skills, needs, and concerns of the infants as they grew and changed. Parents were encouraged to discuss their children's behaviors and to enjoy books with their children. Birthdays and holidays were celebrated by the group. As the variety of these group experiences grew, the early childhood educators took mothers on field trips to a children's museum, a zoo, and a farm.

Our experience shows that the Women and Infants' Clinic can successfully deliver key services (pediatric care, child development, and drug treatment) to mothers and children in one place; our impression is that this small pilot program has had a significant, positive impact on these clients' lives. Eleven of 13 children are still being cared for by their mothers. After more than a year, all the children have received regular pediatric checkups, preventive care, and immunizations. There have been no injuries requiring the care of a doctor or any reports of child abuse. Three children, two of them HIV positive, were hospitalized but, because they and their mothers were involved in the program and assured of good medical and social follow-up, the hospitalizations were shorter than they would otherwise have been. Only one child, also HIV positive, appears to have a developmental delay. Of the mothers, two have totally abstained from cocaine, nine have had 30- to 90-day periods of abstinence, and two have continued to have uncontrolled drug use. These two women were referred for residential placement. We continue to follow the mothers and their children three years after the birth of the index child.

The apparent short-term success of this program is due to many factors. First, we used the one-stop shopping model, collocating key services so that the mothers were not overwhelmed by having to make and keep multiple appointments in different locations with different staff members. Based on our experience, combining drug treatment and maternal and child health services in one setting is critical.

Second, our emphasis on the children and our support for each mother's interest in her child helped to keep the mothers in the drug treatment program. More than one mother said, "I am doing this for my baby." Our impression is that the healthiest part of these mothers is their interest in their children. When programs emphasize mothers' interest in caring for their children, mothers will also benefit. The birth of a baby provides a special window of opportunity because the mothers feel guilty and want better lives for themselves and their child. Thus, mothers reach "bottom" after, not before, the birth of their child, facilitating their involvement in drug treatment.

Third, the pediatric primary care clinic was a nonstigmatizing setting, making it easy for the mothers to come for care. We believe that most drug treatment settings are stigmatizing to women and thus discourage attendance.

Fourth, a relatively small number of professionals provided all of the services so that the mothers were not overwhelmed by having to deal with many individuals in a variety of subspecialities. Combining the roles of case manager, drug therapist, and pediatric nurse made it easier for the women to feel connected to the program.

Conclusion

Even if the model proves to be successful after replication and systematic evaluation, this type of outpatient program will not meet the needs of all mothers; some will need more intensive treatment such as day or residential treatment. The Women and Infants' Clinic, however, could be considered the first level—least intensive and least expensive—of a community program. It keeps women in the system following the birth of their children and provides them with needed evaluation, treatment, and other services. Because it provides, in effect, an extended diagnostic period, mothers who need more intensive treatment can be identified and referred.

The key aspects of our program and our experience can be adapted to many settings, including Head Start programs and public schools. These settings are nonstigmatizing and child-focused. The clinical focus should also be child-focused; attempts to help the mother should focus on her interest in her child.

The direct involvement of a substance abuse specialist is critical. In a school-related program, for example, the mother could receive drug treatment service during the afternoon in a setting near the school, while her child participates in an after-school program. Prior to going home, a combined parent-child group or activity would take place within the school; on some days, it might include making and sharing a meal together.

Training is also vital. Training and effective treatment can occur together when professionals from different backgrounds work together in one place at the same time. In order to facilitate treatment, substance abuse therapists need training on the importance in the lives of drug-using mothers of their children. Specialists in other fields need to learn about addiction and the treatment of addicted families. This includes nurses, Head Start teachers, pediatricians, obstetricians, and social service workers. These individuals have to know about the disease of addiction and about problems of codependency and enabling behavior on their part. Codependency describes patterns of coping among people who are affected by another person's alcohol or drug abuse. These relationships are unhealthy and are characterized by controlling behavior, low self-esteem, lack of trust and intimacy, and self-destructive behavior. Enabling behavior is any behavior that allows another person's addictive behavior to continue. This includes accepting or making excuses for substance abuse and its consequences, denying such use, and assisting with the buying and storing of drugs or alcohol. Professionals engage in enabling behavior when they fail to acknowledge awareness of a patient's drug or alcohol use.

Drug and alcohol abuse can be severely detrimental to children and parents alike. Treatment for addiction in a child-oriented context provides a singular opportunity for promoting children's development while at the same time helping mothers to overcome their addictions. Unless we help the children today, they will likely become the dysfunctional and addicted parents of tomorrow.

Notes

1. Barry Zuckerman and Deborah A. Frank, "Crack Kids: Not Broken," *Pediatrics* 24, no. 89 (1992): 337–339.

2. Linda Mayes, Richard H. Granger, Marc H. Bornstein, and Barry Zuckerman, "The Problem of Prenatal Cocaine Exposure: A Rush to Judgement," *Journal of the American Medical Association* 267, no. 3 (1992): 406–408.

3. Robert Rosenthal and Lenore Jacobson, *Pygmalion in the Classroom: Teacher Expectation and Pupils' Intellectual Development* (New York: Holt, Rinehart, and Winston, 1968).

4. Barry Zuckerman and Karen Bresnahan, "Developmental and Behavioral Consequences of Prenatal Drug and Alcohol Exposure," *Pediatric Clinics of North America* 38 (1991): 1387–1405.

5. *Ibid.,* 1385.

6. Arnold Sameroff and Michael Chandler, "Reproductive Risk and the Continuum of Caretaking Casualty," in *Review of Child Development Research*, ed. Frances Horowitz, E. Mavis Heatherington, Sandra Scarr-Fallatek, and Gerald M. Siegel (Chicago: University of Chicago Press, 1975), 187–244.

7. Zuckerman and Bresnahan, 1392.

8. Barry Zuckerman, Deborah Frank, Ralph Hingson, Hortensia Amaro, Suzette Levenson, Herbert Cayne, Steven Parker, Robert Vinci, Kwabena Aboagye, Lise Fried, Howard Cabral, Ralph Timperi, and Howard Barchner, "The Effects of Maternal Marijuana and Cocaine Use on Fetal Growth," *New England Journal of Medicine* 322, no.17 (1989): 1202–1206.

9. Deborah Frank, Karen Bresnahan, and Barry Zuckerman, "Maternal Cocaine Use: Impact on Child Health and Development," *Advances in Pediatrics* 40 (1993): 65–99.

10. Elizabeth Brown and Barry Zuckerman, "The Infant and the Drug-Using Mother," *Pediatric Annals* 20 (1991): 555–563.

11. Ira J. Chasnoff, Dan Griffith, Kathryn Frier, and James Murray, "Cocaine/Polydrug Use in Pregnancy: Two-Year Follow-Up," *Pediatrics* 89 (1992): 284–289; Ira J. Chasnoff, "Outcome of Children Prenatally Exposed to Cocaine and Other Drugs: A Path Analysis of Three-Year Data," *Pediatrics* 92 (1993): 396–402.

12. Carol Rodning, Leila Beckwith, and Judy Howard, "Characteristics of Attachment Organization and Play Organization in Prenatally Drug-Exposed Toddlers," *Development and Psychopathology* 1 (1990): 277–289.

13. Geraldine S. Wilson, "Clinical Studies of Infants and Children Exposed Prenatally to Heroin," *Annals of the New York Academy of Science* 562 (1989): 183–194.

14. Pamela Bauman and Frank Dougherty, "Drug-Addicted Mothers: Parenting and Their Children's Development," *International Journal of Addictions* 18 (1983): 291–302; Victor Bernstein, Rita Jeruchimowicz, Sydney Mans, and Joseph Marcus, "A Longitudinal Study of Offspring Born to Methadone-Maintained Women: 11 Dyadic Interaction and Infant Behavior at Four Months," *American Journal of Drug and Alcohol Abuse* 10 (1984): 161–193; Kathleen Fiks, Helen Johnson, and Tove Rosen, "Methadone-Maintained Mothers: Three-Year Follow-Up of Parental Functioning," *International Journal of Addictions* 20 (1985): 651–60.

15. Fiks, Johnson, and Rosen, 651–660.

16. Peter Park, "Problem Drinking and Role Deviation: A Study in Incipient Alcoholism," in *Society, Culture, and Drinking Patterns*, ed. David Pittman and Charles Snyder (New York: John Wiley and Sons, 1962); Jan Bays, "Substance Abuse and Child Abuse: Impact of Addiction on the Child," *Pediatric Clinics of North America*

37, no. 4 (1990): 881–904; Daniel W. Behling, "Alcohol Abuse as Encountered in 51 Instances of Reported Child Abuse," *Clinical Pediatrics* 18, no. 2 (1979): 87–91; Sandra J. Kaplan, David Pelcovitz, Suzanne Salzinger, and David Ganeles, "Psychopathology of Parents of Abused and Neglected Children and Adolescents," *Journal of the American Academy of Child Psychiatry* 3 (1983): 238–244; Juan Casado-Flores, Antonio Bano-Rodrigo, and Encarnacion Romero, "Social and Medical Problems in Children of Heroin-Addicted Parents: A Study of 75 Parents," *American Journal of Diseases of Children* 144 (1990): 977–979.

17. Karen Bresnahan and Barry Zuckerman, "Cocaine Use: Impact on Child and Mother," *Pediatric Nursing* 17 (1991): 128.

18. Deborah Frank, Barry Zuckerman, Hortensia Amaro, Kwabena Aboagye, Howard Bauchner, Howard Cabral, Lise Fried, Ralph Hingson, Herbert Cayne, Suzette M. Levenson, Steven Parker, Hillary Reece, and Robert Vinci, "Cocaine Use during Pregnancy: Prevalence and Correlates," *Pediatrics* 82 (1988): 888-895.

19. Barry Zuckerman and William Beardslee, "Maternal Depression: A Concern for Pediatricians," *Pediatrics* 17 (1987): 128.

20. Hortensia Amaro, Lise Fried, Howard Cabral, and Barry Zuckerman, "Violence during Pregnancy and Substance Use," *American Journal of Public Health* 80 (1990): 575–579.

21. Betsy Groves, Barry Zuckerman, Stanley Marans, and D.J. Coen, "Silent Victims: Children Who Witness Violence," *Journal of the American Medical Association* 269 (1993): 262–264.

22. Scott Greer, Howard Bauchner, and Barry Zuckerman, unpublished data.

 **4**

VICTIMS TO VICTIMIZERS

Edwin Delattre

It is in and through each other's lives that we form our sense of who we are, of what is worthy of us, of the habits of life upon which we can rely, of the significance of the lives and rights and feelings of others, of our prospects and possibilities, of our duties, and of our own personal dignity.

For this reason, Aristotle said over 2,000 years ago, "It is a matter of real importance whether our early education confirms in us one set of habits or another. It would be nearer the truth," he wrote, "to say it makes a very great difference indeed, in fact all the difference in the world."[1] "Traditions of civility," Walter Lippmann added in our own century, "are not carried in our genes," and children who live in schools, streets, and homes made perilous and savage by drugs are excluded from those traditions.

All of us are creatures of habit, for better or for worse, and most of our habits are formed by, or at least rooted in, the deep human capacity for imitation. Thus, one of the greatest of twentieth-century teachers, Gilbert Highet, observed that it is impossible to teach children who are allowed to run free, left to their own devices, without restraint or benevolent guidance, in bad surroundings. The behavior they imitate and the habits they form frequently pose insurmountable obstacles to systematic learning, including the acquisition of a reliable sense of self-interest.

It is perhaps unnecessary to describe the forms of deprivation and depravity to which the young are subject in surroundings where levels of illegal drug consumption and drug trafficking are high—where the environment is out of control, streets are unsafe, schools are in disarray, and homes—including those in which adults benumb themselves with drugs—provide no refuge.

Suffice it to say that, where we can see children of drug-addicted teenage prostitutes prowling the streets in the midnight hours, crawling through garbage in search of food, we cannot decently tolerate such stark neglect. Where we see the prostitutes who are scarcely beyond childhood themselves, convinced by their ruthless pimps that only men can transmit or be afflicted with AIDS, we cannot continue to permit death to stalk the young unopposed.

Where we can see children abandoned in crack houses and tenement hallways, while their parent or parents hustle the streets for money to support drug habits; where we can find children hiding under the covers on a bed while a parent sells sex for drugs; where we hear the children begging their teachers at school not to send them home; where we can see children drawn or forced into the drug traffic by urban gangs and more sophisticated criminal organizations—children who are, for all real purposes, finished with formal schooling before they are teenagers; where we can see children as young as six or seven left at home to care for their younger siblings in conditions of hunger and unremitting ignorance, we cannot continue to abide such blatant mistreatment.

We cannot responsibly hope or suppose that these children will form habits that contribute to healthy self-reliance, emotional and physical health, spiritual strength, or anything resembling happiness. From them, the blessings of liberty that our country is intended to secure for each individual are—and threaten to remain—terribly, frighteningly, absolutely remote.

Blessings for each individual. But even our own individuality, as philosopher Edmund Pincoffs explains, depends on and "makes sense only against a background of social organization." "There is," he adds, "no human situation that consists of an aggregate of unrelated individuals. We are social beings. We come into a world that is already organized; we are creatures of organization; we live in each other's lives; we understand ourselves through our reflection in the perceptions of others; we die in the lives of others."[2]

Where the organization of a dwelling or a block, a neighborhood or a city, or a society itself falls under the dominion of drugs, children die. Where children are subjected to the destruction of the social fabric by the ravages of drug trafficking and consumption, their circumstances are at best grim and at worst deadly. The social organization they enter, even before birth, can, and often does, ruin or kill them.

The horrors of children betrayed, tortured, sold into sexual exploitation for the price of a crack rock or a speedball, are perhaps best summarized by a situation I encountered on the streets of Philadelphia.

There, two years ago, three brothers, ages 12, 10, and nine, were taken to a rubbish-strewn lot near their inner-city tenement. The two older boys were shot to death by teenage drug dealers; the nine-year-old escaped when the murder weapon jammed.

He told police at a nearby precinct station of the murder, and explained that he and his two brothers had been given drugs to sell the night before. But their mother had stolen and used the drugs while her sons slept, so the boys could not pay the dealers. They told the dealers that they had been ripped off on the street, but drug traffickers will not believe that tale even when it is true.

When police took the surviving child to his mother and told her of the death of her other sons, her first words were, "If they're dead, where do I get my crack?" Such is the moral standing of children who depend on adults whose lives have been traded away into bondage to drugs. Such are the habits children and youths are invited to imitate, and such is the barrenness of expectation they are offered—by the very people who are most deeply obligated to deserve their love and their trust.

Many such children are largely bereft of exposure to genuinely honorable men—men who take responsibility seriously, who will not abuse women and children, who do not abandon their helpless offspring and ignore parental obligations, and who set standards of fidelity and durable commitment, rather than of promiscuity, within the community. Most children in drug-ravaged settings do not meet enough men—and do not begin to appreciate the women they know—who are secure in their dignity, not threatened by every real or imagined affront, and who rise above pettiness and disproportionate violence in the conduct of daily life.

When these youths believe that someone is "dissin'" them—treating them or their intimates with disrespect—they react. Unable to redress real or imagined affronts with words, without any conception of arbitration by a disinterested and trustworthy party, and mistakenly convinced that their dignity depends entirely on how other people see and treat them, they counter violently. Lacking experience and the desire to temper their reactions to fit the offense, some of them kill. Lethal violence is simpler, reduces the risk of reprisal, and establishes a reputation they believe to be a deterrent to future disrespect. Some of them, of course, acquire a taste for savagery for its own sake; violence, like drugs, hurries their blood, and they grow to like it.

They are tragically deprived of the greatest insights of every human culture in history about personal dignity and accomplishment. Few will learn of Frederick Douglass' insistence, when he was subjected to discrimination, that those who mistreated him besmirched only themselves. Of Rosa Parks, few have heard, or of the kindred courage of Eleazar in defense of the young. Too many are like the six-year-old daughter Martin Luther King, Jr., described in his "Letter from the Birmingham City Jail." Excluded from an amusement park advertised on television because of her race, she had, as King saw, "clouds of inferiority forming in her little mental sky."[3]

What they do learn has an odd kind of coherence to it, very unlike the coherence we have in mind when we speak of a "coherent" curriculum in a school. They learn much about how to harm others and how to get what they want—which often amount to the same thing—but very little about how to do good for themselves or others. In a year, some of them grab enough dirty money through criminal activities to leave the inner city forever; they could easily pay for remedial education or college tuition. Of course, that does not happen—because they have no purposeful long-term vision and thus spend the money on impulse. As one of them said to me, "I just live until I dies."

It is scarcely surprising that children so deprived commonly become their own worst enemies. Philippe Bourgois, who lives and conducts ethnographic research in East Harlem, explains that many of the young in his neighborhood who sell drugs on the streets are able to make a bit more than minimum wage "without having to demean themselves in [legal] jobs they believe compromise their sense of dignity." They drop out of school to enter the crack traffic or, as they say, "to get some of mine's."[4]

There is a special kind of heartache in witnessing the lives of young people whose sense of dignity is so confused that it can be satisfied only by the ruthless exploitation of others even more helpless than they. When I am in their company, I sometimes recall my own early job experience. My first job was in a dairy, when I was 13. My daily task was to put sticks in thousands of popsicles. It was boring, and companionship on the job did not relieve the boredom. It was no affront to my dignity, though, perhaps because I knew that I would not be confined to such work for very long.

For children and youths without such prospects or at least some awareness of them, the allure of essentially depraved criminal organizations can be overwhelming. Not long ago, my research brought me together with several uniformed and plainclothes police, in a chilling fog, outside the main entrance to a multistory tenement. Few lights penetrated the late-night darkness as the police prepared to execute a warrant to search an apartment inside. They believed the apartment to be a stopover place for members of one of the most savage drug-trafficking gangs in America, a leading Jamaican posse.

Then, up the stairs quickly they went, pounding on the door with shouts of "Open up! Police! Open the door! We have a warrant!" No one stood in front of the door for fear of gunfire, but the door was quickly opened, and a fast search of the three rooms revealed only two women, both high on crack. The high did not last through 15 minutes of questioning, although one of the women lapsed into mumbling incoherence.

Coming up the stairs, the smell of our own sweat mingled with the odors of tenement hallways—urine, vomit, garbage, and moldy, crumbling plaster. But entering the apartment, we were struck in the face by a staggering odor of filth and decay. It blurred our eyes.

We learned that the apartment had been used by Jamaican gang members transporting drugs. But the bathroom had not worked for many days—and the sink, toilet, floor, and bathtub were covered with excrement and befouled paper towels. The floor was a soggy swamp of waste that no one was willing to search by hand.

The living room, littered with drug paraphernalia and broken-down furniture, was dimly lit by two bare light bulbs. Oilcloth covered a window, and rotting food, fist-size piles of roach droppings, and crusted stains of semen marked the bed and sofa.

The kitchen sink and counter were piled with dirty dishes wedged all the way up to the cupboards overhead. Touch one dish and the whole congealed tower might tumble down. The freezer door above the refrigerator would not close, and the freezer, running constantly, was filled with one huge block of ice dripping blackened icicles from its face.

Roaches fed on garbage—castoff chunks of fast food—everywhere, on table and counter, refrigerator and floor. They seemed fearless. There were ratholes in the walls and the noises of rats could be heard close by.

One of the women was seated, by now crying; the other flopped, limp against the wall. On a closer look, past scanty clothes as dirty as their surroundings, we could see that they were not women at all, but girls. We learned that they were prostitutes—a fact already known to one of the police—paid to let posse members stay in their place. Their lives obviously revolved around drugs; the police would not arrest them; and the girl being questioned could not conceal that she was shrewdly calculating how much to say in order to satisfy the police and hasten their departure without risking gang reprisal against herself.

Their faces recalled me to Dickens' description of the "heavy darkness" of the slums, and of "the mill that grinds young people old," the mill of "cold, dirt, sickness, ignorance, and want," by which children's faces are made "ancient" and their voices, "grave."[5]

The girl struck a deal for information with the officer questioning her, a threat and a promise were exchanged, and we left. A tenement hallway never smelled so clean. When we hit the streets again, we were less than ten minutes by car from the White House, the Congress, the Supreme Court of the United States, and the beautifully sculpted words on the inner wall of the Lincoln Memorial that celebrate the United States as a country "conceived in liberty and dedicated to the proposition that all men are created equal."

Lincoln's words are not what the city has taught those girls—and countless other girls and boys like them. Criminals such as posse members often achieve hero status in the eyes of inner-city youths. By acquiring wealth and power through ruthlessness, these criminals seem to possess a secret, a shortcut, to fame, fortune, and pleasure.

The shortcut, the quick fix, has enormous appeal for any youth who is a chronic loser, a failure in school, bereft of decent adult male companionship and conversation at home—and sometimes of decent adult female companionship as well. But individual ruthlessness takes daring, even rashness and, for this reason, youths (like adults) who want shortcuts often band together to commit wrongs in greater security and safety.

Not surprisingly, then, youths form and join urban gangs whose levels of behavior seldom rise above the depravity of their meanest and most unlawful members. "Mobocracy," writes columnist Sidney J. Harris, "is the heroism of cowards."[6]

Robert Jackson and Wesley McBride, longtime gang enforcement officers, explain that the tendency of such youths toward remorseless wrongdoing rises in part from their conviction that they are themselves victims of an evil society. When law enforcement authorities and mothers of delinquents come into contact with each other, mothers often make excuses for the children, in "the form of accusations against society in general. Thus, children are taught early that they are not responsible for their actions…By the time the youngsters reach their mid-teens…they truly believe that they are victims and that they have the absolute right, if not the duty, to do whatever they want, whenever they want."[7]

Often their vision of the world succumbs to what Bertrand Russell called "the fallacy of the superior virtue of the oppressed." This way of thinking—that anyone treated badly by another is thereby proven to have personal merit—destroys responsible self-appraisal and thwarts aspiration.

I doubt that anything worse in the way of education can befall girls and boys than to be taught that they are mere victims of society. Such teaching, however well-intentioned or grounded in desperation it may be, diminishes children in their own eyes to such a degree that a realistic and hopeful sense of their own real possibilities for achievement and decency—and for happiness—may be forever obscured to them. Parents and others who thwart youthful aspiration in this way famish the best of human nature within their children. The consequences threaten always to be dreadful, because, as C.S. Lewis rightly explained to teachers, "famished nature will be avenged."[8]

Still, it is impossible to deny that much of what every child born into civilized society deserves as a birthright is denied these children. And, it is both conceptually and practically impossible to believe that children who have been treated as though adults owe them nothing should themselves feel that they owe very much to any other human being.

We cannot find surprising the contempt for others that many of these children feel, however shocking it may be. The refrains are everywhere. Carl Taylor of Jackson Community College has listened to them on the streets of Detroit: "I know that marriage is for suckers...If I get a bitch pregnant, she can go have it or whatever else she want, 'cause the kid don't give a shit. Didn't nobody care about me when I was a baby and I came out cool, so what's the big deal?...If you know a bitch, why marry her? You already got her...When you tired of a bitch [bleep] her and kick her ass to the curb...That's what my old man did to my momma." And Taylor has heard what many of us have listened to throughout the country, a young person saying, "I hate it when I see people walking around happy."[9]

In fact, in the very worst cases, where children are neglected from infancy, we cannot help but see the similarities between them and Helen Keller, whose early learning was blighted by sensory deprivation and exclusion from a community of language users. As Keller herself wrote, "When we walk in a valley of twofold solitude we know little of the tender affections that grow out of endearing words and action and companionship...In the still, dark world in which I lived," she continued, "there was no strong sentiment or tenderness." But she was, as she put it, "restored to her human heritage" by learning words and their meanings. Language, she wrote, "awakened my soul, gave it light, hope, joy, set it free."[10] There was more, of course: Helen Keller learned how much she was loved, and from this she learned both repentance and sorrow.

Crimes of neglect, abandonment, and drug exposure against innocent children even bear resemblance to what Roger Shattuck has called "the forbidden experiment"—depriving a child of all instruction and guidance in order to discover what would become of it, what nature makes without nurture. Children, such as the nineteenth century's Wild Boy of Aveyron, suggest the answer.

That boy, who walked out of a forest at the apparent age of 11 or 12, was later named Victor. Despite the dedication of his teachers thereafter, he never acquired "the enterprise or the imagination to challenge himself to be other than what he was...[and] fell back again into listlessness as soon as he was left to his own devices." Shattuck adds, "The meaning of his life was to stay alive, and he lived that meaning without being aware of it in any sense we conceive of when we use words...Partially because he could not easily conceive of other states of mind outside his own, Victor could not reach a point of view from which other persons' lives and happiness had reality and importance for him." Shattuck draws the right parallel: "A really destitute and neglected slum child, in 1800 or today, is no better nourished than the Wild Boy." All of them are dispossessed of their birthrights—and of the place within a community that every newborn child deserves without qualification.[11]

Shattuck asks, "Was it just too late to reeducate the boy?" He suspects that the answer is yes, and adds, "We could well say that it was just too late for Victor to assemble, become conscious of, and enact an idea of his *self,* of his identity as a separate person. The imagery of sleep that surrounds the Wild Boy stands for the incompleteness of his self-awareness; he never fully awoke to his individual existence."[12]

The lesson of such historical examples—confirmed with a vengeance by what we can see and hear wherever children are dispossessed in our own time—is that it is cruel and sometimes futile to try to do for children at the age of 11 or 12 or in the teen years what should, and could easily have been done in infancy and the preschool years. In practice, it is unconscionable to wait so long to rescue children from conditions that destroy them.

To anything resembling such a condition of existence, we have, as a people, an unconditional obligation to provide alternatives. In the first place, we must reclaim the streets from criminal savagery; take possession of schools currently wracked by drugs and violence; and prevent the suffering of the young who are exposed to parental drug consumption and dependency. In the second place, we must provide for prenatal care, for the highest quality instructional child care in the preschool years, and for the continuing education of illiterate and unemployable parents, including instruction by apprenticeship in child care itself. Bourgois puts the point succinctly:

[All children deserve] streets where they do not have to witness gunfights; hot and cold running water in their homes; heat at recreation centers; public safety officers who do not curse at them when they stand on the corner; child care that is not abusive; schools where they do not have to peer through the keyhole of the bathroom before entering for fear of being raped; principals and teachers who do not smoke crack; regular garbage pickups and mail deliveries; abandoned buildings that are either renovated or ripped down rather than left standing for years; a local economy and job structure that is not perversely distorted by narco-dollars; and supervisors in the entry-level economy who do not subject them to cultural ridicule because of their inner-city ethnic identity.[13]

But these imperatives will not be met everywhere. Failures of nerve and will, as well as of resources, will persist. And evil, as Aristotle rightly observed, remains inevitable. It is not plausible that every child can be provided the birthrights of humanity without our providing alternative safe havens and even long-term placement programs of the most professional quality.

Certainly, the dedication and fortitude of many adults who currently try to safeguard children from exposure to drug use in the home and drug trafficking on the streets command enormous admiration and respect. Child care providers, teachers, church members, drug treatment professionals, and police frequently do everything humanly possible for children in circumstances that remain overwhelming. Grandparents and great-grandparents often echo the words of a 68-year-old great-grandmother named Mary, described by Linda M. Burton of Pennsylvania State University. Mary cares for the eight children of her 36-year-old drug-addicted daughter, four of whom are mentally or physically handicapped: "I ain't no different than any of the other grandmommas in my neighborhood that has a dopehead for a kid. We all have to take care of our children's mistakes. If we don't, ain't nobody else gonna do it. Who cares how it affects us? I'm real sick. I got heart trouble and diabetes. I'm tired myself. But there ain't nobody else to do it...I done lost one child to dope. I ain't letting her babies get lost too."[14]

In circumstances where the needs and demands of the young are betrayed by adults, or where those needs outstrip the strength and the health of those who are devoted to them, or where the spirit is willing and the love is boundless but age and weariness have taken an irreversible toll, we will sometimes have to provide, from the beginning, a very different environment. We owe children an environment that enables them to learn good habits by practice, encouragement, example, and loving instruction. Fed, clothed, housed, safeguarded from disease and rapacity, provided with opportunities for play that inspire curiosity and sharing, children can reach toward the life, liberty, and pursuit of happiness that so many grandparents are desperately seeking to provide.

Children still need safe havens, even after they have reached their teenage years, even though they know a great deal about sex, violence, drugs, and the dark side of human nature. They need places that give them a chance to grow up, to learn to take themselves and their abilities seriously. We need to give them such places in their own neighborhoods—boys' clubs, girls' clubs, and other comparable safe places to go that will provide them with supervision, guidance, and encouragement.

When I was president of St. John's College in Santa Fe, New Mexico, the Boys' Club was feeding a thousand boys and girls a day in the summer, offering them the best places for play and safe, healthy, instructive activities. At the college, we were offering bilingual storytelling hours, reading programs, outdoor activities, and the like.

The circumstances of many of these children were perceptibly improved by such refuges from unsafe homes and streets. Safe havens belong everywhere that children are in real danger, for as many hours as they can be sustained.

Where we cannot provide the young with such havens, where the conditions are simply uncontrollable, we will have to face the question of residential facilities located away from their neighborhoods. In educationally sound group facilities—boarding schools and preschools, if you like, orphanages, if you prefer—they will learn to read, listen, write, and speak. They will learn the habits of self-discipline that promote safety and contentment, in the company of adults they can trust to be loving, attentive, temperate, honest, fair, compassionate, and dedicated to their well-being.

This will not be easy to do well. We will need to pay attention to the experiences of the best boarding schools, group homes, child care centers, kibbutzim, summer camps, and outdoor programs in existence. We will be challenged to provide the necessary education and training for the personnel of such facilities—and to provide the linkages to colleges, universities, and employers essential to the children's later opportunities.

Long-term placement of children in such settings will not be cheap, and it will not be without powerful opposition, including charges of interference with parental rights, racism, undermining the ethnic and cultural heritage of minorities, sexism, and tyranny. I am not unsympathetic with the fears and concerns that lie behind such charges, and I believe we are obligated to make sure that they never come true.

I view long-term placement as a last resort in social policy, but not as a step to be taken late in the life of a child imperiled by parental drug use and a hostile environment from which the child cannot be protected. Deciding to undertake long-term placement in the name of the birthrights of the young is a judgment of the most profound consequence, but when we have due regard for the fact that we become who we are in each other's lives, then, as others have said before me, "the ordeal of judgment cannot be shirked."[15]

Notes

1. J.A.K. Thomson, trans., *The Ethics of Aristotle: The Nicomachaean Ethics Translated*, 2.1 (Hammondsworth, Middlesex, England: Penguin Books, Ltd., 1953, 1958), 56.

2. Edmund L. Pincoffs, *Quandaries and Virtues: Against Reductivism in Ethics* (Lawrence, KS: University Press of Kansas, 1986), 7, 8.

3. Martin Luther King, Jr., "Letter from Birmingham Jail," in *A Testament of Hope: The Essential Writings of Martin Luther King, Jr.*, ed. James M. Washington (San Francisco, CA: Harper & Row, Publishers, 1987), 293.

4. Philippe Bourgois, "Growing Up: What Opportunities for the Young?" *The American Enterprise* (May/June 1991): 31.

5. Charles Dickens, *A Tale of Two Cities* (London: Oxford University Press, 1970), 28.

6. Sidney J. Harris, "Gangs Make Martyrs of Losers," in *Understanding Street Gangs*, ed. Robert K. Jackson and Wesley D. McBride (Placerville, CA: Custom Publishing Company, Fifth Printing, 1990), 1.

7. *Ibid.*, 11.

8. C. S. Lewis, *The Abolition of Man* (New York: MacMillan Publishing Company, Inc., 1947, Thirteenth Printing, 1975), 24.

9. Carl S. Taylor, *Dangerous Society* (East Lansing, MI: Michigan State University Press, 1990), 43–60.

10. Helen Keller, *The Story of My Life* (New York: Airmont Publishing Co., Inc., 1965), 18–21.

11. Roger Shattuck, *The Forbidden Experiment: The Wild Boy of Aveyron* (New York: Washington Square Press, 1981), 63, 65, 170, 198.

12. *Ibid.*, 188.

13. Bourgois, 33.

14. Linda M. Burton, "Caring for Children: Drug Shifts and Their Impact on Families," *The American Enterprise* (May/June 1991): 35, 36.

15. *Trop v. Dulles*, 356 U.S. 86 (1958).

Section 2:

Treating Drug-Addicted Mothers

 *5*

A COMPREHENSIVE PUBLIC HEALTH APPROACH

Richard S. Schottenfeld
Richard R. Viscarello
Judy Grossman
Lorraine V. Klerman
Steven F. Nagler
Jean A. Adnopoz

Drug use is highest among the populations under age 45, so that the vast majority of the drug addicts or those most in need of drug treatment are of child-rearing age. Many are already parents.[1] Despite the large number of drug abusers who are parents, protecting children has not traditionally been a major focus of drug treatment. Even the incidence of child abuse by drug abusers was not routinely reported by many drug treatment programs until changes in federal confidentiality guidelines eliminated the conflict between them and state child abuse reporting requirements.

Rather than being family-centered and oriented toward supporting appropriate parenting and improved family functioning, drug treatment programs have historically been oriented toward males functioning outside of family roles. They have also focused on the individual as drug user because they were designed primarily to support the goal of abstinence or reduction in alcohol and illicit drug use. In theory, other goals of drug treatment include reduction in criminal activity and improved vocational, medical, psychological, and social (including family and parenting) functioning. In practice, however, few treatment resources are devoted to these goals.

One concrete example of the lack of attention paid to assessing the ability of drug users to parent or protect their children is the Addiction Severity Index (ASI). The most widely used clinical assessment instrument, the ASI devotes only part of one item out of 123 to assessing problems between drug users and their children.

The recent cocaine epidemic and the accompanying changes in the demographics of drug users are primarily responsible for the current interest in protecting the families and children of drug users. The large number of cocaine users includes many women who bear primary responsibility for child-rearing. Media reports of the devastating effects of cocaine use during pregnancy, of parental desertion, and of abuse of children by parents binging on cocaine have contributed to the concern about the children of drug abusers.

Although drug-abusing pregnant women should receive the highest priority for services, the reality is that they are often excluded from treatment. An estimated 105,000 pregnant women are in need of drug treatment annually, while only about 30,000 currently receive it.[2] Many hospitals report having no place to refer pregnant women for drug treatment. Many programs do not accept pregnant women because of inadequate medical resources and concern about liability.

Most drug addicts do not intend to harm their children and are not deliberately indifferent to their needs. In fact, they often experience enormous shame and guilt about the problems their drug use causes their children and actively strive to retain care of them. Compulsive drug users continue to use drugs despite the adverse consequences, however, simply because loss of control over the impulse to use is one of the characteristics of drug dependence.

These facts provide the framework for this paper. Since treatment must be based on an understanding of the causes and consequences of addiction, the first section of this paper presents three models of the etiology and perpetuation of addictions, thus delineating the principles underlying drug treatment.

The second section describes family-centered treatment programs. Since treating drug-using women and protecting children of drug users are relatively new objectives of treatment programs, controlled studies have not yet documented which treatments are most effective, what services are or are not necessary, or what outcomes can be expected from different treatments for the wide spectrum of drug-using parents. This is a particular problem with regard to cocaine abuse treatment, which has been less intensively studied than treatment for heroin addiction.

The paper concludes with a discussion of a community-based approach to protecting the children of parents who use drugs heavily.

Models of Addiction

Medical, behavioral, and social models are often invoked to understand the etiology and perpetuation of addictions.

The Medical Model

The medical model stresses the importance of (1) genetic factors that predispose persons to addiction, (2) the addictive properties of the drug itself, (3) the lasting central nervous system changes caused by drug use (protracted abstinence syndromes), and (4) the use of drugs to self-medicate depression, anxiety, irritability, rage, or other dysphoric or intolerable affects or emotional states. Treatments based on the medical model include the use of medications to block the rewarding effects of drugs, to relieve acute withdrawal and protracted abstinence syndromes, and to treat underlying psychiatric disorders.

The Behavioral Model

According to the behavioral model, both classical and operant conditioning contribute to addiction and high rates of relapse. Drug use is strongly reinforced because of its pharmacologic effects on pleasure and reward centers in the brain (operant conditioning). Each dose of a drug produces some level of euphoria (positive reinforcement), and, after the initial dose, subsequent doses counter the "crash" or dysphoric state associated with rapidly decreasing drug levels or withdrawal (negative reinforcement). In a classical conditioning model (Pavlovian conditioning), drug craving can be triggered by exposure to conditioned cues (situations, events, places, drug paraphernalia, as well as positive and negative emotional states associated with drug use). Treatments based on a behavioral model include contingency contracting (in which rewards are achieved for remaining abstinent while negative consequences result from drug use) and relapse prevention training.[3]

In relapse prevention training, patients are taught to identify (1) high-risk situations for using drugs, (2) the role of conditioned cues and other factors in precipitating craving, (3) cognitive processes that are likely to lead to relapse, and (4) coping skills and techniques to avoid relapse.

The Social Model

The social model emphasizes the importance of drug availability, peer pressure, and social stress. As dependence becomes more pronounced, the drug user abandons social and vocational roles that might otherwise serve as alternative sources of enjoyment and satisfaction. Those who use drugs most heavily often isolate themselves from contact with family members or peers who do not use drugs. In treatment, those attempting to reduce drug dependency are encouraged to terminate contact with their drug-using peers, relatives, or dealers, since contact with them will likely lead to relapse. Community reinforcement (which fosters involvement in socially productive and rewarding activities that compete with drug use), fellowship activities, and self-help groups are some of the principal treatment approaches used to deal with social determinants of relapse.

Treatment of Drug Dependency

Because drug addiction and relapse result from a combination of medical, behavioral, and social factors, optimal treatment often involves a combination of pharmacological, behavioral, and psychosocial interventions.

Pharmacological Interventions

Pharmacological interventions for addictive disorders are generally targeted to achieve one or more of the following objectives: (1) block, diminish, or reverse the "high" or acute effects of drug use; (2) manage symptoms associated with intoxication (e.g., cocaine-induced paranoid psychosis); (3) manage withdrawal; (4) block or diminish craving; (5) ameliorate symptoms associated with protracted abstinence; and (6) treat underlying psychiatric disorders that might otherwise contribute to the likelihood of relapse.[4] In the treatment of opiate addiction, for example, methadone maintenance prevents opiate withdrawal and, at a high enough daily dose, also blocks the euphoric effects of heroin (cross-tolerance); craving for heroin diminishes markedly since the heroin high is blocked, and heroin is effectively "not available." Naltrexone (a pure opiate blocker), and disulfiram (which deters alcohol abuse because users know that ingesting alcohol will lead to severe headache, flushing, and protracted vomiting) are useful when patients are compliant with the medication. Unfortunately, no effective substitute maintenance agents or blockers of cocaine intoxication are currently available. The development of a cocaine-blocking agent would modestly improve cocaine treatment. Treatment could then be further enhanced if medication were coupled with other approaches. Strategies to improve compliance and to prevent dropout early in the intervention play a critical role in improving the effectiveness of pharmacological blockage and pharmacotherapy in general.

Psychological Interventions

Behavioral and psychosocial interventions can be used alone or to enhance pharmacological treatments. Psychosocial interventions for drug abusers are based on an understanding of the precipitants of drug use and relapse and the factors associated with sustained abstinence, including (1) involvement in productive social and family roles and leisure activities; (2) alternative sources of satisfaction and positive, health promoting experiences; (3) commitment to spiritual or religious values; (4) desire for abstinence; (5) repair of medical and social damage caused by addiction; (6) restoration of self-esteem and competency; and (7) prolonged supervised probation (monitoring with negative contingencies for return to drug use).[5]

Structural Interventions

Structural interventions, such as confinement in a hospital, residential therapeutic community, home, or prison, may be necessary to (1) initiate abstinence; (2) safeguard suicidal, psychotic, or violent patients; (3) remove a patient from social pressures fostering cocaine use; and (4) initiate rehabilitation and social reintegration into drug-free activities and groups. Repeated failures in outpatient treatment programs may indicate a need for confinement and more intensive interventions.

Hospitalization or residential treatment, however, may have a devastating impact on the children of drug abusers. Few residential programs have the capacity to treat entire families or to house children, and there are long waiting lists to enter programs that offer these services. Consequently, residential treatment usually requires that children be separated from their parents. All too often, siblings are separated from each other. Although parenting by drug addicts may not be optimal, disruption of parent-child and sibling relationships may cause even greater harm to children. Thus, there is an urgent need to increase the capacity of family-centered residential treatment programs.

Less intensive structural interventions include day treatment or partial hospitalization programs. These programs can be enhanced when they offer child care together with parent support and education, use community reinforcement approaches that foster drug-free social interactions, and provide access to supervised, drug-free housing and other incentives for abstinence.

Family-Centered Treatment Programs

Treatment for drug-abusing parents must encompass the drug abuser's role as a parent, taking into consideration the developmental needs of both parent and child as well as the quality of the parent-child interactions. Because the most severely drug-dependent parents suffer from problems in multiple domains, interventions must involve the family, the social network, and the community, in addition to the individual drug-using parent and the child. Thus, treatment for the most severely drug-dependent parents and their children requires a multifaceted approach. This can be attempted within standard drug treatment programs, but the chances of success are probably enhanced when specialized programs are developed.

Within Drug Treatment Programs

In many communities, enhancing services within existing drug treatment programs to improve the parenting skills of drug abusers may be the only way of protecting their children. The need for such family-centered drug treatment programs was shown by the results of a recent survey by the APT Foundation.[6] About 10 percent of the more than 500 women active in the unit's methadone clinics and cocaine program were asked about their need for and interest in child-oriented services. Of the 58 respondents, 95 percent had children, 62 percent had children five years old or younger (66 percent had children over age five), and 85 percent had custody of their children. Eighty percent of the children under age five were cared for by their mother at home during the day. Only 16 percent of the women were married and living with their spouse, another 23 percent lived with a partner, and 61 percent were single parents. Thirty percent reported being the victims of childhood physical or sexual abuse.

Many of the women reported being concerned about some aspect of their children's lives, citing behavior (32 percent), health (27 percent), and learning ability (27 percent). Twenty-one percent felt that they needed assistance in dealing with child protective services, indicating contact with our agency. Although on-site child care and parenting programs were not available, half of the women with children five years old or younger reported that they would always bring their child to the program if child care were available; almost all of the other mothers reported that they would use child care services some of the time. Eighty percent of the women expressed interest in attending a parenting program if one were available.

These statistics document the importance of routinely providing family-centered services in drug treatment programs. The children of drug treatment clients are at high risk for abuse and neglect, and, eventually, for their own drug abuse. Because their parents are already involved in a drug treatment program, on-site services provide access to these children without costly outreach activities. Family-centered services serve as a motivating factor for those seeking treatment and they can also help parents to respond to their children's needs, experience positive parent-child interactions, and deal with their guilt about the damage they may have done to their children. Providing such services is a first step to safeguarding children at risk.

A Specialized Program

With funding from the National Institute on Drug Abuse and the Administration for Children, Youth, and Families, the Mothers Project has developed a specialized program for drug-abusing mothers and pregnant women and their children in New Haven, Connecticut. Intake into this program is through the

Yale-New Haven Hospital's Women's Center, which provides prenatal care to the pregnant women. As part of this program, and with their consent, participating women are routinely screened for alcohol and other drug use. Cocaine-abusing women are eligible for specialized treatment in the program. Centered on a community-based day treatment site, but also working directly in client homes, the program offers six hours of structured daily activities, including group, family, and individual therapy, relapse prevention training, leisure and exercise activities, and education about pregnancy, parenting, and the effects of drug use. Contingency contracting is used to reward women for abstinence, as documented by twice weekly urine toxicology and self-reports.

Family Support Services

Women who have successfully raised families in the same community as the cocaine-dependent women entering the program are recruited as family support workers and are supervised by and teamed with a master's-level social worker. Family support workers initially seek to engage women in their role as mothers. While acknowledging cocaine dependence as a major focus of concern, the family support workers endeavor to build a relationship with the mothers. This relationship focuses on the mothers' strengths and positive attributes and their wishes for their children, born and yet to be born. Through this active and accepting process of home-based outreach, women in the program are encouraged to form positive alliances from which behavioral changes can take place. The medium for this relationship-based approach is the concrete assistance that family support workers provide: case management services, including helping mothers gain access to social services; housing, nutrition supplements, and other entitlements; and hands-on assistance with the concrete needs of the women in the program, such as transportation, assisting with home childproofing, and teaching efficient methods of shopping. Family support workers make home visits and see the cocaine-dependent women outside the geographical and time boundaries of the day program. They also function as dropout-prevention specialists by continuing to work with women who stop coming into the treatment program. They are thus able, if necessary, to facilitate the woman's reentry into treatment. Family support workers serve as "buddies" in the community reinforcement approach (i.e., they help cocaine-dependent women develop a drug-free social network by accompanying them to Narcotics Anonymous or Cocaine Anonymous meetings and by facilitating their reinvolvement with stable, nondrug-using family members).

On-Site Child Care

Since the majority of cocaine-dependent pregnant women are responsible for the care of one or more preschool toddlers, on-site child day care is essential to remove what could otherwise be a barrier to treatment. Child day care provides a needed respite for mothers who feel burdened by 24-hour-a-day responsibility for child care.

Child Development Services

On-site child day care creates the opportunity to help recovering cocaine-dependent women observe how trained teachers respond to the needs of their children, learn appropriate parenting skills, and provide appropriate therapeutic interventions to children in need. Many of the women in the program have difficulty maintaining reasonable expectations about their children's developmental abilities. They may become frustrated and respond harshly, even though the child's behavior may be age appropriate. The child development program includes structured play activities for the children, discussions with the mothers about parenting and discipline, and supervised interactions between the mothers and their children. For many mothers, this is the first time they have played with their children or enjoyed mother-child activities.

Child Protection

A community-oriented approach to protecting children of drug abusers must weigh policy alternatives in order to maximize positive outcomes while minimizing costs and adverse consequences. For example, it is unacceptable for drug treatment programs to overlook or fail to report child abuse, but confidentiality must be maintained within treatment programs. Without this safeguard, drug users will avoid treatment or avoid frank discussion of family relations. In developing public policies regarding protection of children of drug addicts, this issue is key. Policies that call for punitive actions, harsh criminal penalties, automatic removal of children from their parents' custody, or termination of parental rights will probably deter some parents from using drugs and protect some children from abuse. Questions remain, however, about how many parents will be deterred from drug use, how many children will be protected, and at what cost. These policies have little deterrent effect on compulsive users—those who cannot control their drug use and continue it despite adverse consequences—and will deter the those who use drugs most heavily from seeking medical treatment for themselves and their children. The growing number of women who deliver infants without registering for or receiving prenatal care (these women are often drug abusers with preterm infants) attests to the critical need for policies and programs that foster utilization of health care and social services.

To protect children of drug users, communities must expand family-centered treatment programs, increase access to services, and improve the services offered so that they support both the parents who are striving to nurture their children and the children who need their parents to care for them. Even with these services, however, not all of those who are addicted to drugs will cease their drug use or be able to provide safe and nurturing environments for their children.

Notes

1. Beatrice A. Rouse, "Trends in Cocaine Use in the General Population," in *The Epidemiology of Cocaine Use and Abuse*, NIDA Research Monograph 110, DHHS Publication No. (ADM) 91-1787 (Rockville, MD: Alcohol, Drug Abuse, and Mental Health Administration, 1991).

2. U.S. General Accounting Office, *Drug Exposed Infants: A Generation at Risk* (Washington, DC: U.S. Government Printing Office, 1990).

3. Kathleen M. Carroll, "Psychotherapy for Cocaine Abuse: Approaches, Evidence, and Conceptual Models," in *Clinician's Guide to Cocaine Addiction*, ed. Thomas R. Kosten and Herbert D. Kleber (New York: The Guilford Press, 1992), 290–313.

4. Roger E. Meyer, "Prospects for a Rational Pharmacotherapy of Alcoholism," *Journal of Clinical Psychiatry* 50, no. 11 (1989): 403–12.

5. George E. Vaillant, "What Can Long-Term Follow-up Teach Us about Relapse and Prevention of Relapse in Addiction?" *British Journal of Addictions* 83 (1988): 1147–57.

6. Richard S. Schottenfeld, "Survey of Service Needs of Drug-Dependent Women." APT Foundation (unpublished data).

 *6*

Barriers to Successful Intervention

Judy Howard*

Within all cultures and socioeconomic situations, parents have a biologically driven motivation to care for and nurture their offspring. Yet, there are some children who are very difficult to care for and some parents who have priorities that preempt the care and protection of their children.

Heavy use of drugs has a profound impact upon users as well as upon their families. These repercussions are no more tragically apparent than when the user is a mother who has a new baby and other children to care for, as the following case example illustrates:

Susan is a 23-year-old mother of five children (ages five years, four years, three years, 18 months, and three months) who began attending a drug treat-

* The author acknowledges the contributions of the following colleagues: Leila Beckwith, Ph.D., Co-Principal Investigator; Eleanor Baxter, M.A., Early Childhood Educator; Sarah Simpson, M.A., Parent Educator; Jacqui Dickens, M.S.W., Social Worker; Clementine Royston, A.A., Community Liaison; Rachelle Tyler, M.D., Developmental Pediatrician; Carol Rodning, Ph.D., Developmental Psychologist; and Michael Espinosa, Ph.D., Statistician.

ment program prior to the birth of her last infant, who was born preterm following binge cocaine use by Susan.

Susan is struggling with her addiction and the pressure from her significant other to continue to use. She was beaten by him on several occasions when she refused to smoke crack. In spite of the intervenor's efforts to help her separate from this partner and move to a shelter, she has refused. The periodic beatings have continued.

This mother rarely misses a drug treatment meeting and is eager for home visits by professional staff members. Contrary to her reports that she is curtailing drug use, however, her behavior, appearance, and positive urine toxicology screens indicate otherwise. Her drug use continues.

When off on a binge that may last two to three days, she leaves the children locked in the apartment, sometimes without food. The environment is deemed unsafe, and the five children are placed in foster care. Susan drops out of drug treatment.

Staff members feel helpless and inadequate in their efforts to improve this family's chances of surviving as a healthy, nurturing unit.

Parents who use drugs heavily comprise a group that has enormous difficulty consistently engaging with their children. The reasons for this are complex. Just as other parents of newborns with problems express feelings of guilt, denial, anger, and sadness about their baby's medical fragility, chemically dependent parents also struggle with such feelings. Furthermore, their infants demonstrate very difficult behaviors such as extreme irritability or lethargy, poor sleeping patterns, and ineffective sucking that interferes with weight gain.[1] Caring for these children is difficult.

Another compounding problem relates to the past experiences of these parents in their own family of origin. These experiences often influence the parents' current functioning. Common wisdom dictates—and current scientific evidence is now beginning to demonstrate—that people parent the way they were parented.

Our recent work with pregnant addicts confirms that an alarming percentage have suffered complicated and emotional hardships as children and adults. For instance, of 58 women interviewed, 72 percent had been physically or sexually abused, 66 percent came from households in which one or both parents used drugs, 55 percent had multiple caregivers while growing up, and over 74 percent experienced violence during their lives. The cumulative effect of such past experiences upon the self-esteem of these women and their ability to provide for the needs of others must be significant.[2]

A second important factor must be considered in addition to this kind of hardship. These women are involved with substances that interfere with thought processes and, thus, with consistent parenting responses. The nature of addiction, in and of itself, propels users to consider their own needs first—obtaining their next fix is their primary goal.[3] Thus, attending to the ongoing and daily basic physical requirements of a newborn infant or young child, not to mention the child's emotional need for nurturing, seems incompatible with the heavy use of drugs.

Intervention with Parents

This paper describes the efforts of a home-based early intervention program serving newborns of mothers who used drugs heavily throughout pregnancy. The model of intervention was based on encouraging four basic behaviors in parents:

- enjoyment of the infant;

- sensitive and responsive caregiving;

- engagement with the infant in mutually satisfying interactions; and

- appropriate and interesting activities to enhance the child's development.

We also report on systematic research data from naturalistic home observations about how parents who use drugs heavily, as compared to a nondrug-using control group, responded to their infants. Finally, we present results of a standardized stress test that assesses how these children, as toddlers, used their parents as comfort figures.

In 1986, the National Institute on Drug Abuse funded a research project that evaluated the efficacy of early intervention upon the developmental outcome of infants and young children who were exposed prenatally to drugs.

Forty-seven full-term infants without medical complications surrounding their deliveries were selected from a county hospital in the inner-city of Los Angeles. Those infants who had been exposed prenatally to drugs were identified on the basis of positive urine toxicology screens. The hospital informed child protective services that these infants were from environmentally high-risk families. The 37 infants in the control group were from parents who did not use drugs, who were of the same ethnic group, and who lived in the same neighborhoods. The majority of participating families received Aid to Families with Dependent Children.

All families were enrolled in the home-based intervention program beginning immediately following the infant's discharge home from the newborn nursery. The intervention staff was composed of three professionals with master's degrees in early childhood education, parent education, and social work. In addition, a fourth intervenor with an Associate of Arts degree functioned as community liaison. She was familiar with the community agencies and family networks that proved particularly helpful in locating the drug-using mothers when they disappeared during binges.

The combined professional skills of the intervenors included backgrounds in early childhood education, experience with children from low-income families and developmentally disabled children, promoting parent-child interaction with biologically at-risk children, knowledge about the substance abuse culture and treatment programs for substance abuse, and knowledge about community agencies that served special-needs children and youngsters involved in child protective services. The intervenors shared their combined professional expertise at a weekly case conference meeting, as well as during informal encounters in their adjacent offices.

The intervenors' personal attributes were as important as their professional skills: persistence and dedication to serving their assigned families; a stable life pattern; empathy for these families; a thick-skin sensitivity that prevented them from personalizing the often critical, hostile, or rejecting behaviors of the drug-using mothers; and an ability to deal with crises that often included violence.

Each of the intervenors was assigned a caseload of no more than 25 families, which included both drug users and families within the control group. Intervenors made weekly home visits to each of their families during the first month, and then bi-weekly visits during the remaining two years of the program. Telephone contact was also frequent.

The prearranged home visits lasted about one-and-a-half hours and only rarely was a mother not available. In the initial home visit, intervenors assessed the specific areas of infant's health and development, health and development of siblings, parents' health, physical environment, family resources and budget, details of the family health care plan, and status of the drug treatment program for parents. Each intervenor supported the individual mother's participation in her drug treatment program. The subsequent home visits always focused on the intervention goals and objectives that were established during the preceding visit.

In addition to the general categories of intervention described above, the staff was involved with the biological mother's concerns about the men in her life, birth control, and up-to-date information about the status of court and child protective services action. Furthermore, the needs of the family for clothing, food, toys, health care, and appropriate community services were also discussed. The staff always brought toys for the siblings, which made it easier to spend time focused on the mother and child. During the second year of intervention, the staff arranged field trips that included picnics in parks, visits to restaurants, and trips to theme parks.

The intervenors also spent time identifying drug treatment programs in the community and ensuring that space was available for immediate treatment. Each mother was notified about the programs and was transported to them for the initial interview. Our staff helped the mothers decide about the appropriateness of the programs (outpatient versus residential) for their current situations. Even with this support, only about 15 percent of the mothers remained abstinent for one year. (One mother maintained sobriety without treatment.) We were unable to predict which mothers, based on their background history, family supports, and years of substance abuse, had the best chance of remaining abstinent.

Observations about Intervention

The intervention staff found that the more dysfunctional the chemically dependent family, the more difficult it was to focus intervention on the infant. It became clear that the drug-using mother's personal needs had to be dealt with before she and the intervenor could focus on the infant. The mothers wanted to talk about their drug addiction and treatment, the men in their lives and their often abusive relationships, and their conflicted relationships with their own families of origin.

The mothers' problems that emerged over the two years that these families participated in the program presented serious obstacles to successful treatment. There were violent episodes between family members, as well as gang violence inflicted upon the families (whether or not they were involved with gangs). Random neighborhood violence was also common. Not infrequently, our efforts were sabotaged by other family members who resented the attention given to the mother, and resented the mother's interest in changing her life-style. The men in these women's lives also often resented the women's efforts to take charge of their lives. This resentment sometimes resulted in battering. In other families, our intervention efforts were thwarted by drug pushers who terrorized family members. For example, a few of our mothers "charged" their purchases of drugs and were subsequently unable to pay. Family members were beaten and, in one case, a drug pusher poured gasoline around the home in which the grandmother and children lived.

Besides the environmental situations with which our intervention staff had to contend, there was also the problem of the drug users' lack of organization and follow-through about all activities not related to drug procurement, including the safety of their children. For example, at the end of the intervention period, some mothers and their children participated in a field trip to the Los Angeles Children's Museum. The intervenor reported that one mother proudly called out to her that she was tying one of her children's shoelaces so that he would not stumble and fall, while she was unaware that her six-month-old was toppling off a wall upon which she had placed him.

Hours were spent preparing the mothers and their children for trips to community agencies, as well as to UCLA for research appointments. Over time, the intervenors learned that these mothers did not incorporate verbal information about organization of daily routines, and many were also unable to read. The mothers tended not to rise in the morning, nor did they consistently provide food or clean clothes for their children. If the mothers were to keep appointments with community agencies, the intervenor would not only have to provide transportation, but would also have to arrive at the family's residence at least one hour early to help dress and feed the children before departure. Occasionally, the intervenors made unannounced home visits. Not infrequently, they found the mothers high on drugs and had to ensure that an adult who was not using drugs was present to care for the children.

In trying to help the women budget their limited incomes to cover household expenses and their children's needs, the intervenors discovered that some mothers were sacrificing their children's needs to buy drugs. One woman reported, for example, that she felt very guilty because she had used money that had been earmarked to buy shoes for her children to buy drugs. Several other mothers bartered their Women, Infants, and Children food stamps to drug dealers in exchange for drugs.

In contrast, the parents who did not use drugs, although they had similar limited incomes and also struggled with housing, furniture, and clothes, responded differently to intervention. They worked in collaboration with the intervenor, followed through on suggestions, and were able to generalize information, especially concerning child safety.

Developmental and Attachment Results

The children exposed to drugs in utero had depressed developmental scores beginning at six months and continuing through 24 months of age. On average, their scores were at the low end of normal, while the children of mothers who did not use drugs had average developmental abilities. Furthermore, the children of mothers who used drugs heavily had impaired physical growth. Over 60 percent of those either at birth or at six months of age had head growth below the tenth percentile, whereas only one child in the control group had such low growth. Although drug exposure in utero is associated with intrauterine growth retardation, many of these children had normal physical growth in weight and height. Their decreased head circumferences, however, reflected interference with brain growth. These findings regarding the children's physical growth show the biological influence of heavy maternal drug use during pregnancy.

The postnatal environmental influence of heavy maternal drug use was examined by systematic, standardized measures of caregiver behaviors toward the infants at home. One member of the research staff, a postdoctoral fellow in developmental psychology, unaware of whether the mothers did or did not use drugs, visited each home at an appointed time for one hour when the infants were three months and nine months of age.

The results of these observations showed that the groups differed in parental behaviors. At both time periods, mothers who used drugs heavily were significantly less sensitive, responsive, and accessible to their infants than the control group mothers. Moreover, their physical contact was poorer in both quantity and quality, and they demonstrated less acceptance of the infant than did those in the control group. In spite of the ongoing intervention, the behavior of the drug-using mothers deteriorated in all of these aspects during the six-month period. We believe that the behaviors observed during these home visits represented a higher quality than might have been ordinarily shown, since it has been our experience in observing parents that the majority do their best when being observed.

When the infants were 15 months of age, another standardized measure was administered. They were videotaped for 20 minutes in the laboratory to record for assessment their responses to their mother's presence, departure, and reunion. This approach, developed in 1973, specifically evaluates the quality of the child's attachment to the parent. The majority (64 percent) of the children of parents who did not use drugs showed normal secure attachments. This finding is totally consistent with middle-class children and biologically high-risk preterm children. Secure attachment is the hallmark of normal emotional development during infancy.

In contrast, 100 percent of the children living with the drug-using mothers who had not become abstinent during intervention showed insecure attachments demonstrated by a variety of behaviors including avoidance, fear, and anger toward their mothers. Such an extraordinarily high percentage of insecure attachments has only previously been seen in abused and neglected children. Research has shown that insecure attachments in young children are not pathognomonic but are associated with later problems in cooperating with adults and interacting with peers, and with decreased enthusiasm and motivation in problem-solving tasks and increased aggression.

Seven mothers who had used drugs heavily became abstinent during the intervention, and half of their eight children demonstrated secure attachments.

In fact, within the group who used drugs heavily, the only children who showed secure attachments were those whose mothers had been sober for at least six months before the testing procedure.

Since the children of the drug-using mothers were involved with child protective services, we knew that changes in caregivers was a possibility and wondered whether it was the reason for the large number who demonstrated insecure attachments. Of those children who had formed insecure attachments with their mothers, however, the majority (75 percent) had not experienced a change in custody.

Conclusion

Our research regarding the impact of early intervention and supportive services for low-income families who used drugs heavily and those who did not indicates the following:

- During the first two years of life, children growing up in poverty whose parents are drug free can experience nurturing environments that promote secure attachments and normal physical and developmental growth.

- Compromised physical and developmental growth in many children is associated with the heavy use of drugs by the mother throughout pregnancy and during the first two years of the child's life.

- The mothers' abstinence from future drug use is unpredictable (based on knowledge about family background, family supports, and duration of drug use).

- Heavy use of drugs interferes with a parent's ability to respond consistently and sensitively to the child, decreasing the formation of secure attachments.

- Heavy use of drugs by a mother interferes with the professional's efforts to get her to focus on the needs of her child.

- Our home-based intervention program, although provided by a committed and skilled staff, was not able, over time, to assist nonabstinent parents who used drugs heavily to consistently provide caregiving that was both stimulating and nurturing.

Finally, we are unsure of how to measure the success of comprehensive services to parents who use drugs heavily. Addiction is a chronic, relapsing health disorder that has proven difficult to treat under any circumstances. Further, when parents of young, dependent children are addicted to alcohol and other drugs, intervention services are required not only to promote sobriety, but to enhance parenting skills that foster healthy child development. This is a new field and further examination and refinement are needed.

Notes

1. Sherry Deren, "Children of Substance Abusers: A Review of the Literature," *Journal of Substance Abuse Treatment* 3 (1986): 77–94; Anthony J. Hadeed and Sharon R. Siegel, "Maternal Cocaine Use during Pregnancy: Effect on the Newborn Infant," *Pediatrics* 84 (1989): 205–210; Gladys C. Vargas, Rosita S. Pildes, Dharmapuri Vidyasagar, and Louis G. Keith, "Effect of Maternal Heroin Addiction on 67 Liveborn Neonates," *Clinical Pediatrics* 14, no. 8 (1975): 751–757; Judy Howard, Vickie Kropenske, and Rachelle Tyler, "The Long-Term Effect on Neurodevelopment in Infants Exposed Prenatally to PCP," in *Phencyclidine: An Update*, Research Monograph No. 64, ed. Doris H. Clouet (Rockville, MD: National Institute on Drug Abuse, 1986), 237–251.

2. Josette Escamilla-Mondanaro, "Women: Pregnancy, Children, and Addiction," *Journal of Psychedelic Drugs* 9, no. 1 (1977): 59–68.

3. Rebecca Black and Joseph Mayer, "Parents with Special Problems: Alcoholism and Opiate Addiction," *Child Abuse and Neglect* 4 (1980): 45–54.

 *7*

THE NEED FOR
BETTER RESEARCH

Robert Apsler

Is drug abuse treatment effective? Answering this seemingly straightforward question is difficult for two related reasons. First, simply defining terms is complex. For example, *drug treatment* is actually a collection of programs with very different orientations, objectives, staffs, settings, procedures, and clients. Consequently, research conducted on one program may be of little use in drawing conclusions about others.

Second, few high quality studies have assessed drug treatment effectiveness. Furthermore, these few well-designed experiments (1) focused on adult male narcotics users, (2) concentrated on a single type of treatment, that is, methadone maintenance, and (3) studied only highly motivated addicts. As a result, many conclusions about treatment effectiveness are limited to the specialized circumstances under which the research was conducted.

What is Drug Abuse Treatment?

No one process or combination of procedures constitutes drug abuse treatment, nor do the various types of drug treatment programs appear to have much in common other than the generic objective of combating drug abuse. Most descriptions of drug abuse treatment resort to a crude classification system consisting of three or four categories.[1] For example, Gerstein and Harwood identify the following four major types of drug treatment:

- *Outpatient methadone maintenance* is usually provided in ambulatory programs that require daily visits to obtain methadone hydrochloride. This narcotic analgesic produces a stable, noneuphoric state without the psychophysiological cues that precipitate opiate craving. Many programs also provide counseling and other social services.

- *Residential therapeutic communities* typically involve nine to 12 months of participation in a residential setting. Therapy consists of highly structured blends of resocialization, milieu therapy, and behavioral modification practices. Clients progress through a hierarchy of occupational training and responsibility within the therapeutic community that ultimately leads to community reentry.

- *Outpatient nonmethadone treatment* is a heterogeneous group of programs that vary in their treatment processes, philosophies, and staffing. Treatment typically involves one or two visits per week for individual or group therapy/counseling and lasts an average of six months. Clients' drug preferences are varied, although they tend not to be dependent on opiates.

- *Inpatient/outpatient chemical dependency treatment* involves three- to six-week residential or inpatient treatment based on the Alcoholics Anonymous (12-step) model of personal change and the belief that vulnerability to dependence is a permanent but controllable disability. Daily educational lectures are combined with small task-oriented groups and other services.[2]

There are several problems with this classification system of drug treatment programs. First, the programs within each major category differ markedly from each other.[3] For example, methadone maintenance programs differ in the size of the methadone dose, the number and type of additional services provided, the frequency of urine testing, the strictness of enforcing rules, whether they permit methadone to be taken home, and so on.

Second, important program differences sometimes cut across the major categories. For example, various formal and informal "therapies" are practiced across drug treatment programs. Treatment goals also vary. Some programs focus on illicit drug use and criminal activity; others target the overall functioning of clients. Some programs demand abstinence from all illicit drugs; others assist their clients in gaining control over their drug use. Some programs differ in whether they focus on a particular drug and, if they do, on which drug they target. Some programs rely heavily on professional practitioners; others employ ex-addicts. Programs also differ markedly in the clients they serve. Those in the private sector tend to serve employed drug abusers; those in the public sector serve large numbers of indigent clients.

Third, independent self-help fellowship groups, such as Narcotics Anonymous and Cocaine Anonymous, are missing from the classification system, even though some activities in these groups appear similar to activities in certain formal treatment programs.

Which treatment—or treatments—are we talking about when we ask whether drug abuse treatment is effective? Do we mean all drug treatment? Presumably not, since the term *drug abuse treatment* covers such a broad spectrum of clients, drugs, settings, and procedures that it has little meaning. Instead, most efforts to evaluate drug abuse treatment have been directed at the major categories of treatment described above. Yet, those efforts to classify treatment programs have produced gross categories that reflect only a small portion of the extensive variation among drug programs. In fact, the differences within each major category of programs are so great that information about the effectiveness of a few examples of a particular category may tell us little about other programs in the same category. Considerable caution must therefore be taken when attempting to generalize the results obtained from a test of one program to another program.

Who Are the Clients and What Are Their Objectives?

The common references to clients of drug programs as *drug abusers* and *drug addicts* obscure vast differences among these individuals—differences that may be related to treatment effectiveness. Some examples were mentioned above, such as differences in employment status and drug preference. Perhaps of greater importance, clients differ in their reasons for being in treatment and in their willingness to cooperate with programs.

Smart observed that drug users often enter treatment because of a crisis in their lives.[4] As a result, their objectives may be limited to overcoming the current crisis. In Rogalski's words, "After a few days on the unit—when the patients were feeling physically better, their self-esteem and cohesiveness had returned, and their mates and employers were calmed by their presence in a program—many patients would admit that they had little intention of stopping all drug use."[5]

Many clients are forced, either directly or indirectly, into drug treatment. Anglin and Hser reported that the vast majority of drug program clients were compelled to enter treatment by family, legal, or employer pressure, or a combination of the three.[6] Pressure from the criminal justice system was the strongest motivation for seeking public treatment, according to a 1979 to 1981 national sample of public program admissions.[7]

In sum, drug treatment programs treat a wide range of individuals, many of whom want only immediate relief from a crisis, or no treatment at all. Providing effective treatment to unmotivated individuals is clearly a formidable undertaking.

What Is Effective Treatment?

Definitions of effective drug abuse treatment vary in two important ways. First, strongly held views divide the treatment community on whether abstinence from illicit drug use is necessary. One position holds that treatment should be considered successful only when total abstinence from illicit drug use is achieved. In fact, some deride methadone treatment as substituting addiction to methadone for addiction to other narcotics. Conversely, others argue that treatment is successful if it reduces illicit drug use to the extent that clients can lead productive lives and not engage in criminal activities.

The other important difference in definitions of effectiveness is the number of behaviors or areas of client functioning included in the definition. Effective treatment is commonly viewed as synonymous with cessation of just two behaviors: illicit drug use and criminal activities. Others argue, however, that a broader definition of effectiveness is necessary to describe clients accurately. For example, Hall proposed that seven categories are important: (1) drug abuse, (2) illegal activities, (3) employment, (4) program retention, (5) social functioning, (6) intrapersonal functioning, and (7) physical health and longevity.[8]

One example of the importance of a broad view of effectiveness is the observation of Hubbard and his colleagues that treatment did little to integrate clients into the legitimate economy.[9] Thus, it is not surprising that the large reductions in illicit drug use and criminal activity observed immediately after treatment disappear within three to five years.

Another example is the large increase in alcohol consumption frequently observed among treated opiate users.[10] Riordan et al. contend that this "alcohol consumption may present a greater threat to successful rehabilitative outcome than continued use of opiates."[11]

Treatment Outcomes vs. No Treatment

For an evaluation of drug abuse treatment to document a program's effectiveness, it must show that client improvements would not have occurred without the program. This may seem obvious, but few comparisons between drug abuse treatment and no treatment have been conducted. For example, two massive longitudinal studies of treatment effectiveness involving many programs and thousands of clients have been conducted, yet neither included a no-treatment comparison.[12] Both studies argue that drug treatment is effective, but neither convincingly demonstrates that treating drug users is more effective than not treating them.

Although little is known about drug users who do not enter treatment programs, there are indications that some users reduce or even end their drug use largely on their own. For example, Wineck noted as long ago as 1962 that some heroin users "mature out" of their drug use.[13] More recently, Brown et al. observed large reductions in drug use among drug abusers waiting one to six months to enter cocaine treatment.[14]

The phenomenon of people ending their use of highly addictive legal substances on their own is well documented. For example, a large study found rates of quitting smoking about the same for smokers quitting on their own as for those attending treatment programs.[15] Estimates of remission from alcoholism and alcohol problems without formal treatment range from 45 percent to 70 percent.[16] No comparable estimate of quitting by oneself is available for drug users. Nor is there any way of distinguishing between drug abusers who can recover on their own and those who need the assistance of treatment.

Other drug abusers successfully adapt to an addict life-style. Nurco et al. interviewed 402 male narcotic abusers sampled from subjects who became known to the Baltimore City Police Department between 1952 and 1976. They found some addicts who "were skillful at avoiding incarceration and appeared to function well in a life-style that involved obtaining income from illegal sources to purchase heroin."[17]

Effectiveness of Methadone Treatment

The strongest evidence that drug abuse treatment can be effective comes from two randomized clinical trials of methadone treatment. The first, conducted by Dole et al., randomly assigned 32 highly motivated criminal addicts to either a methadone treatment program or a waiting list group that received no treatment. All 16 addicts on the waiting list quickly became readdicted to heroin, as did four others in the treatment group who refused to participate. In addition, 18 of these 20 untreated individuals (the 16 on the waiting list and the four who refused treatment) were reincarcerated within seven to ten months. In the treatment group, only three of the remaining 12 addicts were reincarcerated during this period, and heroin use decreased substantially.[18]

A rigorous test of a methadone maintenance program in Sweden provides more recent evidence of treatment effectiveness, although the stringent client selection criteria limit the generalizability of the findings. Heroin addicts became eligible for the methadone maintenance treatment program only after they (1) had a history of long-term compulsive abuse with (2) repeated failures to stop, in spite of documented serious attempts to do so. Gunne and Gronbladh randomly assigned individuals meeting these eligibility requirements either to treatment or no treatment. Two years later, 12 of the 17 drug addicts assigned to treatment had abandoned drug use and started work or studies, while five still had drug problems (two of the five had been expelled from the program). Conversely, only 1 of the 17 addicts in the no-treatment group became drug free, while two were in prison, two were dead, and the rest were still abusing heroin.[19]

In sum, these two studies demonstrate that methadone treatment has the potential for reducing narcotics use and criminal behavior among highly motivated addicts. To what extent, then, do these findings apply to methadone programs in general? The answer is that we don't know, and we must remain skeptical for at least three reasons. First, despite the existence of other compelling demonstrations of methadone treatment's effectiveness,[20] few randomized clinical trials have been conducted on methadone treatment.[21] Second, a U.S. General Accounting Office survey of 15 methadone programs in five states questioned the efficacy of those programs. It found that the use of heroin and other opiates ranged from 2 percent to 47 percent of patients enrolled in the clinics, many clients had serious alcohol problems, few comprehensive services were offered to patients despite high rates of unemployment, and clinics did not know whether clients used the services to which they were referred.[22] Third, many programs administer doses of methadone much smaller than those known to be effective.[23] Finally, no one knows how many methadone clients are as highly motivated as those in the successful demonstrations described above.

Effectiveness of Other Types of Treatment

Almost all published treatment research deals with narcotics users. Investigations of cocaine treatment are under way, but results are not yet available. Even restricting the focus to narcotics users, little is known about treatment modalities other than methadone maintenance. Thus, we simply do not know whether other types of treatment are effective, and if so, how effective.

Therapeutic Communities

Observational evaluations of therapeutic communities have produced promising results, yet important questions remain unanswered. Two large-scale longitudinal studies involving many of the drug treatment programs mentioned earlier reported substantial reductions in drug use and criminal activity among therapeutic community clients who remained in treatment for at least several months.[24]

However, therapeutic communities are highly selective in two ways. First, they appeal only to clients willing to enter a long-term residential setting. Second, most addicts who enter therapeutic communities quickly drop out.

Thus, the potential of therapeutic communities to influence drug addiction may be restricted to a small and select group of individuals. Furthermore, there is almost no research about the factors that influence success and failure in therapeutic communities.[25]

Chemical Dependency Treatment

Almost nothing is known about the effectiveness of this form of treatment, even though it has become the dominant approach of privately financed inpatient and residential programs.

Outpatient Nonmethadone Treatment

This category consists of many forms of outpatient treatment, which vary greatly in duration and theoretical orientation. Little is known about their effectiveness individually or as a group.[26]

Long-Term Follow-Up of Treated Addicts

Despite their potential value, long-term studies of drug treatment program clients are both rare and hampered by severe methodological problems. For instance, investigators must rely heavily on subjects' memories. They must be alert to possible distortion and varying degrees of truthfulness in the subjects' reporting on their illicit drug use and criminal activities that occurred over long periods of time.[27] Disentangling the role of treatment from other factors is further complicated by the well-known phenomenon of many drug users entering different drug programs for varying amounts of time.

Vaillant's classic study followed 100 addicts from New York City who entered a federal prison-hospital in the early 1950s. Eighteen years later, the number who had died was much greater than would be expected on the basis of age alone. Among the living, the number of abstainers had increased markedly, while the percent who were active heroin users had declined. These results have little bearing, however, on the long-term effectiveness of current forms of drug abuse treatment, which were unavailable when Vaillant's subjects received their treatment.[28]

In another study, Simpson and Sells interviewed 4,627 clients five to seven years after entering treatment and found that both daily use of opioid drugs and criminal activity declined substantially.[29] Unfortunately, several methodological problems raise questions about their findings.[30] For example, the investigators interviewed only 61 percent of the target sample. Outcomes for the missing subjects may have been much poorer than for those who were located.

Summary

Complex issues and a paucity of research greatly restrict our knowledge about the effectiveness of drug abuse treatment. Federal support for treatment research increased only recently following a decade-long decline that began in the early 1970s.[31] As a result, little has been added to the already sparse knowledge base that existed in the early 1970s regarding the effectiveness of drug abuse treatment. Fortunately, the recent growth in federal funding has already increased the number of randomized clinical trials of drug treatment that are under way or in the planning stage.

Most treatment research has focused on methadone maintenance. The results show that methadone treatment is effective in certain specific circumstances, that is, when highly motivated clients receive appropriate doses of methadone and are provided with auxiliary services. The effectiveness of methadone treatment under more typical circumstances, however, is less certain. Therapeutic communities appear to be effective with the select group of clients who choose them and who remain in them for long periods. Too little is known to draw conclusions about other forms of narcotics treatment or treatment for abuse of other drugs. Similarly, little information exists about the long-term outcomes of drug abuse treatment and about what happens to drug abusers who never enter treatment.

Several research priorities are clear. First, randomized clinical trials are needed to investigate the effectiveness of treatment for abuse of drugs other than narcotics (including the abuse of multiple drugs), other forms of narcotics treatment besides methadone maintenance, and the factors that influence treatment effectiveness, such as staff characteristics and comprehensiveness of services. Second, more long-term follow-up studies of treatment effectiveness must be conducted despite their great expense and difficulty. Finally, additional study of untreated drug abusers is important in order to learn about their treatment needs and to find out what can be done to help more of them end their drug use without formal treatment.

Notes

1. M. Douglas Anglin and Yih Hser, "Treatment of Drug Abuse," in *Drugs and Crime*, ed. Michael Tonry and James Q. Wilson (Chicago: University of Chicago Press, 1990); Dean R. Gerstein and Henrick J. Harwood, eds., *Treating Drug Problems: Volume I* (Washington, DC: National Academy Press, 1990).

2. Gerstein and Harwood, 133–174.

3. Robert L. Hubbard et al., *Drug Abuse Treatment: A National Study of Effectiveness* (Chapel Hill, NC: The University of North Carolina Press, 1989).

4. Reginald G. Smart, "Reflections on the Epidemiology of Heroin and Narcotic Addictions from the Perspective of Treatment Data," in *The Epidemiology of Heroin and Other Narcotics*, ed. Joan D. Rittenhouse, NIDA Research Monograph 16 (Washington, DC: U.S. Government Printing Office, 1977), 180.

5. Carol J. Rogalski, "Factor Structure of the Addiction Severity Index in an Inpatient Detoxification Sample," *International Journal of the Addictions* 22, no. 10 (1987): 982.

6. Anglin and Hser.

7. Gerstein and Harwood, 112.

8. Sharon M. Hall, "Methadone Treatment: A Review of the Research Findings," in *Research on the Treatment of Narcotic Addiction: State of the Art*, ed. James R. Cooper et al. (Rockville, MD: National Institute on Drug Abuse, 1983), 575–632.

9. Hubbard et al.

10. Dennis D. Simpson and Saul B. Sells, "Effectiveness of Treatment for Drug Abuse: An Overview of the DARP Research Program," *Advances in Alcohol and Substance Abuse* 2 (1983): 7–29; Paul Cushman, "Methadone Maintenance: Long-Term Follow-Up of Detoxified Patients," *Annals of the New York Academy of Science* 311 (1978): 24; William H. McGlothlin and M. Douglas Anglin, "Shutting Off Methadone: Costs and Benefits," *Archives of General Psychiatry* 38 (1981): 885–892.

11. E. E. Riordan et al., "Successful Detoxification from Methadone Maintenance: Follow-Up Study of 38 Patients," *Journal of the American Medical Association* 235, no. 24 (1976): 2607.

12. Saul B. Sells, ed., *Effectiveness of Drug Abuse Treatment*, vols. 1 and 2 (Cambridge, MA: Ballinger, 1974); Hubbard et al.

13. C. Wineck, "Maturing Out of Narcotic Addiction," *U.N. Bulletin on Narcotics* 14 (1962): 1–7.

14. B. Brown et al., "Waiting for Treatment: Behaviors of Cocaine Users on a Waiting List," in *Problems of Drug Dependence, 1988: Proceedings of the 50th Annual Scientific Meeting, The Committee on Problems of Drug Dependence, Inc.*, ed. Louis S. Harris (Rockville, MD: National Institute on Drug Abuse, 1988), 351.

15. Sheldon Cohen et al., "Debunking Myths about Self-Quitting: Evidence from 10 Prospective Studies of Persons Who Attempt to Quit Smoking by Themselves," *American Psychologist* 44, no. 11 (1989): 1355–1365.

16. Institute of Medicine, *Broadening the Base of Treatment for Alcohol Problems* (Washington, DC: National Academy Press, 1990), 154.

17. David N. Nurco, "Addict Careers. III. Trends across Time," *International Journal of the Addictions* 16, no. 8 (1981): 1371.

18. Vincent P. Dole et al., "Methadone Treatment of Randomly Selected Criminal Addicts," *The New England Journal of Medicine* 280, no. 25 (1969): 1372–1375.

19. Lars Gunne and Leif Gronbladh, "The Swedish Methadone Maintenance Program," in *The Social and Medical Aspects of Drug Abuse*, ed. George Serban (Jamaica, NY: Spectrum Publications, 1984), 205–213.

20. M. Douglas Anglin et al., "Consequences and Costs of Shutting Off Methadone," *Addictive Behaviors* 14 (1989): 307–326; William H. McGlothlin and M. Douglas Anglin, "Shutting Off Methadone: Costs and Benefits," *Archives of General Psychiatry* 38 (1981): 885–892; John C. Ball et al., "Reducing the Risk of AIDS through Methadone Maintenance Treatment," *Journal of Health and Social Behavior* 29, no. 3 (1988): 214–226.

21. Robert Apsler and Wayne M. Harding, "Cost-Effectiveness Analysis of Drug Abuse Treatment: Current Status and Recommendations for Future Research," *NIDA Drug Abuse Services Research Series*, no. 1 (Rockville, MD: National Institute on Drug Abuse, 1991), 58–81; Gerstein and Harwood; Sharon M. Hall, "A Review of the Research Findings."

22. Janet L. Shikles, *Preliminary Findings: A Survey of Methadone Maintenance Pro-*

grams (Washington, DC: Statements of the U.S. General Accounting Office before the House Select Committee on Narcotics Abuse and Control, House of Representatives, August, 1989).

23. Gerstein and Harwood, 149-150.

24. Dennis D. Simpson et al., "Follow-Up Evaluation of Treatment of Drug Abuse During 1969 to 1972," *Archives of General Psychiatry* 36 (1979): 772–780; Hubbard et al.

25. Gerstein and Harwood, 163.

26. *Ibid.*, 168–169.

27. Yih Hser et al., "Evaluation of Drug Abuse Treatment: A Repeated Measures Design Assessing Methadone Maintenance," *Evaluation Review* 12 (1988): 548–550.

28. George E. Vaillant, "A 20-Year Follow-Up of New York Narcotic Addicts," *Archives of General Psychiatry* 29 (1973): 237–241.

29. Simpson and Sells.

30. Apsler and Harding.

31. Gerstein and Harwood, 192–194.

SECTION 3:

CHILD WELFARE'S NEW BURDEN

8

THE CLIENTS AND THEIR PROBLEMS

Beverly W. Jones

The theme of this paper is the changing child welfare clientele and its new service needs. I write from the perspective of an administrator of a local department of social services responsible for the delivery of child welfare services. Most of my professional career has been in the public child welfare arena (social worker, line supervisor, and administrator), with the exception of a few years during which I was in Washington, D.C., with the Child Welfare League of America and the American Public Welfare Association. So it is the operation of child welfare programs that I know best. On most days, this is the work that I love and that I do best.

Goals and Ingredients for Success

Safety, protection, and permanency are the major outcomes that should be achieved for children in our child welfare delivery system. To attain them, child welfare agencies must have adequate staffing levels; well-trained professional staffs; reasonable caseloads; a continuum of services and programs; flexible funding; automated management information systems; a responsive, well-trained judicial system; accountability mechanisms; and a network of community resources.

These characteristics describe the department for which I work. We have ten supervisory units in child welfare, with a ratio of one supervisor to six or seven workers. Seventy percent of the staff have either B.S.W. or M.S.W. degrees, and at least five years of experience in child welfare. Training and staff development are available on a monthly basis from the School of Social Work at the University of Maryland. The average caseload is 25 families; the highest is 33. "Automation" is our director's nickname. All staff members (clerical, line worker, supervisor, and administrator) have or will soon have a terminal on their desks. Child protective services intake is fully automated at this time. By the end of this fiscal year, we will be fully equipped with electronic mail, electronic case records, and the like.

Within the Child Welfare Division, the department offers a full array of services: Single Parent Service (Adolescent Pregnancy), Service to Extended Families with Children, Intensive Family Service (Family Preservation), Child Protective Service (Intake and Continuing Service), Foster Care (Specialized Reunification Unit), and Adoption. In addition, the department has a Professional Foster Care Program, two literacy centers, a drug/alcohol screener and assessor, specialized sexual abuse treatment groups, and a young fathers program. Furthermore, the department is considered a leader in the community and works well with other agencies.

If we have all of these ingredients, we must be successful. Right? Wrong. Although I believe that our agency is an excellent one, we are not doing as well as we should in providing safety, protection, and permanency. I say this because, in recent years:

- the number of new child protective cases has increased;

- the foster care population has increased;

- the length of stay in foster care has increased;

- the length of time to achieve permanency for children has increased;

- the number of children entering foster care from the Intensive Family Service (IFS) program has increased;

- the number of cases moving from IFS to child protective services has increased;

- recidivism within the child protective caseload has increased;

- court involvement has increased; and

- adoption as the permanency plan has become more common.

Obstacles to Success

Why have we fallen short? One explanation is that the needs of children and their families have increased not only in number but also in complexity. I had been away from day-to-day operations for approximately five years (1984 to 1989). My return to the trenches took on a form of culture shock. The differences in the clientele that we are expected to serve are significant and striking. For example:

- *Substance Abuse.* Polydrug use is the theme. Alcoholism is now supplemented with, not replaced by, other drugs.

- *Violence.* The use of violence—and its acceptance—are commonplace. Spousal abuse and child abuse are frequently present, and family members often fight with each other. Neighborhoods are beset with violence. There are many places that my staff members will not go alone, and some where they will go only with a police escort. Staff safety is a critical problem and often goes unaddressed.

- *Poverty.* Families have become poorer than they were 10 years ago, not only in terms of material goods, but also in spirit. Helplessness, hopelessness, despair, and depression are masked by rage and hostility. The internal strengths and resources of clients have dwindled and, far too frequently, are all but nonexistent.

- *Absence/Presence of Men.* I smile when I hear people talk about the lack of a male presence in homes. The men are there. We usually do not see them. I refer to them as the "shadows." Their impact is significant, however, and we need to find a better way to relate to them.

- *Extended Family.* The extended family is becoming an endangered species. We are finding that other family members are exhausted; they often cannot help or are as equally inadequate as the parents.

Some case examples defy the notion that there is a quick fix for most families, or that family preservation is the appropriate goal for all families:

- Mr. and Mrs. A. (34 and 28 years old respectively) were reported to the police and the Maryland Department of Social Services for sexual exploitation of children. A film developer called in the report after developing film. Mr. and Mrs. A. have eight children, ranging in age from two to 14. Over 500 sexually explicit pictures of all the children with the As were found. Extended family members came forth and were ruled out as custodians. The children are in foster care, the parents are refusing to work with the agency. They simply want their children returned to their care.

- Patti is a 14-year-old girl who called the agency to say that her mother had pulled a knife on her and threatened to kill her if she did not leave the house. A worker went out to the house immediately. The mother refused to have Patti home that evening; the father is homeless and lives on a park bench in Annapolis. The mother is being physically abused by her live-in female lover. Patti wants her mother to leave the situation because she is tired of being ridiculed by her classmates. Family members have taken Patti in before but will not do so now because Patti's mother and lover disrupt their lives by fighting and cursing.

- Nicki is a nine-month-old girl whose mother is a long-standing polydrug user (alcohol, cocaine, PCP, marijuana, and barbiturates). At birth, Nicki was diagnosed as having fetal alcohol syndrome. The mother says that she does not know the identity of Nicki's father. Family members will not assume care of Nicki, believing that adoption is the best plan for her. After nine months of chasing after the mother, she has entered a drug treatment program as an inpatient. The anticipated length of stay is at least 18 months. Nicki is in a high-risk adoptive home. Do we pursue reunification or adoption?

• Gregory is a 16-year-old boy who was sent to live with his paternal grandparents by the state of California. Both parents are incarcerated in California for possession and distribution of cocaine. Both have extensive histories of substance abuse. The grandparents asked for Gregory's removal after he took their boat out without permission. They pressed charges and he was placed on probation for one year. Services were offered but the grandparents refused. Gregory is in foster care.

Poor agency track records on permanency, worsening social problems, and cases resistant to treatment add up to the sad but realistic conclusion that many of these clients are going to be with us for a long time. The complex problems facing today's families are not easily solved and drug- and poverty-related patterns of neglect and abuse are hard to break. These families need supervision and services over the long term. What does this mean for agency practices?

A New Model of Ongoing Services

Traditionally, the principal child welfare services have encompassed child protective services, foster care, and adoption. Child protective services, unfortunately, are far too often thought of as investigations only. It is as if an investigation is an end rather than a means to an end. In most discussions about the status of public child welfare programs in this country, we begin the conversation with investigations in the child protective services program and immediately shift to the foster care program. This is most disturbing, given that most of the children who have contact with child protective services do not enter the foster care system. In my own county of Anne Arundel, Maryland, only 15 percent of the children enter foster care, a figure on a par with the rest of the nation.

If this is true, then what happens to the other children and families? The options include: (1) closing the case after a child protective service investigation, perhaps after making a referral to a community service agency; or (2) opening the case for ongoing services after a child protective service investigation.

For the second option to come into play, a decision must be made that the risk of maltreatment is significant and requires a service program. Many refer to these cases as "involuntary service cases." Juvenile court action takes place in some situations, resulting in the agency being awarded an order of protective supervision (legal language varies by state). Such orders allow children to remain with their biological parents while the agency and parents carry out certain activities, such as participation in a drug treatment program, weekly urinalysis, weekly visits with the family by the social worker, parent aide services, and the like. This program component has received little attention and is too often misunderstood. I believe that this is where our local and national scandals (child fatalities) have occurred, and where we must begin to concentrate our efforts. Most of the families about which we are talking are in this service arena, where we encounter those who use drugs heavily.

In seeking to help this group, the following questions confront us: "What service or combination of services should be offered to drug-addicted parents whose children remain in their custody? Does the list change when the children are removed from the parents' care? For how long should the services be offered?"

Regarding the last question—length of service—the problem of addiction looms large. Ups and downs are to be expected and treatment planning must anticipate relapses and plan for them. Although it may be said that recovery is lifelong, this does not mean that an agency remains involved with a family until a child reaches the age of majority. It does mean, however, that services must be available and accessible quickly and easily, particularly during periods of stress or relapse. Treatment planning and implementation revolve around assisting drug-addicted parents to know when they are in trouble and what to do about it. Services are episodic and focused. When the agency is reasonably sure that a child is in a safe and protected environment, child protective services should be terminated.

Recommendations

What services are essential to this population? Service delivery must focus on substance abuse treatment as it relates to the population of women of childbearing years and their families. But there are major obstacles to a woman's successful completion of treatment. First, the woman's caregiver role and her obligations to her children, partner, and extended family can take precedence over her personal need to seek treatment. Second, the relationships in a woman's life often make her dependent and place her in failed, even abusive, situations that may encourage substance abuse. Third, the threat of legal actions and of losing custody of their children keeps many women from seeking treatment. Fourth, as single parents without adequate social support, substance-abusing women do not have the child care available that would allow them to enter treatment. Last, the neighborhoods and communities in which these families live are often beset with violence that reaches into their own households.

Based on this understanding, programming for this client population must include the following services:

- *Child care* that offers a range of options, including on-site child care at a treatment program, purchase-of-care options for parents in treatment, and linkages to existing programs such as Head Start.

- *Housing* for the mother and her children. The usual continuum of care for drug-dependent women lacks this vital component, which is necessary for many substance-abusing women trying to become and stay drug free. For many women who complete a residential treatment program, the return to the home environment means confronting substance abuse by partners or other family members. This bodes ill for women trying to remain drug free. A transitional housing program where women in recovery can live *with their children* would allow these women to support one another in a drug-free environment while they get their lives in order and make progress in their recovery.

- *In-home interventions* (such as Intensive Family Services and Healthy Start) should be expanded in range and availability. Objective evaluations and testimonial evidence from programs such as Illinois' Project SAFE indicate that outreach, home visiting, and case management are critical elements in identifying substance-abusing women and linking them to treatment programs. The lives of these women are generally chaotic and without a meaningful support system. The bonding that can occur between the woman and the home visitor or caseworker, especially when that individual is from the woman's community, is a powerful component of treatment. Case management is essential because the needs of the woman and her family are many and cut across various social service systems and programs. In many jurisdictions, public health or community health nurses are already making home visits and providing case management.

• *Pregnancy testing and family planning* services should be incorporated into substance abuse treatment programs serving women. We know that substance abusers, particularly women, generally do not access the health care system for more than emergency and episodic treatment. They do not avail themselves of existing family planning services or even pregnancy testing because of the chaotic nature of their life-styles. The provision of on-site pregnancy testing and family planning services at drug treatment programs offers the opportunity to prevent unintended pregnancies and the likely births of drug-exposed infants. More importantly, we should be less ambiguous and more straightforward about the importance of family planning and contraception.

• *Family-oriented treatment services* rather than those that focus only on individuals are needed. If any impact is to be made on the mother's substance abuse problem, treatment planning must include the partner or significant others in her life. Relationships with men, children, and family play a significant role in the life of a substance-abusing woman— the nature of these relationships is often a cause of her abuse or an impediment to her seeking treatment.

• *Pregnant adolescent girls* need specialized substance abuse treatment services. Treating adolescents is often very different than treating adults. There are some separate substance abuse treatment programs for adolescents, but these programs are ill-equipped and their staffs are insufficiently trained to meet the unique treatment needs of pregnant adolescent girls with addiction problems.

Lastly, if we are to successfully confront the difficulties of substance-abusing parents, three principles must guide our actions. First, any approach to the problem should include an integration of the medical, legal, and social welfare systems. Second, treatment should be child-centered and family-focused; this should be the guiding philosophy in the development of policies and programs. Third, treatment should be accessible and available in a manner that is neither bureaucratic nor rigid.

The vast majority of our clients are in the child protective services program. Clinical observations tell us that the cases are becoming more difficult and are requiring services of greater intensity and duration. The families are now more demanding, more chaotic, and more complex. The concept of minimal services should no longer be the standard if, in fact, we are serious about serving this population of children and families. What is needed is sound casework based on the principles of a family-focused practice. We must increase caseworkers' capacity to visit the family consistently and regularly. The standard should be weekly visits, not visits whenever caseworkers have the opportunity. The provision of services should include parenting education, parent aide or homemaker services, respite care, and child care. We must be able to deliver these services despite ever-increasing budget deficits. In short, to serve substance-abusing parents and their children properly, we need more money.

9

THE CALL ON
AGENCY RESOURCES

Barbara J. Sabol

For better or for worse, large urban centers such as New York City tend to be in the vanguard of social change—what happens in New York City is usually a precursor of what will happen in other parts of the country. Unfortunately, New York City is in the forefront of a number of urban America's problems—air and water pollution, violent crime, unemployment, child abuse and neglect, school dropouts, teenage pregnancy, and increasing poverty.

New York City's Human Resources Administration (HRA), the largest human services delivery system in the country, is the safety net for over 1.7 million Public Assistance- and Medicaid-eligible New Yorkers. On a recent day, HRA provided basic income supports and medical care to over a half million children living in families on public assistance and provided child day care services to almost 45,000 children; it provided preventive services during the prior 12 months to over 70,000 children and about 30,000 families, despite the financial crunch faced by New York City. Still, over 10 percent of the children in foster care in the country—47,500—are in New York City.

New York was one of the first cities to be afflicted by the dual ravages of crack/cocaine and AIDS. The children of the poor are those most at risk.

Homelessness, substance abuse, crime, neglect and abuse, and AIDS are all related to the poverty in which children live. With a palette of statistics, I want to paint a picture of the devastation children face because of the substance abuse epidemic and its impact on HRA from 1990 to 1991. Although the following facts hardly draw a comprehensive portrait, they forcefully depict a torturous reality for many children in our inner cities. While the examples I give are primarily about New York City, they yield a picture of the problems that have developed in all of our cities and in many of our suburban and rural communities.

The Crack Epidemic

Infants exposed prenatally to drugs constitute a large proportion of the children reported as abused and neglected in many cities. In New York City, 4,643 babies were reported in 1988 to our Child Welfare Administration because of positive drug toxicology—30 percent more than a year earlier and 268 percent more than in 1986, when we first began to track this information.

As overwhelming as these figures are, they may not show the full extent of the crack epidemic. Neonatal toxicology testing at a large number of hospitals in New York City and elsewhere is a major source of allegations of substance abuse-related child abuse and neglect. Cocaine, however, shows up in a newborn only if the mother has ingested the drug shortly before giving birth.

Without neonatal testing or maternal self-reports of drug use during pregnancy, most instances of infants exposed prenatally to crack would initially go undetected. Most infants exposed to crack look healthy at birth.[1]

We may never know the true number of babies born after prenatal exposure to crack and other harmful drugs, including alcohol. Besharov estimates that 10 percent to 20 percent of newborn infants in low-income urban areas around the country are exposed to drugs before they are born and that nationwide, two percent of all newborns are exposed to drugs in utero.[2] The Comptroller for the state of New York estimates that the number of newborns exposed prenatally to drugs in New York City between 1985 and 1989 is not 10,000, as reported in Health Department statistics, but could be as high as 22,000.[3]

Indiscriminate neonatal urine toxicology testing can also be destructive.

False positive results could lead to the wrongful removal of a newborn from its mother's custody. In New York City, we revised our testing regulations so that testing is now mandated when one of the following high-risk indicators is present:

- There is a history of past or present maternal drug use.

- The mother admits current substance abuse.

- The mother exhibits behaviors during labor or delivery that are indicative of substance abuse (e.g., bizarre behavior, slurred speech, unsteady gait, inappropriate affect, or confusion).

- The newborn shows signs of drug intoxication or withdrawal, seizures, or other neurological symptoms.

In addition, further review may suggest the need for testing if the mother has reported no prenatal care, the baby was not delivered in the hospital, there is an abruptio placenta, the baby has congenital syphilis, or there is a history of maternal syphilis.

We do know many of the immediate effects of maternal and often paternal substance abuse. In New York City, in the 12 months from October 1987 through September 1988, there were over 7,100 abuse and neglect reports related to substance abuse. In one month alone during this period (January 1988), there were 659 allegations related to substance abuse—over 21 allegations every single day of the month—almost one an hour. As shown in figure 1, the growth of substance abuse-related allegations between July 1985 and January 1991 has been quite dramatic, especially with respect to instances of neonatal withdrawal.

The repercussions from this extraordinary increase in allegations of substance abuse-related child abuse and neglect were immediately seen in the growth of the foster care caseload. In the early 1980s, New York City had begun to expand its use of preventive services and was able to slowly reduce the number of children who were placed into foster care. Figure 2 shows that, in July 1985 (just before the eruption of the crack epidemic), fewer than 16,700 children were in foster care in New York City. In April 1991, over 49,000 children—an increase of almost 200 percent—were in foster care in New York City. During the peak 12-month period of this crack crisis, between July 1988

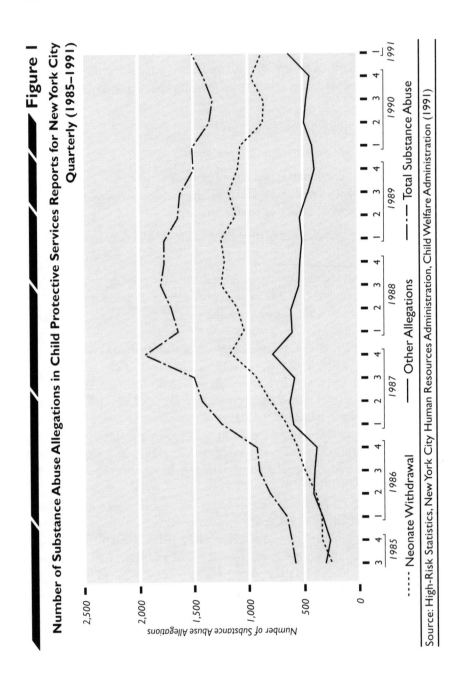

Figure 1

Number of Substance Abuse Allegations in Child Protective Services Reports for New York City Quarterly (1985–1991)

Source: High-Risk Statistics, New York City Human Resources Administration, Child Welfare Administration (1991)

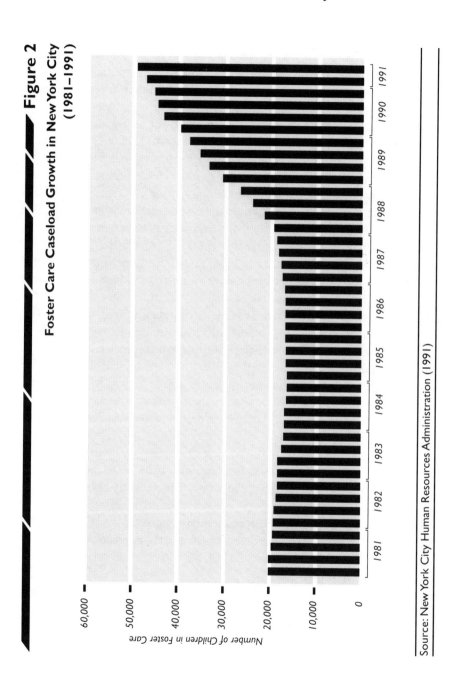

Figure 2

Foster Care Caseload Growth in New York City (1981–1991)

Number of Children in Foster Care

60,000
50,000
40,000
30,000
20,000
10,000
0

1981 1982 1983 1984 1985 1986 1987 1988 1989 1990 1991

Source: New York City Human Resources Administration (1991)

and June 1989, there were 20,900 new admissions into foster care, as shown in figure 3. Although some portion of the increase in foster care placements stems from the increasing number of families and children living in poverty, the unparalleled increase is undoubtedly due to the drug epidemic.

Not only has the caseload grown exponentially, but we are also witnessing a dramatic shift in the composition of the population of children entering care. The innocent victims of the crack epidemic are the very young children. Figure 4 shows that, in 1988, fewer than one in three children in foster care was under the age of six; in 1990, almost one-half of the children in foster care were five or under. Three out of five children who entered foster care in 1990 were under the age of six at the time of admission, as shown in figure 5.

The level of difficulty of the average caseload has also shown a marked increase over the past years. In early 1988, just under 30 percent of the child protective service cases were categorized as high-risk; in June 1990, 48 percent were so designated. High-risk cases are defined as those with child fatalities with surviving siblings in the home or community, drug withdrawal or fetal alcohol syndrome infants, reports of serious or suspicious physical injury, child malnutrition or failure to thrive, current or previous residents of battered women's shelters, children of drug- or alcohol-abusing parents or caregivers, parental or caregiver mental illness or mental retardation, children under seven years of age left alone and unsupervised, and sexual abuse allegations. Allegations in these high-risk cases take longer to investigate and longer to serve.

Not only is the number of high-risk cases in caseloads increasing, but so too is the complexity of the cases. Families with children in foster care because of substance abuse-related difficulties are more likely to have multiple problems than those whose children are in care for other reasons. The multi-problem nature of substance abuse cases requires greater supervision of the families, more home visits by the caseworkers, and the provision of more (and more intensive) services to the family. Thus, the current caseload is, per capita, more expensive to serve.

As the city's overall caseload grew, the caseloads of individual child protective caseworkers also expanded dramatically. In a single six-month period from June to December 1987, the caseloads of child protective workers increased by 25 percent, reaching a high of almost 36 cases per worker. The

Figure 3

Foster Care Population Admissions and Discharges in New York City
(1987–1991)

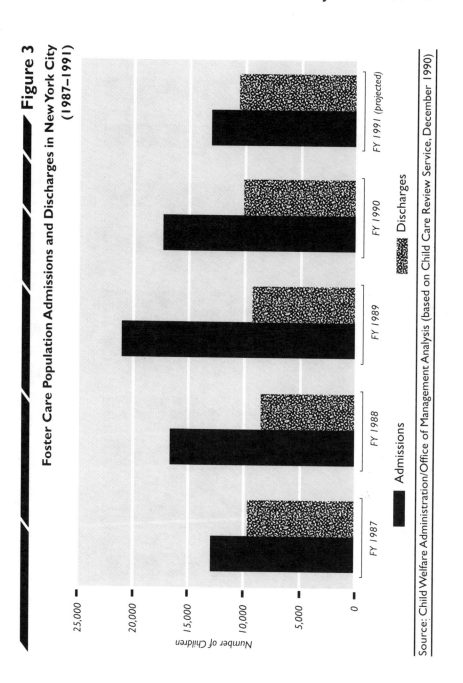

■ Admissions

▨ Discharges

Number of Children

25,000

20,000

15,000

10,000

5,000

0

FY 1987   FY 1988   FY 1989   FY 1990   FY 1991 (projected)

Source: Child Welfare Administration/Office of Management Analysis (based on Child Care Review Service, December 1990)

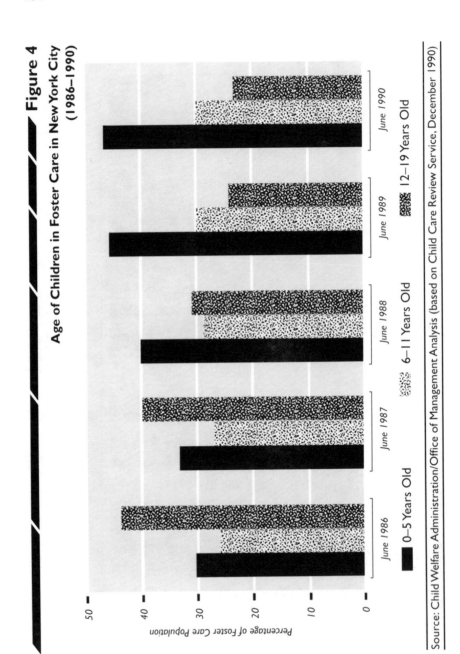

Figure 4

Age of Children in Foster Care in New York City (1986–1990)

Percentage of Foster Care Population

June 1986 | June 1987 | June 1988 | June 1989 | June 1990

■ 0–5 Years Old   6–11 Years Old   12–19 Years Old

Source: Child Welfare Administration/Office of Management Analysis (based on Child Care Review Service, December 1990)

Figure 5

Age of Children at Entrance into Foster Care in New York City
(1986–1990)

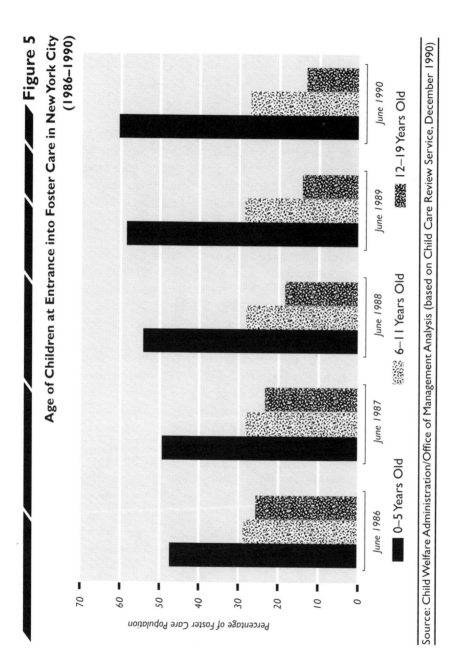

Percentage of Foster Care Population

June 1986   June 1987   June 1988   June 1989   June 1990

■ 0–5 Years Old   ▓ 6–11 Years Old   ▓ 12–19 Years Old

Source: Child Welfare Administration/Office of Management Analysis (based on Child Care Review Service, December 1990)

number of new allegations the workers had to investigate grew by 40 percent during the same time period. In December 1987, our child protective caseworkers were handling an average 9.5 new allegations a month.

Child protective staff turnover skyrocketed. By the fiscal year ending in June 1988, the turnover rate was 59 percent; the next year, it was 62 percent. We were able to convince the budget authorities in New York City that we needed to do more than simply replace all staff members who resigned—we had to hire sufficient new staff members to bring caseloads down to reasonable levels or we would have no child protective workers left at all. We increased the total number of child protective workers from 617 in January 1988 to 1,091 in October 1990. We brought the individual caseload down to 12 cases per child protective worker with just over four new cases a month. Subsequently, the turnover rate showed a small decrease to 52 percent in FY 1990. In the 12-month period ending in June 1991, turnover dropped to 30 percent.

Obviously, when workers have fewer cases, they have more time to devote to each case, more time to conduct thorough investigations and document their work, and more time to arrange for service delivery. A recent analysis demonstrated a number of benefits from this reduction in caseload and stabilization of the work force. First, the percentage of indicated/founded cases has increased steadily from 38 percent in January 1988 to 49 percent in October 1990.[4] In the same time period, the percentage of cases referred for day care, homemaker services, and preventive services had increased slightly. The percentage of cases remaining in the child protective services units for more than six months—as opposed to being closed or transferred to more intensive service-oriented units—has concomitantly declined. Any increase in the size of the caseload—due to either increases in the number or severity of reports or to the loss of staff—will have a negative impact on our workers' ability to perform their jobs.

Nevertheless, I am happy to report that, since 1991, we have begun to see a very small reversal in these trends in New York City. Between 1989 and 1991, the number of admissions into foster care has declined by 38 percent and the number of discharges has increased by 14 percent. In addition, whereas substance abuse was known to be involved in seven out of 10 child fatality cases that we reviewed in 1989, drugs were known to be involved in only half of the cases we reviewed in 1990, as shown in figure 6.

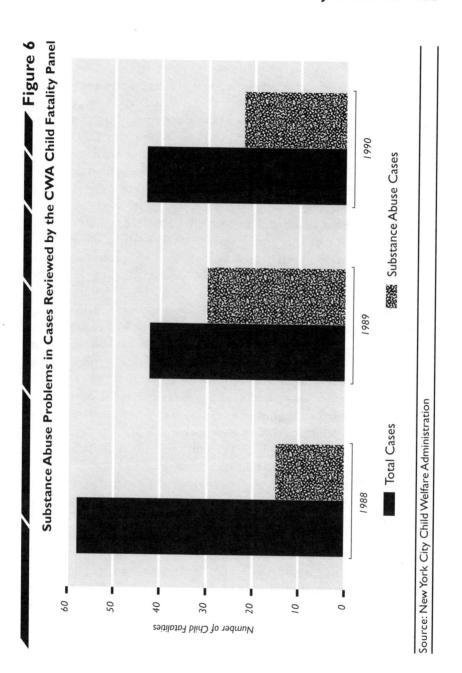

Figure 6

Substance Abuse Problems in Cases Reviewed by the CWA Child Fatality Panel

Number of Child Fatalities

1988   1989   1990

■ Total Cases   ▨ Substance Abuse Cases

Source: New York City Child Welfare Administration

The AIDS Epidemic

Although I have spent a considerable amount of time discussing the scourge of the crack epidemic in New York City, the HIV/AIDS epidemic, especially as it relates to women and children, is a related and equally urgent crisis. The incidence of AIDS among women and children in New York City is closely linked to drug use, although not necessarily to crack or cocaine. Statistics show that 61 percent of women with AIDS in New York acquired the virus by injection with contaminated needles; another 25 percent got it via sexual transmission, often from male IV drug users.[5]

Between December 1986 and December 1990, while the number of persons with AIDS in New York City grew by more than 300 percent, the number of women and children with AIDS grew by more than 400 percent. In January 1991, there were 30,600 New Yorkers with AIDS (as defined by the Centers for Disease Control). Of these, 4,300 were women and 735 were children. Most of these women were in their peak childbearing years—between 20 and 39 years old. By December, 1993, the number of children with AIDS had climbed to 1,261, a further increase of 72 percent. AIDS has become the number one killer of women in the 25 to 34 year-old age bracket. It is the second leading cause of death for children between the ages of one and 14.[6]

Many of these children have been placed in foster care and, in coming years, we expect their number to grow dramatically. Seventy-eight percent of all reported cases of pediatric AIDS in New York involved children infected in utero. The number of women and children infected with AIDS is believed to be five to nine times greater than the number of reported cases.

The vast majority of women and children with AIDS are people of color. Fifty-one percent of women reported with AIDS in New York were African-American, 33 percent were of Latino origin, and 15 percent were Caucasian. Fifty-two percent of the children under the age of 13 with AIDS were African-American; 38 percent were Latino.

The death of children with AIDS is not the only way in which this disease affects the very young; many children have been orphaned because of AIDS. Over the next several years, it is estimated that 10,000 New York City children will lose both parents to AIDS, and between 60,000 and 70,000 children will lose one parent to AIDS.

In sum, AIDS and the onslaught of crack—symptoms of society's larger problems—have taken away from too many children their fundamental right to a strong family in which to be nurtured and a strong community in which to live.

New York City's Response

Our philosophy is that the child welfare system should be attuned to children's needs and that, whenever possible, children should be helped in the context of the family. Because our first priority must always be to keep families together, we are working to enhance family resources and capabilities—even in those families damaged by substance abuse—both to prevent foster care placement where possible and to minimize its impact and duration when placement is unavoidable. To the extent feasible, we believe that foster care should be used as a way to strengthen families, not to replace them.

When placement is unavoidable, our priority is to place children with other relatives. If this is not feasible, foster care placement should be within the same community in which the family resides and an all-out effort must be expended to ensure that siblings are kept together. While children are in foster care, our efforts must turn to the provision of those services that will aid in the reunification of the family. If all else fails, children should not languish in foster care, and permanency planning for adoption must be undertaken.

The Family Rehabilitation Program

The Family Rehabilitation Program (FRP)—one of our key preventive initiatives— provides concurrent, intensive case management, preventive services, and drug treatment services for families in which substance abuse is the major protective issue. The program is designed to allow mothers with substance abuse problems to obtain treatment while their children remain with them.

The target population is families in which children are at risk of being placed into foster care because one or both parents are substance abusers. Primary attention is focused on families reported to the Child Welfare Administration with allegations of babies born with positive toxicologies or in which the contributing factor of the allegation of abuse or neglect is parental substance abuse, and in which there is at least one child six years or younger in the home.

The FRP is based on three important programmatic themes. First is the conviction that effective treatment of the parent's drug abuse requires the provision of a broad array of services to the family. In addition to drug treatment, each client is provided with such services as individual, group, and family counseling, as well as parenting and home management skills, education, and medical and mental health care assessments and referrals.

The second theme is the importance of providing intensive case management of the services mentioned above. The drug treatment providers are encouraged—in fact, required—to maintain close contact and share information about progress in treatment with the FRP caseworker. To allow the FRP workers the time and flexibility to work intensively with their families, the caseload ratios in the FRP have been limited to 1:9.

The third theme is the value of using a range of drug treatment modalities, including acupuncture, self-help groups, and counseling, in a variety of outpatient and day treatment settings. An integral part of the FRP will be an evaluation of the wide assortment of modalities used, to determine which program or combination of services works best for each client.

The Preventive Housing Subsidy Program

This program, currently funded solely by the city and state, provides financial assistance in cases in which a lack of housing prevents the discharge of children from foster care. We also began to provide similar subsidies to families with children at risk of placement.

Between FY 1989 and FY 1994, the program has assisted a total of 1,200 families in obtaining adequate housing and has enabled 2,623 children to be discharged from foster care. In addition, as part of the State Preventive Housing Demonstration Project, the Child Welfare Administration is expected to provide housing subsidies to 539 families whose children are at risk of being placed in foster care. In FY 1993, due to staffing shortages, the Child Welfare Administration issued preventive housing subsidies to only 67 families.

The New York/New York Connect Program

This program provides coordinated services to pregnant or parenting women who abuse drugs, alcohol, or both, and who live in three communities in New York City: Bedford-Stuyvesant in Brooklyn, Central Harlem in Manhattan, and Mott Haven in the Bronx. The Connect program is designed to improve access and expand the delivery of human services to pregnant women, women who have recently given birth, and the families of these women.

The Target Cities Initiative

Under this program, run by the U.S. Department of Health and Human Services, states may seek support in behalf of one city in which drug abuse problems have reached crisis proportions. We are that city in New York State. The objective of the Target Cities Initiative is a comprehensive and coordinated system of substance abuse services in the South Bronx and northern Manhattan. What makes this program unique is that it targets pregnant women among its priority populations.

The Family Preservation Program (FPP)

This program, based on the Homebuilders model started in December 1991, provides intensive in-home counseling and support to families with children at imminent risk of foster care placement, as well as follow-up preventive services and mentors. FPP served 954 families with 2,509 children in FY 1993, compared with 247 families with 684 children in FY 1992, making it the largest municipal family preservation program in the nation.

The Hospital Babies Unit

Each of the zones of the Child Welfare Administration's decentralized Office of Field Services has a Hospital Babies Unit. Child protective service caseworkers in these specialized units investigate cases reported by hospitals of newborns with positive drug toxicologies. The workers become familiar with and establish a rapport with the different hospitals and the staffs in their zones. The hospital staff and the child protective workers meet regularly to inform each other of their operations. As all babies in these units are considered to be at high risk, the unit supervisors work even closer with the child protective caseworkers than is the norm in nonhospital cases.

The Foster Parent Training Program

This program teaches parenting skills to all foster parents—including kinship foster parents—and those biological parents who need the service. The program also provides special-needs training to the foster parents of children who were born with positive toxicology.

The Pre-Discharge Conference Pilot Program

Under this program for babies born with positive toxicologies, conferences encompassing hospital representatives, Child Welfare Administration case-workers, and parents are conducted in order to share vital information concerning the medical needs of those babies born with positive toxicology who are to be discharged to their parents.

The Child Protective Workers' Training Academy

The Child Welfare Administration developed the specialized Satterwhite Child Protective Services Training Academy to provide substance abuse training courses to our new child protective caseworkers and refresher courses to more-experienced employees. After undergoing an intensive month-long training program at the academy, new caseworkers spend three additional months in special training units in their field locations. During this period, the caseworkers are closely supervised.

During the initial 20-day training, new workers learn about child protective practices, child development, legal and social services, interviewing techniques, and high-risk assessments. The new workers are taught how to handle the requisite paperwork and the critical procedures they will have to follow when it becomes necessary to remove a child from the home.

Following these first 20 days, there are two days of intensive training on substance abuse. The training includes viewing a video called *Crack Street, USA*, role-playing a crack mother, and learning about the indicators of drug use and withdrawal, the addictive personality, stages of addiction, the effects of maternal substance abuse on fetal development, the process of assessing an allegation of substance abuse, drug treatment programs, guidelines for engaging the addictive client, clinical management, alcohol as a drug, signs and stages of alcoholism, the "alcoholic" family, and family roles.

The academy also provides training on substance abuse to the caseworkers in the voluntary agencies from which we purchase preventive services.

Early Permanency Planning Project for Children of HIV-Positive Parents

A collaboration between the Child Welfare Administration and the Division of AIDS Services, this project seeks preadoptive homes for the children of women dying of AIDS. The purpose of this pilot program is to ease the child's transition to a new home and to ease the mother's concern about her child after her death. When such homes are found, the preadoptive parents will meet with the mother and the child.

The Need for More Resources

We can succeed in diminishing the devastating effects of crack and other debilitating symptoms of poverty if we pull together and work together; if we dedicate our energy, intelligence, imagination, expertise, and a sizeable portion of our resources.

But let us be pragmatic. We will need significant amounts of federal funding to enable the massive supports we need to provide. Although New York City has responded gallantly to the drug epidemic, much more still has to be done. We must have more drug treatment programs that are sensitive to the needs of women. Most of the existing drug treatment programs were developed to deal with male heroin addicts. Drug treatment experts have found, however, that "methods that work with men often backfire with women. Women will not be spoken to harshly or in a condescending manner."[7] In addition, most detox programs will not accept pregnant women because "they are not equipped to deal with prenatal medical needs" and because they are concerned about their liability. We must have drug treatment programs that will accept pregnant women and women with young children. To reach this goal, Congress must expand Medicaid coverage for services in all licensed drug treatment centers, regardless of modality. Medicaid has to be expanded to cover comprehensive family-centered residential substance abuse treatment services for Medicaid-eligible women and their children.

Currently, those who receive "drug-free" treatment counseling services are eligible for Medicaid reimbursement only if the services are provided in a hospital facility or under the supervision of a doctor in an outpatient setting. Those who receive residential substance abuse treatment services are not eligible for Medicaid reimbursement. This is not an effective use of federal, state, and local resources—residential programs are often less expensive and deal with substance abuse more directly than inpatient hospital programs. Residential treatment is often the modality of choice for cocaine-addicted, low-income pregnant and postpartum women. Nevertheless, nationwide, the availability of these services in no way meets the demand. "Only 11 percent of pregnant substance abusers get into treatment."[8]

Services for this population should be comprehensive, with a family-oriented approach that includes health care services, parenting skills training, vocational assistance, housing advocacy, domestic violence counseling, HIV education, and education in nutrition and budgeting. For these residential treatment programs to be most effective, they must also assure day care for the children and a therapeutic nursery to provide developmental skills training for infants exposed prenatally to drugs.

The current child welfare system, designed over ten years ago, no longer reflects today's realities. When the Adoption Assistance and Child Welfare Act [P.L. 96-272] was enacted by Congress, the nation's child welfare systems were not faced with the ravages of HIV/AIDS, homelessness, and drugs. As a result of the massive increase in the number of children in foster care, we have been forced to operate within a system that is unresponsive to the needs of children, that does not offer the flexibility to address appropriately the needs of children and families, and that often unfairly sets penalties for failing to meet standards that are no longer realistic. We need substantial increases in funding for the Title IV-B Child Welfare Services program and set-aside funds for families in crisis due to substance abuse.

Conclusion

The crack epidemic has greatly increased the vulnerability of the children in this country and, while the years of peak usage appear to be behind us, the crisis does continue. With respect to HIV/AIDS, each year brings more cases of HIV-positive and AIDS-infected women and children.

New York City is committed to helping these families in need. Although we have been able to develop many innovative programs and we are still in the process of developing new initiatives, much more has to be done. All of urban America needs the legislative mandate and the federal dollars that are prerequisite for serving and saving these children and their families.

Notes

1. See Zuckerman, Chapter 3 of this volume.

2. Douglas J. Besharov, "The Children of Crack: Will We Protect Them?" *Public Welfare* (Fall 1989): 6-11.

3. Eleanor Bachrach, Deputy Comptroller, New York State, "A Preliminary Analysis of the Impact of Prenatal Exposure to Crack in New York City," Report 22-91 (Albany, NY: Office of the Comptroller, February 7, 1991), 5.

4. Human Resources Administration/Child Welfare Administration, "Analysis of Reduced P/D Caseloads on Service Delivery," internal memo, July 1, 1991.

5. Commissioner Barbara J. Sabol, "AIDS, Drugs, and the Family," keynote address, Fifth Montefiore Symposium on AIDS, New York City, April 22, 1991.

6. *Ibid.*

7. "Should We Take away Their Children?" *Time*, 13 May 1991, 62-63.

8. "Innocent Victims," *Time*, 13 May 1991, 59.

10

African American Children in Foster Care

Clarice Dibble Walker

African American children have been disproportionately represented in the foster care system for more than a decade. In recent years, even larger numbers of these children have been entering or returning to the child welfare system—largely due to the deepening crisis of parental drug use. The most recent data available (FY 1990) showed that African American children constituted 40.4 percent of the total population in foster care, but only 15.1 percent of the total population of children under 18.[1]

This paper presents the findings of a study of African American children who entered the foster care system in 1986 and our analysis of the potentially devastating impact of substance abuse on this population and on the African American community itself.[2]

The analysis is based on data from an earlier National Black Child Development Institute (NBCDI) two-and-one-half-year study that profiled 1,003 African American children who entered foster care in five cities (New York, Miami, Houston, Detroit, and Seattle) during calendar year 1986. Additional analyses were performed to compare the children who entered foster care with parental drug abuse as a factor contributing to placement with those who entered care for other reasons. Differences in these two segments of the foster care population were tested and described along many variables, including family characteristics, child characteristics, reasons for placement other than parental drug abuse, services offered during placement, the role of relatives, and discharge outcomes. The differences in the total sample of children were based on data collected approximately 26 months after the children's entry into foster care. In addition, updated data on the discharge status of children in New York City were analyzed four and one-half years after their entry into foster care.

It was hypothesized that the children who came into care with parental drug abuse problems would come from multiproblem families, with few financial and social supports. It was also hypothesized that, because of the lack of direct child welfare programs to deal with many parental problems, the lack of caseworker resources, and the lack of available and suitable drug treatment programs for pregnant women and mothers in many cities, the children, particularly those from homes with parental drug abuse, would tend to stay in care for long periods of time.

Our research led us to three major conclusions:

- Child welfare agencies were not achieving permanency for most children, particularly for those from homes with parental drug abuse.

- Services that deal with the problems contributing to placement in foster care were either unavailable, or insufficiently brokered or coordinated with other organizations.

- Placements with relatives were often available and represented a significant resource for children.

The Study Population

Characteristics of the Children

Children entering care from families with drug-abusing parents were younger than those entering care for other reasons. The median age of the children from families with drug-abusing parents at initial placement in foster care was 4.7 years, compared to 7.5 years for other children.

Characteristics of the Families

Families in which parental drug abuse was a problem were more likely to be poorly housed and to receive Aid to Families with Dependent Children (AFDC) prior to placement than were other families with children in care. Fifty-three percent of the drug-involved families were headed by single parents and 85 percent received AFDC. The mothers in such families also had less education than those from nondrug-using families: 67 percent had not completed high school. Inadequate housing and poverty were cited as placement factors twice as often in families with drug abuse as for the other families.

Reasons for Entry into Foster Care

Child neglect was the primary reason for placement significantly more often for children from families with parental drug abuse problems than for other children; *child abuse* was more often associated with placement of children from the nondrug-abusing families. Parental mental health problems and child behavioral problems were more likely to be factors contributing to placement for children from families without parental drug abuse.

The Lack of Permanency

Barriers to Reunification

Among the most commonly reported barriers to reuniting children with parents was the continued drug abuse of the parent. This prevented reunification in 63 percent of the parental drug abuse cases that had not been discharged by the end of the study. Drug treatment referrals, however, were made by the agency for only 60 percent of all drug-abusing parents at some time during the study period of 26 months. It is likely that even fewer actually received the services to which they were referred.

We found that drug treatment programs had limited availability, accessibility, and effectiveness, and did not provide mothers with the treatment they needed. Many of the treatment slots available may not have been suitable for pregnant or parenting women. For example, then New York City mayor David Dinkins reported in 1990 that there was only one residential drug treatment program in that city that served young mothers with their children. Half of the programs did not accept pregnant women; only one-third treated pregnant women with Medicaid coverage; and only 13 percent provided detoxification for crack-addicted pregnant women eligible for Medicaid.[3]

Lengthy Stays in Foster Care

Children are remaining in the child welfare system for long periods of time. Despite P.L. 96-272's mandatory goals and guidelines, long-term foster care appeared to be common among African American children placed in foster care in 1986. This was particularly true among children from families with drug-abusing parents. Even after 26 months, 72 percent of the children of substance abusers in the total sample were still in foster care. By contrast, 49 percent of the children whose parents did not abuse drugs were still in care. Reunification with biological parents was almost twice as frequent for cases with no drug abuse as for parental drug abuse cases. Adoptions, guardianships, and other nonreunification discharge options were rare in general for cases with parental drug abuse. Children from families with parental drug abuse, however, had more frequent placements with relatives.

Other research has demonstrated a declining probability of reunification of children with biological parents over time. The results of our study's examination of New York case discharge records in late 1990—four and one-half years after placement—were thus very disturbing. More than half of these children had never been discharged. Fully 63 percent of children whose parents had been drug abusers were still in care. Their chances for reunification with their biological parents are undoubtedly poor.

African American children, like other children, should not remain in what is intended to be "temporary" care for such lengthy periods of time. Over ten years ago, Congress mandated that children should be moved into a situation of permanency as quickly as possible, whether by returning them to their homes, placing them in the care of relatives, or freeing them for adoption. The psychological and emotional harm of prolonged stays in foster care has been well-documented. Children have only one childhood. If that childhood consists of regular, constant, reliable, loving relationships, it is likely that the child will develop a sense of belonging, a necessary ingredient for good citizenship as an adult. If those conditions do not exist, then the child's future may well be in doubt.

Evidence is growing that children in foster care whose parents are substance abusers have experienced interruptions in the bonding and attachment process and have not had the opportunity to build relationships. Many of these children entered foster care at a very young age—50 percent of our study population was under the age of 4.7 years. This characteristic of the population portends serious problems for the future unless special attention is given to the needs of these at-risk children and their families.

Underutilization of Adoption

Indisputably, not every child can be reunited with biological parents; in such instances, adoption should be an early consideration and should be utilized when appropriate. The study's findings show, however, that only 9 percent of the total sample's children of drug-abusing parents were adopted within 26 months after placement; only 17 of the New York sample's 226 children had been adopted after 54 months in foster care. We are concerned that child welfare agencies appear to continue to have difficulty in achieving adoption for African American children, particularly for those children with emotional, physical, or behavioral problems. We are also convinced that adoption delays are not all related to the child's problems. Failure to make early decisions and a lack of aggressive adoptive planning frequently cause children to languish in the system.

A survey by the Child Welfare League of America Adoption Task Force reported a significant increase in the percentage of minority children who are free for adoption, awaiting adoption, and yet unadopted. From 1981 to 1982, 37 percent of the waiting children were minorities. In 1989, minority children represented 51 percent of this population. African American children represent the majority of those minority children who have not been adopted. Obstacles to the adoption of these children must continue to be examined. This will be especially important since, by all reports, one impact of substance abuse in the child welfare system is that an increasing number of vulnerable and troubled children are in need of homes.

The Role of Kinship Care

In many instances, children in foster care have relatives who are available and willing to provide assistance and care. These relatives frequently need financial support and family support services, however, to assist them in their caregiving roles. Placement of children with relatives is a care option that is rapidly growing in many jurisdictions, especially New York, California, and Illinois.[4] This option is fueled by two perspectives. Advocates have been persuasive in making the case for the power of the extended family to provide care, continuity, and a sense of identity and family belonging for the child who is being separated from the biological parent. At another level, agencies have experienced severe shortages of family foster parents in recent years and have turned to relatives for needed foster homes.

Kinship placements are not without controversy, however. Should relatives be used as foster parents and should they should receive foster care payments and the same types of services or training rendered to nonrelative foster parents? Critics question whether any foster care payments should be made to relatives. They fear disincentives for reunification with biological parents given a reimbursement for foster care that is presently higher (albeit still inadequate) than the payment level for children under AFDC. The argument goes that drug-abusing parents will relinquish their children to grandparents or aunts for the sake of added income in the kinship network.

Our study revealed that relatives were an important resource for the children and the foster care agencies. The relatives were obviously concerned about the welfare of their grandchildren, nieces, and nephews before any offers of foster care payments were considered. They were able and willing to provide help to the children of substance abusers, usually in the form of a foster placement in 60 percent of the cases in which the agency considered them a resource. When relatives did not assist, it was usually due to a lack of personal financial resources. Foster care payments would remove this obstacle.

When appropriate and supported by the agency, relative placements may promote uninterrupted bonds between the child and parents, as well as the relatives. Such relationships are important to a child's physical, social, emotional, and cultural well-being. If agencies encourage strengthening familial bonds, relatives may also continue to function in beneficial roles for the family after reunification.

Reducing the Need for Placement

The services that parents need in order to reduce the likelihood of placement are too often unavailable, inadequate, insufficient, or not coordinated. Just as continued substance abuse is a barrier to the return of children to their parents, so too are inadequate housing and a lack of financial resources. These problems often lack easy solutions. According to the case plans reviewed in the study, when inadequate housing was identified as a problem, the parent was expected to improve the housing conditions, usually an unattainable goal given the poverty status of the parent. Public housing—with its years-long waiting lists— is usually not a resource, especially in urban areas where there is no visible coordination between housing authorities and child welfare agencies. The dependence of foster care agencies on public housing agencies to provide housing for the poor is usually futile.

In addition, mothers whose children are in foster care lose their AFDC payments, which, for many, is their sole source of financial support. Some parents may be able to obtain employment only in menially paid jobs. If so, they are more likely to lose or retain their previous housing during the child's placement than to be able to upgrade it.

Parenting education, a service that is frequently provided directly by the child welfare agency, was offered to only 48 percent of the substance-abusing parents and to 34 percent of the other parents in the study. Considering that 85 percent of the drug-abusing parents and 70 percent of the nondrug-abusing parents had abandoned, abused, or neglected their children prior to placement, the need was clearly much greater.

Conclusion

Our study of African American children in care confirms that children are entering the child welfare system at earlier ages and that they are remaining for long periods of time. They are frequently without the services that give children a chance for a stable, permanent home with their parents or with an adoptive family. Many children of substance-abusing parents are often enduring the distress of chaotic family environments without appropriate agency interventions. This must not continue.

Caring for children must become a priority for this nation and for the agencies charged with this responsibility. African American children need the same things that other children need: stimulation to promote cognitive, social, and emotional development at every stage; a sense of security from responsive and protective caregivers; and opportunities to learn. Their parents must be given every opportunity to build an economic base that will be the primary source for meeting their children's needs and to have some of their own needs met through constructive, intensive, multidimensional services. This could be achieved for many troubled families with personalized, longitudinal case problem-solving with the family unit within a coordinated, multi-institutional service network. If, however, after being given appropriate supports, parents cannot provide the ingredients needed for the healthy growth of their children, we can no longer ignore reality. We must explore alternative families for the children.

The costs of intensive comprehensive programs using multidisciplinary professionals will undoubtedly be great. The costs will be greater, however, and we will pay more if we leave children in distress at home without protection, if we leave children in foster care and abandon their parents prematurely to the ravages of drug abuse, or if we fail to provide an adoptive home when such a need is indicated. Without an honest attempt to remedy the situation, we can expect to go on paying enormous sums for postnatal care in our public hospitals for infants exposed prenatally to drugs, for special or remedial education and other needed therapies for these children, and possibly for a lifetime of institutional costs—foster care, criminal justice, homeless shelters, and mental institutions. The financial costs of comprehensive effective family services programs and other strategies seem to make sense when faced with these alternatives.

Notes

1. Toshio Tatara, *Characteristics of Children in Substitute and Adoptive Care: A Statistical Summary of the VCIS National Child Welfare Data Base* (Washington, DC: American Public Welfare Association, 1993).

2. Clarice Walker, Patricia Zangrillo, and Jacqueline Smith, *Parental Substance Abuse and African American Children in the Child Welfare System* (Washington, DC: National Black Child Development Institute, 1991).

3. The Honorable David Dinkins, Mayor of the City of New York, *Testimony before the Subcommittee on Children, Family, Drugs, and Alcoholism* (Washington, DC: U.S. Government Printing Office, February 5, 1990).

4. U.S. House of Representatives Committee on Ways and Means, *Overview of Entitlement Programs (1993 Green Book)* (Washington, DC: U.S. Government Printing Office, 1993), 935.

THE INSUFFICIENCY OF STATUTORY PROTECTIONS

Ramona L. Foley

Three years ago, I received a phone call from a family court judge in a small rural county in upstate South Carolina. As a judge with 14 years experience on the bench and a strong reputation as a child advocate, he expressed his concern and frustration over a case that he had heard earlier in the day. Briefly, the case circumstances were as follows:

Lucy had entered protective custody one year earlier due to a report of being physically abused by her mother. During the 60 days allowed for the investigation, Lucy had five placements. This quick succession of placements did not reflect improved behaviors and less restrictive environments for Lucy. On the contrary, she had run away twice, stole from the other foster children, and been sexually provocative in conversation with and verbally abusive to the foster parents and emergency shelter staff.

After available placements in the small county had been exhausted, Lucy was returned to her mother. Shortly thereafter, the agency received several reports of Lucy being out all night drinking. Lucy reentered foster care, but this time she was hospitalized for medical evaluation and detoxification at a medical university. Upon release, she entered a community-based crisis stabilization unit followed by a community-based residential treatment program. After running away four times from the treatment unit, Lucy was court-ordered to a reception and evaluation unit of the juvenile correctional system. She tested positive for cocaine and had contracted gonorrhea. So, in addition to nine out-of-home placements in a year, Lucy had documented evidence of alcohol and substance addiction, was sexually promiscuous, and often ran away from her placements. The judge recognized that incarceration in the juvenile correctional system was not the answer. He simply wanted to know what was.

None of the problems presented by Lucy's case was remarkable in and of itself. In fact, these problems are fairly common among our special-needs teens of today. But what was remarkable about Lucy is that she was only 11 years old and her 11 years had not been spent in poverty or on the streets of a large city. She had spent her formative years in a community where the main occupation is farming and where it is still considered safe for 11-year-olds to walk to the corner grocery to spend a quarter.

Although problems related to the heavy use of drugs are more prevalent in urban areas, it must be noted that the resources tend to be more prevalent in those areas as well. A referral that might be routine in cities such as New York stretches the imagination as well as the budget of a social service agency in a rural area.

Lucy is only one example, but she epitomizes a number of critical difficulties that we face in foster care today. The safeguards against foster care drift that were built into P.L. 96-272 simply do not meet the needs of children like Lucy—children whose best chances for treatment and stability often lie within the system rather than in reunification or adoption. This paper discusses five aspects of the problem and makes recommendations concerning the federal mandate, the change in the foster care population, the foster care providers, public sentiment, and the philosophy of the foster care system.

The Federal Mandate

The Adoption Assistance and Child Welfare Act of 1980 (P.L. 96-272) has played a major role in reducing foster care drift, that pivotal term of the 1970s and early 1980s. Having seen firsthand the faces of children in foster care whose cases remained in the backs of file drawers, I strongly maintain that the implementation of P.L. 96-272 forced open the file drawers and demanded a level of accountability previously unknown in the foster care system. It forced agencies to review their caseloads, resulting in the return of many children to their biological families and the placement of others for adoption.

In the early 1980s, this was not as difficult as it might seem. In many cases, we could no longer resurrect the reasons why the child was placed in foster care initially and, with the process of placement being somewhat loose, we had loaded our foster care caseloads with some rather fetching, blue-eyed, blonde-haired preschoolers. So, an admission of the system must be that many children were in foster care in the 1980s who would not have been in the system had their families had the benefit of intensive in-home services.

Although in-home services and "reasonable efforts" to preserve families have kept some children with their families, and although P.L. 96-272 is still useful in arousing the public's interest in unfit and uncaring parents and in keeping children out of foster care, P.L. 96-272 has not eliminated the problems in foster care. The law obviously could not have been written with the increasing number of children in foster care that the 1990s has seen. Challenging our caseworker to see how many times she can prepare for a third-party case review will not significantly alter Lucy's life course. And, while I remain a strong advocate of third-party review and monitoring, I have come to realize that foster children such as Lucy demand much more from the system than the application of the safeguards of P.L. 96-272. In-home services did not keep Lucy out of foster care nor will six-month reviews reunite Lucy with her family. On the contrary, in spite of the required case plan, which, like most others, indicates "return home," the indication in Lucy's case is that her mother is a longtime substance abuser who provides little if any parental supervision and that return to her will not be a viable option for Lucy.

Although P.L. 96-272 can provide a quantitative analysis of how many safeguards can be applied, it does not consider the quality of what occurs in the child's life experience. In a time of scarce resources, is it more important for the worker to perform the paperwork for a six-month review of a child who is to remain in foster care, or is that worker's time better spent in direct contact with the child (for example, working with the child on the child's life book or on matters that the child identifies as critical)?

A second legal mandate that deserves mention is that of independent living services for teens. For foster children over 15 years of age, these services have added emphasis to efforts toward self-sufficiency and independence. But again, legislation may become obsolete in terms of the changing population. As we prepare foster children to live on their own by the age of 18 or 21, the trend in society has shifted; fewer of our own children are moving out and becoming self-sufficient at that age. One must question if this is a realistic goal in foster care.

The Changing Foster Care Population

A second issue we face with long-term foster care, as well as with foster care in general, is the change in the foster care population. Perhaps the foster care system that has evolved with P.L. 96-272 would be totally adequate in the 1990s if only we could have kept the same families and children that we served in the early 1980s. The analogy might be that we are continuing to sell a product that no longer meets the needs of the consumer. The problems of the families that entered our services system in the 1970s seem almost benign in retrospect. Today's families are far more dysfunctional, less likely to be two-parent, and less apt to be receptive to increasingly short-term intervention. Families like those of the 1970s may be increasingly unlikely to become part of the foster care system because their needs are met at the front end of the system with family preservation and in-home services. Consequently, it is the difficult and more needy families that end up in the foster care system.

We must be careful, however, not to assume too quickly that all families are provided the safety net of family preservation. In South Carolina, 45 percent of the children who enter foster care are entering primarily because of neglect. In addition, approximately one-third of those children who enter will return home or to relatives within the first six months of out-of-home care. With statistics such as these, one suspects that all that can and should be done to avoid placement in foster care is simply not being accomplished.

The foster care population provides a snapshot of society's current problems. Substance abuse, AIDS, physical violence, and severe emotional disturbance are all ills of the general population and are therefore, not surprisingly, characteristics of our families and of the children in foster care. Foster children of the 1960s and 1970s drifted in the foster care system due to a lack of attention. Today's foster children, however, are not ignored; they receive mandated attention from courts, third-party reviewers, guardians ad litem, and so on, yet many remain in care on a long-term basis. Why?

The answer lies in the inadequacy of services to reunite families, the need for long-term residential treatment for foster children along with compatible outreach for the families, and the failure to recognize that the foster care system cannot in six months resolve a generation's toll of family dysfunction.

Foster Care Providers

Just as the foster care population has changed, so too have foster care providers. Although foster care providers represent many of the broader attitudes of the general public, there is the advent of providers who recognize the extreme level of dysfunction of many of the families and, therefore, the level of service that is required for the children needing foster care. Programs previously recognized as shelters for the abused and neglected find themselves serving fewer victims of abuse and neglect. Many of these providers have totally and successfully revamped their programs, recognizing that children may be with them on a long-term basis rather than as an emergency and may have tremendous needs for intensive services. Programs to serve the children of substance abusers, children who are themselves substance abusers, sexually assaultive children, and severely emotionally disturbed children are examples of the specialized programs being developed in the private sector.

Foster parents have changed as well in that the traditional "mom and pop" arrangement has become atypical. We are realizing that what is needed from foster parents is professional parenting, which, as a professional service, costs more money. One has to wonder if the high cost of good foster parenting is also motivating the new trend toward kinship care. As professionals, we have always subscribed to the use of relatives for out-of-home care. But, with fewer foster parents available to the foster care program and with increased fees for those who do take on that role, kinship care becomes an increasingly attractive option to the taxpayer as well as to the frustrated professional.

Public Sentiment

Public sentiment with respect to foster care is a fourth issue. We seem to still be selling the public on the notion that foster care is about children being abused and neglected. Although the notion is certainly true to some extent, we are acutely aware that the public has far less sympathy for substance abusers, the severely emotionally disturbed, promiscuous adolescents, and HIV-positive children and youths. As a result, we continue to promote foster care for "victims" of abuse and neglect, encouraging communities to open shelters and fund programs the brochures for which present heartwarming snapshots of a five-year-old girl with tears on her cheeks. What might the public's reaction be to a brochure depicting a 12-year-old setting fire to his house or a 10-year-old sniffing cocaine? We recognize that the image of foster care has become so controversial that it seems self-defeating to confuse the matter further with the truth.

Foster Care Philosophy

A last critical consideration concerns the philosophy of foster care. Over the past 20 years, we have evolved from a philosophy of short-term care (that turned out not to be so short-term) to permanent plans (that have turned out to be less than permanent). We cannot go backward in our thinking. We must still advocate keeping children with their own families when at all possible and moving children from foster care into permanent families through reunification, placements with relatives, and adoptions. But for the growing number of foster children for whom these desirable plans do not evolve, the philosophy of foster care and how we explain it publicly are of crucial importance. If we believe what years of practice have taught us—that is, that a child's self-esteem and sense of worth are intricately altered by removal from the family—can we not also believe that we are sending the wrong message when we sit face to face with the child at periodic reviews and question the family's commitment to having the child returned or the fact that no family wants the child as a permanent member? If our philosophy is that, through consistent and periodic review, we should continue to pressure the foster care system to remove the child from foster care, are we not also implying that to remain in the system in long-term care is in and of itself a negative outcome? And, more importantly, does the foster child in long-term care somehow sense that he or she is, after all, the failure? How many adoption searches and recruitment brochures must a foster child experience before the system is willing to relax its compulsion with case closure and admit that, for many long-term foster children, our energy is better expended toward the quality of life in care?

Recommendations

In closing, I would make five recommendations concerning long-term foster care.

1. In terms of the federal mandate, an in-depth review of P.L. 96-272 could result in recommendations to accommodate the changing needs of children in foster care in the 1990s.

For example, while objective monitoring is a critical aspect, monitoring under P.L. 96-272 is closely associated with the single goal of permanency. For many of our foster children, especially those in long-term care for reasons of substance abuse and emotional disturbance, permanency is secondary to the goal of good physical and mental health and emotional well-being. The energy invested in these cases should be directed toward the specific needs of the child, not toward justifying continued foster care. It is critical that we examine foster care in terms of our expected outcomes of the system and not just in terms of numbers of reviews.

Also, in considering P.L. 96-272, it is important that placement of children in long-term foster care not be construed as a negative. For a growing number of our troubled foster children, it is the only alternative. Consideration should be given to recognizing this fact and perhaps encouraging states to categorize this population as a small but significant group to target for special services. States should not be penalized for having the average length of time children stay in foster care increased by children for whom an enormous percentage of the state's resources are being invested in direct service. These children are not drifting in care. Rather, care is the only place for them.

Still another aspect of P.L. 96-272 that bears scrutiny is the bias against group care. Group care providers have recognized this bias since the earliest days of P.L. 96-272. As practitioners, we should include group care as part of the essential array of services for the substance abusers, the sexually assaultive, the physically aggressive, and so on. It is unrealistic to expect that all these problems can be resolved through day treatment programs coupled with family foster care. Our experience indicates that "least restrictive" has come to mean the necessity of three or four foster family placements prior to the child receiving the specialized services that may be available only in a specific group setting. Group care providers have voiced their concern about the philosophy of "least restrictive," indicating that their success rate with a child is greatly enhanced if the child has not been through numerous less restrictive settings before entering group care.

Independent-living services are critical for the majority of our long-term foster care placements, but there is nothing magic about the age of 21 just as there was nothing magic about the age of 18. Transition into other programs becomes essential for many of our former foster children. The linkage should be encouraged and explored in creative ways if the ultimate goal of independence is to be achieved for young adults exiting long-term foster care.

2.   With respect to the changing population of children and youths in long-term foster care, linkages of child welfare services, mental health services, drug and alcohol treatment services, and Medicaid are essential.

In South Carolina, we have worked with Medicaid officials to expand essential treatment services for foster children. Specifically, funding for therapeutic foster family care, residential treatment, and community-based group care treatment is being shifted into a plan for Medicaid reimbursement. This will ensure that the individual treatment needs of foster children are being met through individual treatment plans. States must consider these alternatives as foster care funds are depleted and the needs of foster children increase.

In terms of other needs of the long-term foster care population, we should explore consistent and objective ways of obtaining feedback from the children in state custody. A clear message we have heard consistently since South Carolina's first foster children's conference in 1982 has been: "I want to be involved in decisions regarding my life. I should have something to say about what happens in my future." We should find ways to allow foster children this input. Their perceptions and recommendations regarding treatment programs, contacts with caseworkers, agency policies, and so on, are essential to those of us in policy-making positions. Exit interviews, toll-free phone numbers, and written surveys are all examples of ways in which we could hear from children in foster care.

3. With respect to our foster care providers, we must also be open to their concerns and recommendations regarding continued commitment to the foster care program.

In South Carolina, our challenge in recruitment is being overshadowed by our challenge in retention. As we place children who have increasingly difficult problems, we need to explore the reasons for placement disruption as well as reasons for foster caregivers leaving the system. Even if we had the money, throwing additional funds into foster care payments would not remedy the problem. We must explore and adequately provide for innovative approaches such as respite care for foster caregivers and incentives for attending specialized training. These services have been demonstrated to be effective, but they are not routinely available throughout public agency foster care.

Stability in long-term foster care could be enhanced by therapeutic work with the foster child and the foster caregiver. Although training of foster care workers has expanded, much of this mandatory training relates to policy, legal mandates, and liability matters. Too few workers have the clinical skills to help children in long-term care deal with the loss or peripheral involvement of their parents, attachment and bonding with their foster caregivers, or the children's own emotional problems. Clinical skills are essential if the foster care system is to substantively improve the quality of life of those children whose life circumstances do not allow them any placement besides foster care.

4. In terms of public sentiment, we must move away from defensiveness about our foster care programs.

The problems of the children and families in the foster care system reflect the problems of our society in general. Therefore, while these problems are consistently highlighted by the media, as practitioners we have been reluctant to defend the use of foster care and especially the use of long-term care. Very little attention is paid to those children who remain in or exit from the foster care system with a recognized degree of success. For example, the public is not told about the 19-year-old we have had in foster care since he was a preschooler who is currently enrolled in college on a full scholarship. We should be more assertive about some of the positive outcomes of the foster care system.

5.   Finally, related to public sentiment is the philosophy of foster care.

Most of our agency manuals still define *foster care* with terminology such as *time-limited* and *goal-focused toward permanency*. We need to examine these definitions with a realistic perspective of today's problems and today's client population. Continuing to use obsolete definitions results in system failure each time we do not meet the outcomes implied by "time-limited service delivery" or "permanent placement with plans that promise return home."

To fail to explore these and other alternatives would be a critical disservice to those children and families who must rely on the foster care system on a long-term basis.

SECTION 4:

REORIENTING CHILD WELFARE

IMPLICATIONS FOR POLICY-MAKING

Wade F. Horn

From 1982 to 1991, the number of children in the United States living in foster care increased by 63.4 percent, from approximately 262,000 to 428,000 children.[1] This dramatic increase is not due to an increase in the rate at which children are entering foster care, but rather to a significant decline in the rate at which they are exiting from care.[2] This pattern suggests that children entering foster care are coming from more seriously disturbed families than previously, necessitating longer stays in foster care. Perhaps even more importantly, this pattern also reflects the difficulty child welfare agencies are having in adjusting to the changing characteristics of children in need of foster care and the families from which they come.

Almost everyone agrees that, compared to a decade ago, children in substitute care today are far more likely to come from families involved in serious and chronic substance abuse—especially abuse of crack cocaine. The National Institute on Drug Abuse, for example, estimates that more than 4.5 million women of childbearing age are using illegal substances; half a million of them are using cocaine.[3] Prenatal exposure to crack can cause severe developmental damage.[4] Some drug-affected children remain in hospitals even though they are no longer in need of in-hospital medical care. Others are placed in foster care. Many leave the hospital with their parents, but later come to the attention of the child welfare system because of neglect or abuse. Once in foster care, these children are spending increasing amounts of time in foster care placement.

Despite the acknowledged relationship between the increase in the prevalence and severity of parental substance abuse and the increase in the foster care population, few child welfare agencies are taking assertive steps to manage this change in their client population. Whether implicitly or explicitly, many child welfare agencies continue to adhere to a social work model that views a trip to foster care as an opportunity to "fix" the family. When this "fixing" is done, the child returns home. Under such a model, the average expected number of trips into substitute care is one.

This model works reasonably well in cases of children suffering from chronic neglect or episodic abuse due to environmental stress. For such children, time spent in foster care is time that social workers can spend working with the families, helping them to alleviate current environmental stressors and get their lives in order, and teaching them better parenting skills. When these children return home, their families are seen to have an enhanced capacity to care for and nurture them; the expectation is that even with only minimal follow-up services, another trip into foster care will be unnecessary.

As successful as this model can be with these types of clients, it has far greater difficulty meeting the needs of families involved in heavy and chronic substance abuse and addiction. Because child welfare agencies are reluctant to return children of such substance abusers to their homes for fear of recurring abuse, these children are spending increasing lengths of time in foster care. Simply increasing the length of time spent in foster care, however, has not resulted in less risk of recurring abuse. On the contrary, not only is the length of time that children are spending in foster care increasing, but so is the percentage of children who experience more than one episode of substitute care. That is, once sent home, children of parents who heavily abuse drugs are much more likely to experience additional placements into foster care. The model used by most child welfare agencies, designed for less challenging cases, thus becomes a revolving door between home and foster care for children affected by parental substance abuse.

If child welfare agencies are to respond successfully to the current crisis in foster care, what is needed is not more time applying the "single fix" model, but rather the adoption of entirely new child welfare practices. The first step in creating these new models is understanding the different patterns and dynamics of substance abuse.

Differing Patterns of Substance Abuse

All substance abusers are not caught up in equally severe addictions. Some who abuse illegal substances do so only occasionally and in a controlled way. The behavior of these occasional substance abusers may be unlawful, but so long as their use of illegal substances is controlled, they are generally not a danger to themselves or to their children. Of course, every user of illegal substances is at risk of becoming an addicted, chronic user, but until that happens we are unlikely to know who they are, and hence will have little opportunity for intervention.

Parents who use alcohol or illegal substances heavily and chronically are quite a different matter. They are frequently a danger to themselves and to their children, and are therefore quite likely to come into contact with the child welfare system. Of course, they are also the most difficult clients to treat. Complicating the picture further is the reality that such substance addiction is often a relapsing disorder with multiple periods of remission and relapse. Recognizing these differences between occasional users and those who are chronically addicted has profound implications for child welfare practice.

Decision Making

Any use of illegal substances can lead to episodic child abuse or neglect. When occasional users come into contact with the child welfare system, however, their substance abuse problem is most often a co-occurring symptom rather than the immediate cause of child abuse or neglect. In such cases, treatment of the substance abuse itself is unlikely to result in a reduction in the risk of further child maltreatment. Other factors, such as overall familial stress or a character disorder, are much more likely to be the cause of both the child abuse or neglect and the occasional use of illegal substances. Consequently, for the occasional user who has been reported for child abuse or neglect, the primary goal of the child welfare system should be to treat the underlying cause of the child abuse or neglect, and not the substance abuse per se.

It is also true, however, that most of those who are heavily addicted to drugs began as occasional users. Consequently, while drug treatment might not be the primary goal for some clients, neither should their occasional use of illegal substances be ignored. At a minimum, their contact with the child welfare system should be viewed as an opportunity to prevent an intensification of their drug use. Ideally, of course, an attempt should be made to help them stop using illegal drugs altogether.

One service that may prove particularly helpful in such cases is home visiting, particularly when combined with outpatient substance abuse treatment. Home visiting has been shown to help reduce the incidence of child abuse and neglect in low-income families at risk for abuse and neglect.[5] With occasional users of illegal substances, home visiting may also prove valuable as a monitoring tool to help detect a shift toward a stronger and more dangerous reliance on alcohol or illegal substances. This information would be useful both to ensure the safety of the client's children and to provide feedback to the outpatient substance abuse treatment provider regarding the status of the client's drug use.

Of course, when home visiting is used in this way, the home visitor should always inform the client beforehand that one of the purposes of the arrangement is to provide supervision and monitoring of the client. Failure to discuss this could potentially undermine the trust that is so necessary between a client and any service provider, be it a child welfare worker or a substance abuse counselor.

Those who are chronically addicted to drugs are highly unlikely to be adequate parents. Their time and attention is diverted from parenting to accessing and using their drug of choice. Experience shows that these parents are likely to experience multiple relapses, even if successfully enrolled in drug treatment programs. They need dramatically different child welfare service models.

Expedited Adoptions

Within the population of drug-addicted parents, there are at least two significant subgroups. The first can be defined as those so ensnared by their addiction that it is unlikely that they will ever become adequate parents. The goal with this subgroup is to move quickly toward termination of parental rights, and the placement of their children into more long-term, permanent homes through adoption. The second subgroup comprises those for whom drug treatment has a reasonable possibility of success, in terms of both helping the client become drug free and managing any relapses.

It is extremely difficult to determine at initial contact precisely which clients belong in which of these two subgroups. All drug counselors have had the experience of seeing seemingly hopeless clients emerge as treatment successes, and of seeing others, who appeared at the onset of treatment to have a good chance of recovery, slide into long-term drug addiction. Our current technology is simply unable to predict reliably who will be treatment failures and who will be treatment successes. Lacking a high degree of predictive accuracy in such matters, and without prolonged observation of the family, it is all but impossible to differentiate between those parents who should and those who should not be moved quickly toward termination of parental rights.

There is, however, one subgroup of substance-abusing parents who would appear to have little chance of treatment success, at least in the short-term, and for whom the need to move their child quickly toward adoption would seem to outweigh their parental rights. This is the group of substance-abusing parents whose children are born drug affected and are then abandoned at birth or shortly thereafter. These substance-abusing parents have, in effect, given two strong indications that they are unlikely to be adequate parents—they have abused drugs during pregnancy and they have abandoned their responsibilities to care for their children after birth. (The father is almost sure to be equally irresponsible: He has failed to help the mother avoid drugs during pregnancy and has also abandoned his responsibilities after the child's birth.)

In such cases, it is reasonable to move quickly toward termination, for, even if we are able to locate these parents—often a lengthy process in itself—the treatment for their substance abuse is likely to take quite a long time and still be unsuccessful. Given the importance of early parent-child bonding, as well as the critical need for infants to experience consistent and nurturing care during the first year of life, strict time limits should be set for child welfare agencies to petition the court for prompt termination of parental rights and subsequent adoption. The need for rapid termination of parental rights in these cases is reinforced by evidence that many infants can overcome the deleterious effects of prenatal exposure to drugs if they are given a consistent and nurturing environment after birth and by the fact that infants are the children most easily placed in adoptive homes.[6]

Of course, a parent who abandons a drug-affected newborn is different from a parent who continues to be interested in and involved with such a child. Indeed, whenever a child welfare agency discovers a substance-abusing parent, its first obligation must be to attempt to rehabilitate the parent. It is only when the parent of a drug-affected newborn has truly abandoned the child that swift and sure termination of parental rights should be pursued in order to free the child for adoption into a permanent home.

Integrating the Child Welfare and Drug Treatment Systems

Given that heavy use of drugs is likely to be a chronic, relapsing disorder, neither child welfare services nor drug treatment should be viewed as a one-shot cure, but rather as long-term services that help chronic drug users control their relapses and cope with their responsibilities. Child welfare agencies must work more closely with drug treatment facilities to help them develop a greater focus on the needs of the children of drug users. At a minimum, child welfare agencies should advocate for residential treatment programs that allow the children of drug-addicted parents to stay with their parents during treatment. Collocation of drug rehabilitation and child care services will require an adjustment by many substance abuse treatment providers, who often view drug treatment as demanding a client's full attention and energy, and thus the presence of children as an inopportune distraction. But children can be a powerfully motivating force for parents to complete drug treatment successfully, and the effectiveness of drug treatment may actually be enhanced by encouraging parent-child interaction while in drug treatment.[7]

Collocation of drug treatment and child care services has the added benefit of affording an opportunity to teach drug-dependent parents more effective parenting skills. Many drug treatment programs seem to have assumed that, once adults are no longer drug-dependent, they will become adequate parents. Frequently, however, drug-addicted parents have never developed adequate parenting skills in the first place, particularly when their drug dependency is intergenerational. Consequently, enrollment in a residential drug treatment program should be seen as an occasion to teach drug-dependent adults how to be adequate parents.

In fact, drug treatment facilities are now beginning to view their role as one of providing a wide range of comprehensive services to drug-addicted parents. In addition to parenting education, substance abuse treatment programs are increasingly providing these parents with housing assistance, vocational rehabilitation and career counseling, social skills training, health education, and recreational counseling.

Two demonstration projects funded by the Administration on Children, Youth, and Families within the U.S. Department of Health and Human Services reflect this increasing willingness to undertake treatment of these parents in a comprehensive fashion. One of these initiatives involves locating Head Start programs on the drug treatment campuses sponsored by the Office of Treatment Improvement within the U.S. Public Health Service. The Head Start programs are intended both to provide a safe haven for the children of substance-abusing parents while they are in drug treatment and to afford the opportunity for these parents to learn appropriate parenting skills.

The second initiative involves funding a wide array of social services to complement the more traditional substance abuse interventions. This initiative, a specialized version of the Comprehensive Child Development Program, is unique in that it will provide ongoing comprehensive services to substance-abusing parents and their families from the birth of a child until that child enters elementary school.

Despite our best efforts, many children of drug-addicted parents will continue to be placed in foster care while their parents are in treatment or on the streets. Presently, foster care placements are often made without a clear recognition that drug dependency is a chronic, relapsing condition. Given the great likelihood of relapses in severe cases of drug dependency, however, multiple episodes of foster care should be seen as the rule, and not the exception. For children of drug-addicted parents, it will be necessary to ensure both that these children are not moved from foster home to foster home once placed in out-of-home care, and that these children will be placed in the *same* foster care arrangement each time the parent relapses.

Achieving such placement stability is highly unlikely if we are to rely on nonrelative foster care. There is already a severe shortage of nonrelative foster care families in the United States. According to the National Foster Parents Association's Survey of States for 1991, there are about 100,000 foster care homes available to absorb over 450,000 children in need of foster care placement.[8] It is unreasonable to assume that slots in nonrelative foster care homes can be reserved for the possibility of a relapse by a particular parent— if a foster home slot is available, it will be quickly filled by another child in need of immediate placement. The foster care arrangement most likely to afford the stability necessary for children of substance-abusing parents is kinship care, an arrangement in which relatives of the child serve as the caregiver.

We must be careful, however, if kinship care is to be used in this manner. Currently, in many states, maintenance payment rates for kinship care are the same as those for nonrelative foster care. And although in some states, kinship caregivers cannot get payments unless they qualify as foster parents first, both kinship care and nonrelative foster care rates are always higher than AFDC payments. The higher payment rates for kinship care may create a disincentive for parents to complete drug treatment successfully. Families would, in effect, lose income if the parents successfully combated their substance abuse and regained custody of their children.

One way to remove this financial disincentive for recovery from drug dependency is to offer the AFDC rate—rather than the higher foster care maintenance payment rate—to kinship caregivers, along with the full array of in-kind services available to the parents (e.g. Medicaid, housing assistance, child welfare services, etc.). Alternatively, legal guardianship could be pursued whereby the court transfers to the kinship caregiver some, but not all, of the biological parent's rights and responsibilities, thereby making the kinship caregiver eligible for an AFDC payment on behalf of the child. With legal guardianship, the kinship caregiving arrangement is sanctioned both legally and socially, protecting it from inappropriate disruption.

Both kinship care and legal guardianship have the advantage of offering greater stability for children of drug-addicted parents. In other words, the children would know with whom they would be staying in the event of future parental drug abuse relapses. Indeed, recovering parents could even be trained to anticipate relapses, and to seek protection for their children by quickly sending them to the relative for emergency care. The children would clearly benefit from this consistency in out-of-home placements, as contrasted with the deleterious effects of multiple placement arrangements experienced by far too many children in out-of-home care.

In addition to attending to the needs of children while their parents are in drug treatment, there is also a critical need for more comprehensive follow-up services once the parent is discharged from drug treatment. Recovery from drug dependency is never easy, even under the best of circumstances. But when the recovering drug addict is a low-income parent, the chances of long-term success are slim in the absence of continuing supportive services. As with the occasional illegal drug user, home visiting programs might prove helpful in providing much needed long-term support and monitoring changes in the parent's condition. Ideally, home visitors would begin their contact with the family before the parent's discharge from drug treatment, helping to more formally integrate the drug treatment system with the child welfare system.

Finally, if we are to successfully intervene with the children of drug-addicted parents, the child welfare and drug treatment systems must begin to share common outcome criteria. A parent who successfully overcomes his or her drug addiction, but who continues to evidence inadequate parenting skills, can no longer be viewed as a drug treatment success. As drug treatment expands its mission to include a focus on the needs of children, it will have to begin to measure its success or failure in terms of the developmental outcomes of the children.

Of course, expanding the definition of success in this way will make it more difficult to demonstrate the overall effectiveness of drug treatment. Ultimately, however, improving the outcome for the children of drug-addicted parents should be a major goal of the war on drugs. We must focus not only on the effects of drug use on the drug user, but also on the effects that parents' use of drugs has on their children.

Notes

1.	Toshio Tatara, "Child Substitute Care Population Trends FY 82 through FY 91— A Summary," *VCIS Research Notes*, no. 6, August 1992 (Washington, DC: American Public Welfare Association, 1992), 1.

2.	*Ibid.*

3.	*Maternal Drug Abuse and Drug Exposed Children: Understanding the Problem*, U.S. Department of Health and Human Services, DHHS Publication No. (ADM) 92–1949 (Washington, DC: U.S. Government Printing Office, 1992), 3.

4.	Ira J. Chasnoff, Carl E. Hunt, Ron Kletter, and David Kaplan, "Prenatal Cocaine

Exposure is Associated with Respiratory Pattern Abnormalities," *American Journal of Diseases of Children* 143 (1987): 583; Scott N. MacGregor, Louis G. Keith, Ira J. Chasnoff, Marvin A. Rosner, Gay M. Chisum, Patricia Shaw, and John P. Minogue, "Cocaine Use during Pregnancy: Adverse Perinatal Outcome," *American Journal of Obstetrics and Gynecology* 157 (1987): 686.

5.   David L. Olds, "Home Visitation for Pregnant Women and Parents of Young Children," *American Journal of Diseases of Children* 146 (1992): 704-708; David L. Olds and Harriet Kitzman, "Can Home Visitation Improve the Health of Women and Children at Environmental Risk?" *Pediatrics* 86 (1990): 108–116.

6.   Barry Zuckerman and Karen Bresnahan, "Developmental and Behavioral Consequences of Prenatal Drug and Alcohol Exposure," *Pediatric Clinics of North America* 38 (1991): 1387–1406.

7.   Barry Zuckerman, "Heavy Drug Users as Parents: Meeting the Challenge," paper presented at the "Protecting the Children of Heavy Drug Users Conference" in Williamsburg, VA, July 18–21, 1991.

8.   H. Gordon Evans, National Foster Parents Association, Houston, Texas, telephone conversation with author, 20 January 1994.

 *13*

LONG-TERM
IN-HOME SERVICES

Richard P. Barth*

The largest group of children now entering the child protective/child welfare system is composed of the children of drug-using parents. This is a significant change from the recent past, when parental alcohol abuse was a more common problem. The type of drug being used has also changed, with crack cocaine replacing heroin as a chief cause of family destruction.

For decades, the heavy use of drugs by parents has been a common contributor to the need for out-of-home care for children.[1] The recent increase in crack-related cases, however, caused the number of children in care to rise swiftly across the country. Even as recently as 1990, an estimated 80 percent

---

* This work was partially supported by awards to establish the Berkeley Child Welfare Research Center and the National Abandoned Infants Assistance Resource Center from the U.S. Department of Health and Human Services, Administration on Children and Families, Children's Bureau. A Senior Fulbright Fellowship and a Lois and Samuel Silberman Senior Faculty Fellowship Award to the author greatly facilitated this work. The Zellerbach Family Fund and the Wallace Alexander Gerbode Foundation provided invaluable support to the seminar that helped develop the ideas in this paper.

of the children exposed prenatally to drugs who were known to the child welfare system entered foster care—usually about half of them to stay for the long term.[2]

After the initial shock to state and local foster care programs and budgets, however, the criteria for accepting children into foster care began to tighten. The most significant change of the last few years is that the majority of the children of drug-using parents who now come to the attention of child welfare service providers will not enter foster care. These children will typically remain at home. Some will receive services in the home, but these services will be quite brief. Indeed, during recent years—despite the crack epidemic—the likelihood of getting in-home services beyond investigation decreased in California from 23 percent in 1985 to 6 percent in 1992 (see figure 1). At the same time, there was no change in the likelihood of entering foster care following the investigation—this remained at about 13 percent. In Texas, only 29 percent of cases determined to require ongoing services (but not placement) ever receive any services.[3] In child welfare cases involving drug-involved families, a State of California Senate Office of Research study indicated that 64 percent of cases received some services beyond intake. Of those who did receive services, 57 percent received them at home. Out of 100 newborns referred to child welfare services for positive toxicology screens, 73 were expected to remain in homes with some or no services (see figure 2).[4]

We can and must do better at protecting the potential of these very young children in the period of their greatest vulnerability. More children and families should receive services, the services should last longer, and new alternatives should be explored.

What Services Do Families Receive at Home?

Even when family maintenance and preservation services are provided, they are not long lasting. A recent state survey on placement prevention and family reunification programs found that, in 15 states, families receive placement prevention or reunification services from the public agency for an average of only 4.17 months. In California, in-home services last—on the average—less than 90 days. Data from Oregon describe the course of in-home services for drug-exposed children. The cases of approximately 36 percent of 532 drug-

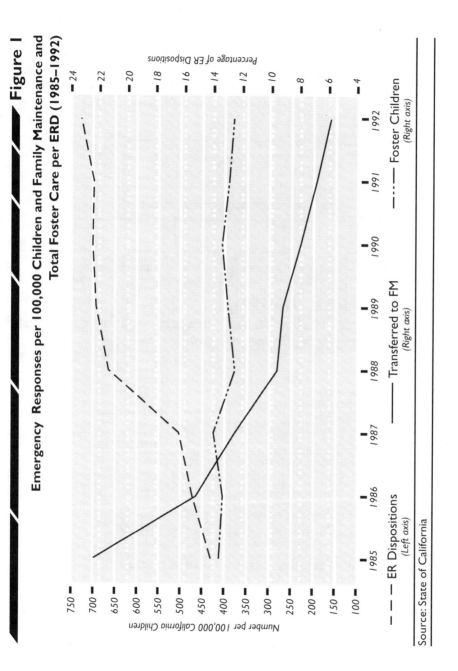

Figure 1

Emergency Responses per 100,000 Children and Family Maintenance and Total Foster Care per ERD (1985–1992)

Source: State of California

━━━━ ╱━━━ ══ ━━━ ══ ══ ━ **Figure 2**

Outcomes of Referrals to CPS for Perinatal Drug Exposure
Caseflow Analysis for Selected Counties (22 Counties Reporting)*

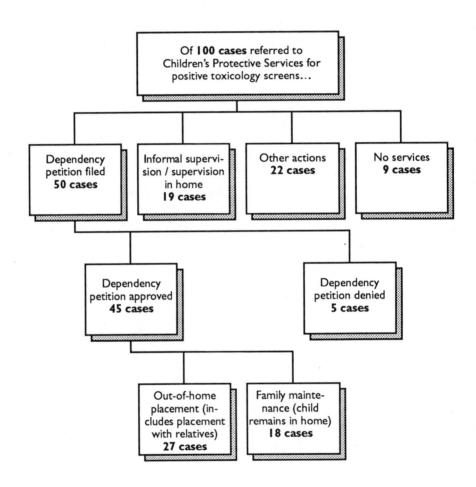

Source: California Senate Office of Research, 1990.

exposed newborns reported to Oregon's Children's Services Division in 1989 were open for less than 30 days, the majority of them only for the purpose of recording the report. A 1988 two-year follow-up study of 346 reports of newborns exposed prenatally to drugs revealed that the average case life was just over nine months.[5]

This brevity of service does not square with the fact that the resolution of drug treatment typically takes at least one year and frequently two—or with the fact that drug-exposed children create great demands on parents—or with drug users' limited capacity to parent. Whereas some parents have fallen from successful roles as parents and providers and need drug rehabilitation, many drug-involved parents need habilitation and must—for the first time—become effective parents and providers. Until they do, their children are in double jeopardy.

The vast majority of children from drug-involved families are probably under the court's supervision and are court dependents. Some families, however, voluntarily accept services. Although parents involved with substance abuse are not known for volunteering for long-term social services, they may do so if day care and counseling accompany this voluntary family maintenance status. Especially appealing to mothers is a mixture of in-home and center-based developmental services that help them to learn how to care for their children. Several service providers indicate that case management that includes the option of in-home developmental services is the key element in retaining drug-involved women in programs.[6] Two recent reports on long lasting—three and four years, respectively—early intervention programs with high-risk families indicate 93 percent and 89 percent continuation rates.[7]

In-home services—whether court-ordered or voluntary—are typically limited to six months with the possibility of extensions to a year. One social worker on a special unit that provides in-home services to parents of newborns exposed prenatally to drugs explained, "Six months isn't even hardly enough. It isn't even a minimum amount of time. We are talking about a program that needs to run a year to 18 months. If they go live in a group home, they get to stay that long and it costs three times as much. Why shouldn't they get 18 months of service at home, too?" In a few cases, supervision extends beyond a year, although many states are reluctant or unwilling to pay for services beyond one year.

In-home services are often continued after a child is reunited with drug-involved parents, although this is—like virtually everything else about child welfare services—not uniformly so. Thousands of children go home and have their cases closed simultaneously. Because child protective services and drug-treatment programs have contracts that cover only clients, drug-testing and the expectation for drug treatment are also usually discontinued at this time—a fact that many drug treatment specialists find disheartening. Thus, when child welfare services end, so does access to ongoing drug treatment.

In theory, if parents fail to meet the conditions of the court order—that is, if they fail to see that their children attend day care or they fail their drug tests—their children can be removed from their care and placed into long-term foster care or put up for adoption. In practice, the social worker and judge may see no better alternative placements for the child, or may find that the unavailability of adequate child or foster care arrangements shares the blame. If so, they will either continue the supervision for another period of time or will close the case. Unless there is an egregious lapse in the quality of care, the child is rarely removed from parental custody. As a social worker told me, "The law has no teeth. I don't know why it is so, but I know it is so." In 1989, only 15 percent of the children in foster care in California had ever received in-home family services.[8]

After case closure, there is little service or supervision. In theory, a judge could order continued supervision (including anything from home visits to random drug testing), services for a second year (although the local child welfare authority and the parent's attorney might fight such an order on the basis that it exceeds the requirements of the law), or both. In theory, the judge might order supervision without services, by insisting on a case plan that only included social worker visits. Judges are unlikely to do this, however, because the assurances of "reasonable efforts" are such that surveillance is expected to be accompanied by services and the rationale for the case plan requires explication of how the services will meet the case goals. Under most case plans, the social worker visits are intended to help oversee the services, not to be the service. To develop ways around this, social workers might close the case and then put a note in their book to develop a suspicion of neglect in three months. They could then use that as an excuse to go visit the family and develop a case to initiate another year or more of dependency family mainte-nance. This is a relatively circuitous and duplicitous route to lengthening follow-up and services. We should develop more legitimate routes to monitoring the well-being of children. Some evidence from studies of reabuse indicate that keeping cases open longer—independent of the social worker's level of effort—is associated with less reabuse.[9]

Implications

This pattern of brief in-home services has implications in three realms related to the child's protection and most probably results in a greater likelihood of (1) reentry of the child into the child welfare system, especially foster care; (2) threats to the child's development; and (3) subsequent children being born who were exposed prenatally to drugs and parents being reported for child abuse and endangerment.

Reabuse

Given the current configuration of family maintenance services, many children of drug-addicted parents will not be protected by the state for very long, if at all. Such lapses in protection may result in reporting at a later point. We have no great data on the re-reporting or reabuse of these children, but descriptive information about the experiences of our general child welfare clientele is instructive. In 1985, 29 percent of the California families receiving preplacement prevention services had received them before. Of all families receiving preplacement prevention services, more than 50 percent had a substance abuse problem. A similar study in 1989 found that the percentage of children who had previously received child welfare services went up to 40 percent and that 88 percent had a substance abuse problem. On average, children received services for four months in 1985 and for six months in 1989.[10] Apparently, cases are staying open a bit longer, but not much.

Eckenrode's data from New York are consistent with California's. He found that there had been a previous case opening for nearly 30 percent of the children on whom a neglect report was filed in 1985—the category under which many drug-related reports go.[11] If this 1989 data paralleled California's, New York's reabuse rates would also now be approximately 40 percent. This may be a worsening of the 30 percent reabuse rate shown in previous studies of in-home services.[12] In short, if we maintain the status quo on the duration and intensity of in-home services, we can expect that 30 percent to 40 percent of children exposed prenatally to drugs will suffer maltreatment that is serious enough to require another report and, hence, a case reopening. We cannot estimate the percentage whose maltreatment will go unreported.

Developmental Outcomes

The evidence about the developmental outcomes of children who were exposed prenatally to drugs is unclear.[13] This is a welcome contrast to the apparent certainty we had just a few years ago that these children were missing part of their humanity and were therefore doomed. Nevertheless, what we now think we know about the variation in possible outcomes is encouraging only if those outcomes are fostered through a habilitative family and school environment.[14] The fewer—or the later—the services, the less the variation. P.L. 99-457 offers the clearest avenue for providing early intervention services for children ages birth to three and their families. The services that could be generated through this law, however, are not uniformly in place and are largely unavailable to families with substance-exposed newborns (unless a severe developmental disability is evinced). The majority of children exposed prenatally to drugs—even if they begin life under the protection of child welfare services—will fall into the developmental chasm between the neonatal intensive care unit and Head Start. In-home child welfare services do not ensure appropriate developmental assessments and interventions. These must be carried out by health and education providers. At least those children who are enrolled in hospital-based perinatal follow-up services will benefit from well-baby visits and pediatric screening during their first year and their developmental gap will be smaller. Without such a program, the pediatric well-baby follow-up rate among children exposed prenatally to drugs in Oakland is 10 percent; with such services, the follow-up rate approaches 70 percent.[15] Even if we lengthened in-home family maintenance services to three years, it would not be enough; social workers do not assist children directly—they just talk to their parents and caregivers. They must have child development services to offer the children.

Repeat Drug-Exposed Births

Women who bear children exposed prenatally to drugs and who have their children taken away or who receive no ongoing family planning and social services may be more likely to have repeat drug-exposed births. In San Francisco, during the first three months of 1991, referrals of newborns exposed prenatally to drugs decreased by 17 percent. Yet, 95 percent of all cases of infant prenatal drug exposure involved women who had given birth to drug-exposed babies in the past. This is an increase from the very high 62 percent repeat figure for all cases in the previous year. In Oakland, the percentage of newborns with traces of cocaine in their urine declined from 15 percent to 9 percent (or, in real terms, from 401 to 240 babies) between 1990 and 1991, but "hard-core addicts continue to have babies at levels only slightly below those of 1988 and 1989."[16] The California Senate Office of Research reports that repeat referrals or petitions are common. Between 20 percent and 40 percent of dependency petitions following positive toxicology screens at birth in California in 1990 were repeat petitions for the mothers. A county administrator reports, "Many petitions we do file on drug babies were filed because this is a second or third pregnancy involving positive drug screens or the mother is a long-term drug user, resulting in CPS intervention and removal of older siblings. We believe this is a common pattern."[17] There is no evidence about whether these mothers had custody of the children previously born to them, although the likelihood is increasingly high that they will in the future.

Extended Services

Extended services do not routinely exist for drug-using parents. But we have enough experience with the current service mix available in at least some communities to know the essential components of such extended services: a perinatal aftercare case management program, extended case management, developmental follow-up, intensive family preservation services, shared family care arrangements that combine characteristics of in-home services and out-of-home care, and informal family support services. Each component is discussed below.

Perinatal Case Management

Many children are now being diverted from foster care and the formal child protective system because in-home services are provided by case managers working out of health care agencies. The Healthy Infant Project (HIP) at Highland Hospital in Oakland targets women whose infants were exposed prenatally to drugs. The mother is contacted soon after birth and, when the baby is discharged from the hospital, the HIP social worker contacts the family at least once a month. This lasts for a year, sometimes two. The follow-up services are funded primarily under Medicaid's EPSDT program and focus on well-baby visits. With EPSDT funding, HIP is allowed to provide only those services designed to encourage well-child medical visits.[18]

With eight different funding sources, HIP has no routine support available for other services. Corporate support for family planning allows HIP to schedule infants' appointments with their pediatricians for the same time as the mothers' appointments with the family planning provider. With consent from the mother, HIP calls the family planning provider to see that the mother is receiving services. HIP also provides parenting classes. HIP does not emphasize drug treatment, partly because its funding sources do not support it, partly because of a lack of adequate facilities, and partly because the antidotes to substance abuse among women are concrete services, health care, and family planning assistance rather than conventional drug treatment. The program also has a parents' support group, a grandparents' support group, and a Cocaine Anonymous group that meet weekly.

The response has been surprisingly good. Upon initial contact, the mothers are told that if they do not participate in HIP, they will be referred to the child protective agency. Past program director Mildred Thompson indicates that this rarely works because "many of the women know that child protective services, which is often overburdened, will not do much, [and] the threat is often ineffective."[19] Still, caseloads of 25 clients allow case managers to engage a high percentage of women and complete necessary networking and collaboration with a variety of providers. Pediatric follow-up visits have improved by 75 percent for the first 250 women served. Providers agree that, once the mother leaves the hospital (or the family maintenance program) without a written contract, it is almost impossible to provide appropriate services for her or for her infant.

Jenny is a 23-year-old woman with four children; two were exposed prenatally to drugs and one is severely developmentally delayed. Jenny is short-tempered and has been known to hit her children. Her boyfriend is assaultive and has been in and out of prison for the last three years. Jenny has a history of heroin use and recently became involved with crack cocaine. Upon the birth of her youngest child (who was cocaine- and opiate-positive), she was referred to HIP. The home visit showed bad—but salvageable—living conditions, lack of patience toward the children, and general lack of interest in following through on pediatric visits. What Jenny wanted most was to get the developmentally delayed child out of the house and into a special program. She was not interested in drug counseling (although she was still using drugs), support groups, therapy, pediatric follow-up, family planning, parenting classes, or even monthly home visits. She accepted the social worker's visits only because a partnership existed between HIP and child protective services that allowed her to keep her child as long as she cooperated with HIP. The social worker found a program for the developmentally disabled child. Over time, the mother began to learn ways to stop hitting her children and to protect them and herself from her boyfriend. The family situation was continuing to improve at the two-year follow-up.

Extended Case Management

Long before we were worried about the children of parents who used drugs heavily, we were worried about the children of adolescent parents. That population, too, has undergone a transition, from being given care and protection in out-of-home care (especially adoption) to being cared for at home. Federal law authorizes comprehensive case management services for adolescent mothers. In California, the Adolescent Family Life Act recognizes the long-term risks for adolescent parents—children with developmental problems, welfare dependence, and closely-spaced repeat births—and provides ongoing case management for over 13,000 adolescents from the time of their pregnancy until they reach age 20—for some mothers a service period of seven years. A recent evaluation found that the program is cost-effective, reduces the rate of unwanted pregnancies, improves birth outcomes for subsequent children (that is, cuts the rate of low birthweight), and increases mothers' connections to health and early education that they could use for their children.[20] This program was developed during tight fiscal times in California. Like Head Start and the Women, Infants, and Children program, this ongoing case management model is compelling enough to have grown (although not necessarily to have prospered) under these harsh conditions.

Developmental Follow-Up

A few clinics provide special outreach, developmental interventions, and parent support groups for drug-involved parents. One such clinic, CARE, at

Children's Hospital in Oakland, endeavors to "empower the mother's capacity to care for the child throughout his or her life."[21] The importance of developmental follow-up is illustrated in Denzel's story:

> Denzel was born prematurely, with low birthweight and serious respiratory and heart problems. During his 31-year-old mother's pregnancy, she drank beer and used $30 to $40 worth of crack every day. The mother was referred from the intensive care unit to the CARE clinic, which eventually referred her to outpatient drug and alcohol treatment services and enrolled her in a support group. The mother sought assistance from the clinic to convince child protective services that she should have custody of Denzel when he was discharged after heart surgery. This was accomplished and the child was discharged home. The mother's continued binge use of cocaine and her inability to fully protect herself and Denzel from her abusive spouse became apparent through her contact with the CARE counselor. With intensive case management support, however, she attended some Narcotics Anonymous meetings and kept all pediatric appointments for Denzel. By Denzel's first birthday, the mother was clean of illicit drugs and Denzel was developing age-appropriate motor skills. At 18 months, Denzel faced a second heart surgery, the mother had filed a protection order to keep her spouse away, and Denzel and his mother were working to improve his language skills. Their short-term progress is significant—as are their needs for sustained developmental services.

Child Care Services

Child care services are the bedrock of developmental services and are essential to the protection of children at home. That the absence of child care is an impediment to successful drug treatment is widely known. Studies have shown that less than 10 percent of drug treatment programs provide child care.[22] Child care is equally critical to the success of family maintenance services, yet in many areas of this country, there are no child care allowances for mothers in family maintenance programs. If there is no guarantee that families can receive child care during family maintenance, then there is virtually no hope that parents will have the chance to rehabilitate themselves.

Meanwhile, more ambitious efforts to develop 24-hour child care and crisis nurseries in order to provide greater protection for children and their families are emerging. Crisis nurseries, respite care, and "child centers" that will become second homes and therapeutic interventions for children who had positive toxicologies at birth are among the most important. These will all eventually provide vital resources to families heavily involved with drugs. These resources would also prove invaluable for social workers who, at best, visit with families every two weeks and typically every month even when the cases are open. The less contact the social worker has with the family, the greater the need for ongoing child care. For now, however, these services are as scarce as grass on a busy street.

Continual case management is also possible through the early intervention services program (Part H) of P.L. 99-457. In concept, drug-affected families could receive assistance in developing an Individualized Family Services Plan and case management support in implementing that plan in order to prevent educational disabilities among their children. In practice, few states have made these families eligible for such care.

Intensive Family Preservation Services

Few drug-involved families receive family preservation services. Those program that exist have begun to show their effectiveness with a somewhat select group of voluntary clientele. Success rates may be as high as 60 percent at one-year follow-up.[23]

The J. family received services from the Ennis Center for Children, a program established under the statewide Families First initiative. Marilyn J. freely admitted her addiction to crack. At 98 pounds, the 31-year-old mother of four was selling food stamps to support her habit. Drug trafficking was taking place in her home, her 13-year-old daughter had not attended school in six months, and her younger children were unkempt and uncontrolled. She was living illegally in a house with broken windows, falling plaster, and bullet holes. Marilyn was told by the police that she had 24 hours to rid her home of drug traffic and child protective services threatened to remove her children. Before her involvement with crack, Marilyn had used heroin but worked as a restaurant manager and owned a house and car. By the end of six weeks of intervention, Marilyn had moved to a four-bedroom house, was enrolled in a drug treatment facility, and was participating in a program for preschool children. Six months after the program's conclusion, Marilyn's improvement was being maintained.[24]

Intensive family preservation programs are also beginning to make a greater effort to link their families with other resources. Services in some areas may be somewhat longer than usual—Homebuilder's programs are typically six weeks in the Bronx instead of four weeks in Tacoma—and may try to ensure that the mother has a plan for the protection of her children if she resumes using drugs. Ideally, such brief services could be welded to longer-term, continuing developmental and case management services. Combining intensive family preservation services with ongoing family support services is a challenge and opportunity of the Family Preservation and Support Act of 1993.

Shared Family Care

Although this paper focuses on children receiving services at home, the question of what it means to receive services at home must be more thoroughly explored. In the United States, we assume a dichotomy between child protection and family preservation for children at imminent risk of harm. We also believe that, if children are at imminent risk, they must be in out-of-home care. But we are already witnessing two exceptions to this rule: first, in a way, intensive family preservation services bring staff members into the home with such frequency that we basically create an out-of-home care bed in the home; and, second, drug abuse treatment group homes that care for mothers and children combine both family preservation and out-of-home care. Both of these programs deserve our continued support, but they have serious limitations. Intensive family preservation programs are quite brief and therefore afford short-lived protection—unless they succeed in making a lasting improvement in family functioning. Group home programs are difficult to establish and expensive to maintain.

We should explore alternative shared family care arrangements that involve "the planned provision of out-of-home care to parent(s) and children so that the parent and host caregivers simultaneously share the care of the child and work toward independent in-home care by the parent(s)."[25] Versions of shared family care can be many and varied, but in all forms are probably used less frequently in the United States than in any other Western country. Although there is some federal, state, and local support for the development of shared family care that places a pregnant mother in a group home with other pregnant mothers, additional models that are more flexible and less costly must emerge.

Most central is the need for foster care arrangements that include mothers and children and cluster housing or supervised living arrangements for drug-involved women and their children. The Children's Home and Aid Society of Chicago and the Human Services Associates of St. Paul, Minnesota, are pioneering programs in which host foster families care for mothers and children together. Project Demand in Minneapolis is using apartment clusters and is placing mothers and children with resource families upon discharge back into the community. This should be just a beginning. Both programs have replicated the long experience of the Europeans in providing foster care for drug-involved families—it can be done. When recovery is not achieved, and the mother returns to her drug use or is afflicted with AIDS, at least the children have some continuity of care with the host foster family. Most foster families become like relatives and provide children with the unconditional commitment and advocacy they need.

Informal Family Support Programs

Although many drug-using parents have relatives and social support networks upon which they can count, many others do not. Los Angeles' Adopt-a-Family program and Sweden's Contact Family program suggest the possibility of boosting informal networks in order to strengthen families and protect children. The Adopt-a-Family program recruits community volunteers to contribute professional and personal services to a family in an effort to give them the extra boost they need to leave an unsuccessful life-style behind. Sweden's program is run by the government and was developed in the 1970s to provide community surveillance of adult substance abusers but has since been modified to focus on provision of personal services.[26] The Contact Family—as it is called—is matched with a vulnerable family. The relationship involves weekly contact and one weekend a month of care for the children in the Contact Family's own home. The Contact Family receives a modest stipend and reimbursement for travel. If the mother is unable to care for her children, the Contact Family acts as emergency foster parents and cares for the children for as long as necessary. Some Contact Families have become foster parents for HIV- infected biological mothers who could no longer care for their children. Contact Families provide significant continuity of care and protection.

Conclusions and Recommendations

The current "system," when it is working at its best, protects the children of drug-involved parents in their own homes when possible. The first wave of services may involve a year or more of in-home follow-up services by the child welfare services system or public health services. These services could segue into a Family Services Plan under P.L. 99-457 that oversees the child's developmental care until age three. These services might then be supplemented by Head Start and the beginning of early childhood education that prepares children for school. Children of drug users who have had this massive array of services strung together have a good chance of making good.

At this time, however, no such system exists and the service cloth is full of holes. The recommendations below are intended to patch some of those holes:

1. If we think of "prevention" only as placement prevention or of prevention of some untoward outcomes for an already born child exposed prenatally to drugs, then we are guilty of small-mindedness. Every program—whether it provides residential or in-home services—should emphasize prevention of subsequent pregnancies through *family planning*. Programs must have the expectation, license, and resources to ensure that women who want to use oral, surgical, or implanted contraception, and are medically fit to do so, receive that contraception.

2. *Intensive family preservation services* should be only the initial response for drug-involved families. Anecdotal evidence indicates that the frequent companionship and tangible assistance provided through intensive family preservation services can help families who basically need brief rehabilitative services rather than long-term habilitative services.

3. Child welfare, drug treatment, and child care providers suggest the importance of *ongoing case management* for children of parents who use drugs heavily. These programs should provide aftercare to the majority of these children after their child protective cases are closed. Ongoing case management can be offered through P.L. 99-457's Individualized Family Services Plan, through a mechanism such as the voluntary case management system for families proposed by the National Commission on Children (1991) and the National Commission on Child Welfare and Family Preser-

vation (1991), or through a program similar in design to California's Adolescent Family Life Act.

4. When they need it, we must find a way to pay for women and their children to live together in *shared family care*. At this time, such an arrangement is neither fish nor fowl—it is not reimbursable under the foster care program and it is not used as a family preservation program. In the meantime, pilot projects and local dollars can be used to support such arrangements and group home services for mothers and children together. Title IV-B Part 2 and Title IV-A could also be used if states plan accordingly.

5. P.L. 99-457 is not now providing significant *early childhood services* to the majority of children of drug-addicted parents. These children fit the spirit of the law, but they do not always fit the letter of the eligibility criterion that states have developed. Fiscal constraints appear to be ruling them out. Although we do not have any evaluations of how those services might benefit the children of such drug users, the accumulated evidence from Head Start, Perry High Scope, and the recent Stanford Study on early intervention with very low birthweight children strongly suggests that much good could come out of these services at this time.[27]

6. Although in-home services should be more enduring, child welfare services should not necessarily be extended to prolong the oversight of drug-involved families. Ideally, child welfare services should end with a family service plan that—as much as possible—guarantees referral to and retention in other *community-based and developmentally focused services*. These service providers should, in turn, ensure that they will inform child welfare services if they are concerned about child maltreatment. In some cases, child welfare services will have to resume a voluntary or court-ordered case supervision. If family maintenance is still appropriate, child welfare services should have the option of providing services and supervision for an additional 12 months.

7. *Child care* for children receiving in-home family maintenance services must be ensured. Every eligible family being served should be entitled to child care. Child care providers can develop the kind of relationship with children that will protect them in the future. When all the other fancier services fail a child, the child care providers will be there.

8. The *permanency planning time frames* should be maintained. The short average duration of family maintenance services (less than three months) is due to fiscal, not statutory constraints. Allowing family maintenance to last longer does not substantially decrease the likelihood of adoption for children. Providing longer periods of protection for in-home services should reduce reabuse and its accompanying harms and costs while improving developmental outcomes. Additionally, if family planning is incorporated into the service, it may reduce repeat pregnancies.

We are learning that children exposed prenatally to drugs are not all doomed to educational and social failure and that most can succeed in their endeavors if given a boost. This presents us with a window of opportunity. These children are going to need our protection and family and community support to avoid the most dreaded outcomes. Because they and their parents are more similar to than different from the children and parents about whom we have been concerned for a long time, we already have in place most of the mechanisms they will need. Now we must see that we have the resources and leadership to work together for this most endangered group of children.

Notes

1. David Fanshel, "Parental Failure and Consequences for Children: The Drug-Using Mother Whose Children Are in Foster Care," *American Journal of Public Health* 65 (1975): 604–612.

2. U.S. Department of Health and Human Services, *Drug-Exposed Infants and Children: Service Needs and Policy Questions*, paper prepared by L. Feig (Washington, DC: U.S. Government Printing Office, 1990); Richard P. Barth et al., *Pathways through Child Welfare Services: From Child Abuse to Permanency Planning* (New York: Aldine De Gruyter, 1994).

3. Sheila B. Kamerman and Alfred Kahn, "Social Services for Children, Youth, and Families in the United States," *Children and Youth Services Review* 1/2 (1990): 1-184.

4. California Senate Office of Research, *California's Drug-Exposed Babies: Undiscovered, Unreported, Underserved* (Sacramento, CA: Senate Office of Research, 1990).

5. Margaret Tyler, "State Survey on Placement Prevention and Family Reunification Programs" (Oakdale, IA: The National Resource Center on Family-Based Services, 1990).

6. Nika St. Claire, "The Child's Developmental Path: Working with the Family," in *Families Living with Drugs and HIV: Intervention and Treatment Strategies*, ed. Richard P. Barth, Jeanne Pietrzak, and Malia Ramler (New York: Guilford Press, 1993), 177–203; Mildred Thompson, "Drug-Exposed Infants and Their Families: A Coordinated Services Approach," in *Families Living with Drugs and HIV*, 238–252.

7. The Infant Health and Development Program, "Enhancing the Outcomes of Low-Birthweight, Premature Infants: A Multisite, Randomized Trial," *Journal of the American Medical Association* 22 (1990): 3035–3042; Sandra L. Martin, Craig T. Ramey, and Sharon Ramey, "The Prevention of Intellectual Impairment in Children of Impoverished Families: Findings of a Randomized Trial of Educational Day Care," *American Journal of Public Health* 80 (1990): 844–847.

8. "Pre-Placement Prevention Services: Emergency Response and Family Survey of Selected Characteristics for Cases Closed during January 1989" (Sacramento, CA: California Department of Social Services, 1990).

9. William Johnson and Jill L'Esperance, "Predicting the Recurrence of Child Abuse," *Social Work Research and Abstracts* 20 (1984): 21–31.

10. "Pre-Placement Prevention Services: Emergency Response and Family Survey of Selected Characteristics for Cases Closed during April 1985" (Sacramento, CA: California Department of Social Services, 1986).

11. John Eckenrode, personal communication, 21 June, 1991.

12. Richard P. Barth and Marianne B. Berry, "Implications of Research on the Welfare of Children under Permanency Planning," in *Child Welfare Research Review*, ed. Richard P. Barth, Jill D. Berrick, and Neil Gilbert (New York: Columbia University Press, 1994), 323–368.

13. Richard P. Barth, "Educational Implications of Prenatally Drug-Exposed Children," *Social Work In Education* 13 (1991): 130–136.

14. Barry Zuckerman, "Developmental Considerations for Drug- and AIDS-Affected Infants," in *Families Living with Drugs and HIV*, 36.

15. Mildred Thompson, "Drug-Exposed Infants," 238–252.

16. Rick DelVecchio, "Bay Area Crack Baby Epidemic Declines," *San Francisco Chronicle*, 3 June 1991, A13.

17. *California's Drug-Exposed Babies*, 18.

18. Thompson, "Drug-Exposed Infants," 238–252; Mildred Thompson, "Healthy Infant Program: An Alternate Approach to Families of Drug-Exposed Infants," *Henry Ford Hospital Medical Journal* 38 (1990): 140–141.

19. Thompson, "Healthy Infant Program," 140.

20. Karen S. Thiel, Marie Weil, Beatrice Ferleger, Wendy Russel, Chul Jo, and Ann Kwinn, "California's Adolescent Family Life Program: Evaluating the Impact of Case Management Services for Pregnant and Parenting Adolescents, Adolescent Family Life Evaluation Project" (Los Angeles, CA: University of Southern California, School of Social Welfare, 1990).

21. St. Claire, 18.

22. Wendy Chavkin, "Drug Addiction and Pregnancy: Policy Crossroads," *American Journal of Public Health* 4 (1991): 483; Karen Portis, "Intake and Diagnosis of Drug-Dependent, Pregnant Women," workshop presented at the NIDA National Conference on Drug Abuse Research and Practice, An Alliance for the 21st Century (Washington, DC, 1991).

23. Richard P. Barth, "Intensive Family Preservation Services to Drug-Using Families," in *Intensive Family Preservation Services: An Instructional Sourcebook,* ed. E.M. Tracy, David A. Haapala, Jean Kinney, and Peter J. Pecora (Cleveland, OH: Case Western Reserve University, 1991), 203–213.

24. Linda J. Morgan and Peg Marckworth, eds., *Intensive Family Preservation Services: Resource Book* (Cleveland, OH: Case Western Reserve University, 1990), 67.

25. Richard P. Barth, "Shared Family Care: Child Protection without Parent-Child Separation," in *Families Living with Drug- and AIDS-Affected Families*, 2.

26. *Ibid.*, 36–42.

27. The Infant Health and Development Program, 3035–3042.

TERMINATION OF PARENTAL RIGHTS

Michael S. Wald

This paper examines some of the issues that must be addressed in developing a statutory structure regarding termination of parental rights.[1] Although the focus of the paper is on termination in cases involving substance abuse by the child's custodial parent, the general framework is applicable to all termination proceedings.

Termination entails a legal finding that all connections between the parent and child should be permanently severed. The parent no longer has any right to regain custody of, or to visit with, the child. The primary rationale for termination is to allow for the adoption of children who have been removed from their parents' custody, after it has been determined that reunification with their parents is not feasible or desirable. Termination may also be appropriate when it is determined that a parent should never have a right to contact a child, even if the child will not be adopted, because any contact is likely to be extraordinarily damaging to the child.

Termination laws are necessary because it is generally undesirable to leave children in long-term foster care, which exposes children to multiple placements and inadequate care. Children need the care of adults fully committed to their well-being. Such care is most likely to be provided by adults who consider themselves the child's "parents." Therefore, it is a goal of public policy to facilitate adoption when children cannot be reunified with their parents. (Other solutions, such as kinship care and legal guardianship, are discussed elsewhere in this book.)

I agree with those people who see a need to change existing termination laws in order to increase the number of terminations and adoptions. In fact, I will advocate an entirely new approach with respect to children in long-term care. There is, however, a major caveat with respect to my recommendations. I believe that the rules regulating termination cannot be viewed in isolation; they are one part of the overall statutory structure regulating state intervention in behalf of maltreated children. Any rules regarding termination that are developed without relating them to all aspects of the child protection system, including the grounds for intervention and the level of services available to parents and children, are likely to be ineffective and unfair.

Current Laws

The availability of termination is solely a matter of state law. Every state has a statute that specifies the grounds for termination. Some statutes authorize termination as an immediate option after children have been made a dependent and removed from their parents' custody. Other states permit termination only after children have been in foster care for a period of time and efforts at reunification have been unsuccessful.

Although these statutes vary substantially, they generally focus on parental conduct or conditions thought to indicate parental unfitness to resume custody. The most common grounds are abandonment, mental illness or disability, incarceration or conviction of crimes, chronic abuse and neglect, severe abuse, alcohol or chemical dependency, and the fact that a child has been out of parental custody for a period of time and is unlikely to return soon. In addition to proving one of the grounds specified by the statute, in most states it also must be proven that termination will be in the best interests of the child.[2]

The ways in which termination proceedings can be initiated also vary substantially. Most statutes require that termination proceedings be initiated by a special petition, alleging one or more of the statutory grounds. Only one state, California, requires that termination automatically be considered by the juvenile court after a child has been in care for a specified period (18 months). In all other states, the decision to seek termination is left entirely to the discretion of the child welfare agency or the would-be adoptive parents. A child can remain in foster care indefinitely without a court considering termination.

Policy Issues

Several major criticisms have been made with respect to existing state laws and procedures regarding termination, especially as they are applied in cases involving parental substance abuse. Some critics believe that termination is too easy, but most assert that termination is too difficult or not initiated quickly enough. The people who believe that termination is too difficult raise two points. First, they argue that requiring reunification efforts in every case is unrealistic since reunification will clearly be futile in some situations. In such situations, it is in the child's interest to be placed in a preadoptive home as quickly as possible. Second, they claim that many states continue to leave too many children in long-term foster care—even after it is clear that reunification efforts have failed—because it is difficult to bring termination proceedings. As a result, children never get permanent homes.

In contrast, other critics believe that termination occurs too frequently. They claim that many terminations could be avoided if states made better efforts to reunify families. They argue that many parents are being deprived of their children because the states are unwilling to invest in the services that are necessary for reunification efforts to be truly meaningful. In addition, they argue that, even if children cannot be reunited with their parents, guardianship, not termination, is better for children, since it allows for continued contact with biological parents.

Unfortunately, there are no systematic, large-scale studies that examine how current termination laws are being applied. Therefore, any analysis of existing laws must rely primarily on anecdotal information and inferences that can be drawn from general statistics. Consequently, in this paper, I propose a framework for approaching termination decisions that requires the exploration of three related questions:

- Are there any types of situations in which reunification efforts should not be mandated, that is, situations in which immediate termination is appropriate following a finding of maltreatment?

- When reunification is required, how long must such efforts continue and what type of services should be provided?

- In attempting to provide children with permanent homes, is it preferable to seek adoption or is legal guardianship a better alternative in most cases?

Using this proposed framework, we can ask two additional questions: Are the existing grounds for termination generally adequate, or should new criteria be enacted? Should there be changes in the procedures by which termination cases are initiated? For example, should there be a set time after which the desirability of termination must always be evaluated by a court?

Termination without reunification efforts should be permissible only in a very limited category of cases—those in which a very young child has been seriously abused (physically or sexually), past treatment efforts have clearly failed to change a parent's behavior, or the parent refuses to participate in a reasonable and adequate treatment program. This proposal is basically consistent with the present law in many states.

I would change entirely the way termination is approached with respect to children who remain in foster care longer than one year. I would replace the existing grounds for termination, which focus primarily on parental conduct, with a statute that considers only two things—the length of time that the child is in foster care and the question of whether termination is beneficial for the child. Moreover, the juvenile court supervising the child's foster care placement would be *required* to consider termination after the child had been in care for a specific period of time, generally 12 to 18 months, depending on the age of the child. The goal of the system would be to have the great majority of children in a permanent home in no longer than 18 months.

Prerequisites to Termination

The rules regarding termination cannot be viewed in isolation. Therefore, my proposals are based on certain judgments about how the entire child welfare system should operate. Although the judgments that follow are not universally accepted, they represent the dominant thinking among child welfare professionals.

First, coercive intervention through child maltreatment laws ought to be permissible only when children have suffered serious physical or emotional harm or there is a substantial likelihood, based on the past conduct of the parents, that they are in imminent danger of suffering such harm. Second, when intervention is necessary, it is preferable to try to keep children with their parents through the provision of services. Children should be removed only if they cannot be protected from serious harm without removal. This preference, which is reflected in P.L. 96-272, is based both on values favoring family integrity and on evidence that the well-being of most children is best protected by leaving them at home, provided that good services are available. Third, in most, but not all, instances when children are removed, every effort should be made to reunite the family. This too is codified in P.L. 96-272. Moreover, it should not be required that parents be able to provide a high level of care before children are returned. The standard for return is whether or not the child will suffer serious harm if reunification takes place.

At present, no system in the country approaches compliance with these general goals, especially in cases involving chemically dependent mothers. Due to the lack of services, punitive ideologies, vague or inappropriate statutes, and poor performance by people in the child protective system, unnecessary interventions occur, removal frequently is not used except as a last resort, and reasonable efforts to reunify families are often not made.

The fact that all existing systems are woefully inadequate poses practical and ethical problems for legislators drafting termination laws and for judges implementing them. Should termination be restricted until the rest of the system functions adequately? If so, children are likely to remain in unstable, long-term foster care, since their parents will never have received adequate services. Yet, if termination is made easier before these other deficiencies are corrected, the system may have little incentive to improve. This is both unfair to parents and, in the long run, harmful to the interests of children.

Although this paper discusses how termination should work in a properly functioning system, I would not support adoption of my proposals until the rest of the system is in place, even if this means leaving some children in long-term care. At this point, I doubt that any state provides adequate family preservation and family reunification services to the great majority of families entering the child protection system. Hopefully, implementation of the Family Support and Preservation Act of 1993 will make total system change possible in the near future.

Termination without Attempting Reunification

No data exist that allow us to determine the percentage of cases in which termination is currently granted without any efforts at reunification. Anecdotal evidence indicates that it is quite rare. Under some states' statutes or case law, it may not be possible to terminate at this stage. In those states that do permit immediate termination, the process is quite haphazard, a situation that is facilitated by the vagueness of many statutes.

As previously indicated, some commentators suggest that, in cases where there is little hope that the parent will be able to resume custody, more terminations should take place without attempted reunification. They believe that it is possible to identify parents whose behaviors are so egregious, or who are so unamenable to treatment, that requiring reunification efforts makes no sense. Therefore, they would adopt an approach such as that of South Carolina, which permits immediate termination if "the parent has a diagnosable condition unlikely to change within a reasonable time such as alcohol or drug addiction, mental deficiency, mental illness, or extreme physical incapacity, and the condition makes the parent unlikely to provide minimally acceptable care of the child."[3] This statute allows a court to decide that the situation is irremediable based solely on the existence of the condition.

Is such an approach desirable? Should there be more initial terminations and, if so, on what grounds? In particular, is it desirable to increase initial terminations in cases involving heavy substance users?

In thinking about the desirability of termination in cases involving drug-addicted parents, it is necessary to keep in mind that two very different groups of cases are now brought into the child protective system. The first group comprises cases in which a child who has been living with a parent is reported to protective services because of actual child abuse or child neglect, as those terms are defined by state law. The substance abuse might be the cause of the parent's behavior, but it is the abusive or neglectful *behavior* by the parent that serves as the basis for intervention.

The second group consists of cases in which the mother used drugs or alcohol during her pregnancy. In these cases, the mother has not abused or neglected the child (the issue of fetal abuse is beyond the scope of this paper). Intervention is based solely on the prediction that the mother is likely to abuse or neglect the child in the future because she used drugs during pregnancy. This second group raises special problems with respect to termination laws, problems beyond those previously discussed. Some people see substance use during pregnancy as especially troubling, in part because of the potential harm to the fetus. It has been argued that we should make less of an effort to attempt reunification in these cases. Many other people, however, feel that the argument goes in the other direction. Because the mother has never abused or neglected a child, they oppose any intervention by child protection agencies; they would leave care to the medical system. If intervention did occur, they would strongly oppose ever allowing termination without services, since the mother has never abused or neglected the child.

I do not discuss the appropriateness of intervention based solely on substance use during pregnancy in this paper. The following discussion assumes that intervention may be appropriate following the birth of the child in at least some instances—for example, where the mother's chemical dependency impairs her ability to provide adequate care for her infant. Thus, the question of immediate termination may arise both in the case of newborns and in cases of older children who have been maltreated by parents who are chemically dependent. It must be remembered, however, that the following discussion is based on the premises previously discussed—that is, intervention is justified only when it is necessary in order to prevent substantial harm to the child and that removal is used only as a last resort.

Factors Favoring Immediate Termination

A number of arguments might be made for allowing courts to terminate parental rights without reunification efforts in some cases in which the mother is a substance user. Perhaps surprisingly, the case is strongest with respect to children who must be removed from their mother's care at birth. The main argument might go as follows:

In many cases in which a child must be removed from a chemically dependent parent because that parent is unable to provide adequate care, the probability is low that the child will be reunited with the parent, unless the parent willingly enters a treatment program. It is claimed that, among crack users in particular, successful treatment is the exception, rather than the rule. Motivation is the critical factor. Therefore, immediate termination ought to be considered unless the mother is willing to accept treatment and there is reason to believe that she can benefit from this treatment.

In support of this position, proponents point to the historically low reunification rate in cases in which the parent is chemically dependent. They contend that the low rate reflects the resistance of substance users to any type of treatment program. Since the probability of reunification is low, and treatment programs are both expensive and problematic as to outcome, it is a waste of resources and harmful to the child to attempt reunification, unless the parent is highly motivated.

The harm that attempting reunification might inflict upon the child may take two forms. First, because infants and young children need to bond with their caregivers, and disruption of these bonds is likely to be harmful, it is undesirable to place infants in temporary foster care. This is especially true for infants who have been exposed prenatally to drugs or alcohol and who may, as a result, have special needs. Immediate termination would make it more likely that the child can be placed with a family that is willing to make the type of emotional commitment to the child necessary to foster the child's normal development.

Moreover, it seems likely that, in a number of cases in which reunification does occur, the parent will relapse and the child will have to be removed again—which can have a potentially devastating effect on the child's emotional growth. It is argued that many agencies now reunify children in clearly inappropriate situations, perhaps because of the mandates contained in state or federal laws. If, overall, few children will be reunited successfully with their parents, then it is best to adopt a policy that protects the development of the majority of children.

Finally, there are cases in which the parent has a long history of substance abuse and previous efforts at treatment have failed. Other children of this parent may have been placed in foster care and reunification efforts for them were unsuccessful. Especially in such cases, it is both dangerous and a waste of time and resources to attempt reunification with yet another child.

Although these arguments apply primarily in cases of newborns, many of the concerns, such as the last one, are relevant in cases involving older children as well.

Factors Opposing Immediate Termination

A number of considerations must be weighed against the previous claims. I am just listing them here, because each requires a lengthier discussion than space permits.

First, immediate termination may be harmful to a large number of children—older children who are strongly attached to their parents and both newborns and older children who cannot be placed permanently. It is generally difficult to obtain sufficient information on one or both of these matters until the child has been in placement for a period of time. For example, it usually requires several months—or longer—to determine whether a child is adoptable. This is especially true with respect to infants who have been exposed prenatally to drugs or alcohol. The time period may be considerably longer if efforts are made to place children with families of the same race, ethnicity, or cultural background. If termination occurs and the child is not adopted, the child is parentless. Moreover, the ideal time to begin reunification efforts has passed.

Second, it is difficult to determine whether a parent is not amenable to treatment unless treatment is attempted. There is little research on which to base guidelines indicating who is amenable to treatment, except in the most extreme cases. Absent guidelines, there is a substantial possibility that judges and social workers will act arbitrarily, basing their decisions on their biases or on poor information.

Moreover, existing data regarding the probability of successful reunification may be misleading. They likely reflect the inadequacy of existing treatment efforts or programs, rather than the true potential for reunification. Current practice is deficient in many ways. Social workers often take punitive views toward these women and expect them to do everything on their own. Many treatment programs are inappropriate; for example, they often fail to recognize that the mother is also suffering from a mental illness that requires separate treatment. Courts and social work agencies often make unreasonable demands with regard to treatment "success." Any relapse is viewed as a total failure, even if the parent is providing adequate care.

A growing body of evidence supports the claim that, if good programs, including residential programs, were in place, family preservation or reunification would likely be the norm. Until such programs are widely available, we cannot obtain reasonable estimates of treatability. There are a number of programs that now provide specialized services to this population. Until such programs are widely and adequately evaluated, we cannot obtain reasonable estimates of treatability.[4]

Third, since our society currently provides very few good treatment alternatives for substance-using parents, especially for pregnant women, it is fundamentally unfair to deprive these women of their children. The lack of fairness is heightened because many of these mothers have grown up in poverty, often in foster care, and have never been given a real opportunity to lead a different life-style. Moreover, permitting termination without requiring reunification attempts would encourage society to continue ignoring the treatment needs of these parents. In the vast majority of cases, a requirement that "reasonable efforts" at reunification be attempted helps commit our society to developing good treatment programs.

Fourth, if good social work practices were followed—including daily visiting, training the parent to handle the child, and using the foster parents to work with biological parents—then many children could become attached to their biological, not foster parents, and temporary foster care would not be so harmful for them.

Fifth, a policy of immediate termination of parental rights in the case of substance-exposed newborns would certainly lead many women to avoid medical care and hospital births, thus jeopardizing their infants. Moreover, if infants are taken away permanently, many women will become pregnant again and avoid the medical system during these pregnancies. Treatment efforts may discourage future pregnancies and improve the mother's parenting skills.

Assessing the Arguments

Overall, I find the arguments against expanding the number of initial terminations persuasive. As a matter of values, and probably in terms of the overall well-being of children, the general legal structure should require reunification efforts in virtually all abuse/neglect cases.

There are, however, three types of case in which immediate termination should be authorized: (1) situations in which a child under three years of age has suffered serious physical or sexual abuse; (2) situations in which a child has been removed previously, good services were given to the parent, the child was returned home, and the child was maltreated again; and (3) situations in which the parent is completely resistant to any treatment. Category 1 is not applicable in the case of newborns; the other two categories might apply in such cases.

I select these criteria because they are the only indicators for which substantial evidence exists that reunification is unlikely, even with good services. With respect to Category 1, good research indicates low levels of success in rehabilitating parents who seriously abuse very young children; this is true regardless of whether the situation involves substance abuse.[5] In light of the substantial harm to the child, there may be cases in which the risks of future abuse outweigh the possible benefits of reunification. In these cases, the parents should have the opportunity to demonstrate that they are amenable to treatment. Absent such a showing by the parent, the court should terminate parental rights, provided that termination is otherwise in the child's interest.

With respect to Category 2, it is especially harmful to children to move them back and forth between home and foster care. If good services have been tried and failed, there is little reason to expect future success. Again, however, the parent should have the opportunity to indicate why services are likely to be successful despite past failures.

Category 3 is the most applicable in cases involving infants who have been exposed to drugs or alcohol during pregnancy. If the mother is unable to provide adequate care for the infant—and refuses treatment services—immediate termination may be appropriate in order to facilitate the immediate permanent placement of the child. Some mothers are so addicted to drugs that they are unable or unwilling to care for their child or to use treatment resources. In some cases, they essentially abandon the child. Termination must be approached cautiously, however, even in these situations. A mother may reject services because of the negative way in which they are offered. Babies may be abandoned because of a failure by the worker to offer support to their mothers when they are in the hospital. Caseworkers may have negative perceptions of women who are substance abusers and may falsely assume that the mother is not amenable to treatment. Thus, each jurisdiction should establish clear guidelines with respect to the actions that must be taken prior to filing for termination.

When reunification is not feasible or desirable, I believe that termination is preferable to legal guardianship as a means of creating stability, unless the child is placed with a relative. Guardianship does not create the same degree of commitment on the part of the adults; adoption is also the best way of making the child feel part of a family, at least for young children. Moreover, many foster parents are unwilling to become legal guardians because they do not want to have continued contact with the biological parent. They may view such contact as harmful to the child or as threatening to themselves. They will keep the child only if they can adopt.

In general, existing laws would allow termination in the types of cases that I recommend. While these laws could, and should, be made more specific along the lines suggested, the major obstacles are administrative, not statutory. Moreover, because the grounds for termination should be related to each state's laws and service structure, as well as to local value preferences, the federal government should not try to dictate a particular statutory structure.

Termination after Extended Foster Care

Although there is only limited evidence indicating whether there is too much or too little termination as an initial disposition, there is more evidence of problems with respect to children who have been in foster care for a period of time. Despite the broadly accepted goal of providing permanent homes, it appears that many children still drift in foster care.[6] The situation may be especially bad in cases involving chemically dependent parents.[7]

From a legal perspective, the problem seems to be primarily one of agency and court practices, since most state laws provide many grounds for termination, including the fact that a child has been in care for one year. Although the laws authorize termination, there is no requirement that a court actually consider termination, regardless of how long the child has been in foster placement. P.L. 96-272 requires that a court review the status of each child who remains in foster care for 18 months, in order to establish a permanent plan.

But the decision to seek termination, or legal guardianship, is discretionary, left to the child welfare agency in every state except California. For a variety of reasons, agencies seem unwilling or unable to institute termination proceedings. Initiating termination actions is time-consuming and requires extra work by the social workers. Given heavy work loads, and predilections against termination, there is an incentive for workers and courts to just leave children in foster care as the "permanent plan."

Even when agencies request termination, the request may be denied because the agency supervising the child has not made reasonable efforts to work with the parent to facilitate reunification. Again, this is not a problem with the statutes; it represents a breakdown in implementation of the statutory structure. Finally, fault concepts may creep into the decision-making. Termination may be refused because the parents are not thought of as blameworthy. Just a little effort by the parent to cooperate with a treatment plan may be enough to avoid termination, regardless of the substantial likelihood that the treatment will be unsuccessful.

Although it is possible that current laws could be made to work properly, I believe that a new approach is needed with respect to children who are placed in foster care and who cannot be returned home despite good services. In place of the current fault-based grounds, termination should be based on only two factors: (1) the length of time the child has been in foster placement, and (2) the possibility that termination will harm rather than help the child. On the first factor, a court would be required to examine the need for termination after the child has been in care for 12 or 18 months, depending on the age of the child. Termination would be the norm if a child under three cannot be returned home within a year of placement; for older children, termination would be the norm after 18 months.

On the second factor, termination would not be permissible in two situations: (1) when the court finds that termination would be detrimental to the child because of the emotional importance to the child of continuing the parent-child relationship, or (2) when the child is placed with a relative and the relative does not wish to adopt. In addition, the court would have to find that there is a substantial likelihood that the child will be adopted.

These proposals are based on data indicating that the length of time in foster care is the critical variable with regard to the likelihood of the child's being returned home, the amount of harm a child is likely to suffer as a result of being in foster care, and the likelihood of finding a permanent placement following termination. Because the harm from lengthy placement is generally greater when the child is younger, and the potential harm from termination is greater for older children, the periods chosen vary with the child's age.[8]

A case could be made for making the period shorter for younger children (six months?) and longer for older children. The exact time frame is not critical; the principle of setting a time frame is. In addition, a statute might allow for earlier termination in cases in which the parent is totally unresponsive to treatment efforts or fails to maintain contact with the child. If the agency has been diligent in its efforts to contact and work with the parent in an empathetic manner and the parent is still unresponsive, then the parent's actions should be construed as the equivalent of abandoning the child.

The exceptions are designed to preclude termination in cases in which the child will be harmed by the termination. Unlike present laws, they focus on the child's needs and perspectives rather than on parental behavior.

Are there any special factors regarding substance-use cases that justify special rules for these specific cases? One question is whether it is appropriate to adopt a system with relatively rigid time frames in these cases, given the highly individualized patterns of drug use, responsiveness to treatment, and parent-child relationships. Assuming that it is decided to use the time frame approach, how much time should be allowed before requiring termination? Is 12 months too long to wait in some cases? Is 18 months too short a period in some cases? What about cases that involve removal of infants or cases in which the mother is making no progress in treatment after six months? What about cases in which the mother is making progress in a residential treatment program, but the treatment requires longer than 18 months? Should a parent's incarceration toll the statutory time frame?

These are difficult questions. Perhaps a more discretionary approach, one that authorizes termination after a set period of time, defines reasonable efforts, but allows agencies and courts to decide whether to initiate and grant termination based on all the factors in the case, would be fairest to parents and most attuned to the needs of each child.

Still, I tend to favor the less discretionary approach. It is just too tempting for courts and agencies to let foster care continue forever when a parent seems to be trying. Yet, there is little reason to believe that allowing treatment to continue for longer than 18 months will make a difference in many cases. There is more reason to fear that extending foster care beyond this point jeopardizes the well-being of many children. The proposed exceptions to termination should cover situations in which the parent has retained a relationship with the child. Moreover, if parent-child residential treatment programs were more widely available, termination would not be an issue in most situations.

It might be reasonable to allow termination after six months in cases involving children removed before their first birthday. These children need to bond with a caregiver as soon as possible. Moreover, earlier termination for very young children might facilitate placing these children in foster homes in which the foster parent is open to adoption. This exception would have to be applied very cautiously, however, with clearly articulated criteria for the point at which it can be concluded that the mother is failing to make any progress toward reunification. The appropriateness of the proffered services, and the sensitivity with which they were offered, would have to be reviewed in detail. In fact, the entire structure I propose is justified only if the system is really prepared to make *meaningful* efforts at reunification. Otherwise, the goal of reunification is a sham and it would be just as well to terminate immediately. To ensure a meaningful process, states must provide adequate procedures for regularly reviewing the status of the reunification plan. Although P.L. 96-272 requires a court or administrative review after a child has been in foster care for six months, in most places this does not occur regularly and adequately.

Conclusion

As I have emphasized throughout this paper, an adequate approach to dealing with child maltreatment cannot be developed piecemeal. Focusing on termination is the wrong place to start. If removal is truly to be a last resort, it might even make sense to allow early termination in the majority of cases in which removal is necessary, but we will never know that until the entire system functions properly.

Notes

1. This brief paper cannot discuss all of the issues related to termination. For a fuller discussion, see Wald, *State Intervention on Behalf of Neglected Children:*

Standards for Removal of Children from Their Homes, Monitoring the Status of Children in Foster Care, and Termination of Parental Rights, 28 Stanford Law Review 623 (1976).

2. Ibid.

3. South Carolina Code Ann. @ 20-7-1572 (1991).

4. See Beatrice Moore, *In-Home Services for Crack-Using Mothers in Detroit* (Washington, DC: U.S. Department of Health and Human Services, 1989); David E. Biegel, Henry L. Zucker, and Kathleen Wells, eds., *Family Preservation Services: Research and Evaluation* (Newbury Park, CA: Sage Publications, Inc., 1990).

5. Michael S. Wald, *Protecting Abused and Neglected Children* (Stanford, CA: Stanford University Press, 1988).

6. Toshio Tatara, "Child Substitute Care Population Trends FY 82 through FY 91— A Summary," *VCIS Research Notes*, no. 6 (August 1992).

7. Toshio Tatara, "Children of Substance Abusing and Alcoholic Parents in Public Child Welfare," final report prepared for The American Enterprise Institute for Public Policy Research (Washington, DC: American Public Welfare Association, 1990).

8. Wald.

LONG-TERM FOSTER CARE

Ruth Massinga

During the last five years, medical practitioners and scientists following the developmental course of children exposed in utero to alcohol, tobacco, and multiple drugs have come to note that child resiliency is a strong determinant of the long-term effects of these substances on the newborn. Clinicians assessing these children report that it is difficult to see any physical effects of the prenatal exposure to drugs in many of the children.[1] Whether many of these children thrive—or fail to thrive—seems to depend on the nature of their environment. Notwithstanding the stresses suffered early on, children who have a "trustworthy environment do a lot better...in terms of their whole behavioral constellation," especially if the decision about the child's permanent home is swift and stable, and the supports provided by the caregivers are dependable and robust.[2]

Indeed, pediatricians and other experts in child development note that the postnatal environment is a key predictor of the well-being of children who have experienced the assault of prenatal drug use by their mothers. Dr. Barry Zuckerman, a noted pediatrician who has followed a significant number of these children, notes that those with "relatively high perinatal stress had good outcomes if their families had a high level of stability...the quality of the home environment, and not the amount of substances taken by the mother while pregnant, was a more important determinant of outcome."[3]

Over the past ten years, during the height of the increase in crack cocaine use in this country, medical, legal, and child welfare policy and practices have supported the view that stabilizing drug-affected children within their biological families should be given first preference, as long as the children are safely protected from harm. This policy position is supported by the fact that significant numbers of such children do thrive within their families—if suitable caregiving arrangements and supportive service strategies are put in place to rehabilitate the mothers and care for the children at the same time.

Nevertheless, the increase in reports of children of drug abusers is having a dramatic impact upon the system that provides care for children outside of their homes, notably through foster care. In 1992, the number of youths in foster care had risen to nearly 500,000, with the largest increase being in infant admissions. (In 1989, infants represented 31 percent of children entering care for the first time in New York City; 25 percent in Cook County, Illinois; and 25 percent in Wayne County, Michigan).[4] A significant factor accounting for these increases was the rise in reports of neglect or abuse associated with one or both parents' persistent drug abuse.

Clearly, family foster homes were the environments of choice for a significant number of children who could not be sustained safely with their parents. The ability of these out-of-home resources to ensure that the rising population of youth would thrive in family foster home environments then became a major public policy concern.

Creating wholesome alternative environments for children is the specialty of the Casey Family Program, a private operating foundation that, as of February 1994, provides long-term family foster care to more than 1,300 children in 23 different localities across 13 states. The aim of the program is to raise these children to maturity, with the skills to form and sustain positive, significant relationships, participate responsibly in the life of their communities, and support themselves economically. Over the last five years, the program's direct service staff members have determined that, while children enter the program between the ages of six and 16, a significant portion of the youths served by the program have a family history of either one or both biological parents being seriously involved with alcohol, drugs, or both. In some of our urban divisions and in reservation communities, referrals of youths for whom parental substance abuse is a significant threat to the ability of the child to remain at home exceeds 70 percent.

Based on 27 years of experience with providing long-term foster care in diverse settings, the Casey Family Program has designed an effective model of long-term alternative care to meet the needs of children affected by drug abuse who are unable to remain in their own homes.

Fostering Families

Which foster family arrangements work for whom and why? For more than 30 years, spurred on by the work of Bowlby, Ainsworth, Freud, and others, we have been increasingly conscious of the importance to healthy child development of attachment between parents (or their substitutes) and children. Dr. Kathryn Barnard, a nurse-practitioner/educator at the University of Washington who has worked with hundreds of caregivers, notes that there is a dyadic, reciprocal responsibility between child and caregiver and describes the responsibilities of the caregiver in relationship to attachment issues as follows:

> Caregivers who are sensitive to the developmental and interactional cues the child provides and who can help the child learn to present its needs clearly are essential. Good care providers are promptly responsive to the distress of a child and they provide a social, emotional, and cognitive growth-fostering environment.[5]

Thus, despite the irritability and confused reactions to environmental stimuli displayed by many young children exposed to drugs in utero, the availability of an anchoring, secure base with stable, caring adults is a critical factor for the adequate growth and development of these children. The adults in these children's lives must act with intentionality to help them learn to provide the cues that will get their needs satisfied.

These skills have been successfully taught by Dr. Barnard and her colleagues to poor or working-class mothers in the Seattle, Washington, area and, in a similar effort reported by Pharis and Levin, to high-risk mothers served by the Clinical Infant Development Program in Prince George's County, Maryland.[6] These women initially lacked social competencies and had multiple problems in functioning, but, over time, within the context of caring relationships, gained appropriate child-centered responsiveness. Dr. Barnard noted, however, that the mothers' acquisition of these abilities was frequently too delayed to meet their child's developmental needs. This suggests that creating a fostering environment that is responsive to both the recovering mothers and their babies would provide a more helpful dynamic mix.[7]

The relevance of these findings is directly related to the often-cited lack of adequate foster families. It is striking that the most commonly promoted and pursued means of achieving success in recruiting, developing, and retaining an adequate supply of caregivers focuses on compensation, respite, child care, and family therapy, as well as enriched child development for both foster and biological children in the home. These are all critical, but do not directly address the caregiver's ability to respond to the cues children provide them about their needs. Critical to promoting lasting commitment from adults to children are demonstrated and persistent attitudes, as well as goal-directed training and support of foster care program staff members that affirms and actively develops increased competencies in child-rearing among all adults, biological and foster parents alike. Increased competence of caregivers seems to correlate with psychic satisfaction in doing the job well, as evidenced by children's increased well-being.

The aim of such an approach would be to focus less on the notion of protecting children from intrinsically "harmful" parents and more on the idea of helping children sustain themselves—and reconcile or resolve issues of loss and disappointment with their biological parents—as they mature and grow stronger in their own, healthy identities.

Describing a changing model that goes from being solely child-focused to fostering families to the extent possible, Kufeldt and Allison promote the following objectives:

- Boundaries between natural families and foster families must be permeable; competition must be absent.

- The task of fostering is significantly different from normal parenting and thus foster parents who take on a fostering families assignment must be viewed as employees.

- The concept of ownership of children needs to give way to shared care.

- Parenting and fostering must be viewed in a community context.[8]

Underlying these competencies is an assumption that biological parents and foster parents are really part of the professional team, with varying roles and responsibilities. Depending on their individual strengths and motivations, the foster parents and the social workers will jointly develop a plan to help children prosper in accordance with their needs as well as those of their families. This can be done by means of differential skills and expertise that now exist or with skills that need to be developed among all team members. Thus, approaching foster parents in relation to their current abilities and recognizing and supporting the need for skill development over the life of the therapeutic relationship are critical and fundamental elements of success.

At its best, long-term foster care incorporates the best elements of the natural family system along with those of the neighborhood and community support systems that will sustain the "as if" extended family, whether related through kinship or cultural affinities. These systems of values and shared responsibilities for the child and family, in which the agency social worker is responsible for assuring long-term, effective child rearing, buffer the tensions and stresses of the caregivers as they learn to respond to the child's changing needs.

Marion Lowe describes the evolving concept of *foster carers*, the term the National Foster Care Association in the United Kingdom substitutes for the term foster parents.[9] These foster carers see themselves as integral to good child care, with a right to help develop clear placement goals, to have access to information about the children in care, to receive adequate support and training from the agency, and to take an active role in decision-making. The attendant obligations for foster carers are to safeguard the child; to be a cooperative partner for parents, social workers, and other professionals involved with the child; and to continually assess their work in order to improve their skills, attitudes, and behaviors.

Within the Casey Family Program, the most fully developed manifestation of this emerging model is on Native American reservations, where all foster parents are related by a cultural definition of shared responsibility for children and family members (and often by blood) and by a recognition of shifting roles based on competency and planned changes. Such a program model has begun to thrive in kinship and affiliation networks in the south and southwest among African Americans and Latinos, and among religious Caucasian families in the midwest and Pacific northwest. What is not clear are the conditions and costs of large-scale replication of such a model in urban areas of concentrated, long-standing poverty that have been compounded by racial oppression.

In many ways, the large increases in placements with relatives have given us some time and opportunity to refine new systems of family fostering and have provided some of the conceptual and practical modeling for changing roles and responsibilities. In many major cities, relative care constitutes a growing and major portion of the foster parent group. Statewide in California, relatives care for 37 percent of children placed in out-of-home settings[10] and account for 50 percent of all foster care placements in New York City.[11]

Nationally, about half of cocaine-exposed newborns are discharged to a relative, usually the maternal grandmother. These affiliations force the field to reexamine and define the best, most developmentally sound child-rearing environments for children. Not surprisingly, relatives are frequently well-suited to nurture children, especially older children who cannot be reunited with natural parents but whose continuation of ties with their biological family is a very high priority. Social workers require new learning in how to support relative care, including how to help older caregivers acquire different behaviors to address the complex physical and emotional needs of their young charges. Letting go of mutually unhelpful stereotypes allows the caseworker and the relative foster carer to forge a collaboration of mutual respect and reinforcement.

Implications for Programs

Dr. Jim Whittaker of the University of Washington School of Social Work lists the following program guidelines that emerge from family-based services models:

- Establish a service continuum with expanded capacity for individualized case planning.

- Promote confidence and the basic developmental needs of children in "normalized" settings by teaching practical life skills and providing environmental supports as opposed to encouraging and treating pathology.

- Renew emphasis on family supportive and family strengthening approaches.

- Support a reemerging view of the foster family as a part of the social environment, living in a reciprocally sustaining manner within the community.[12]

As Mary Jo Bane indicates:

The key to the success of these (effective) programs lies in the quality of interactions that go on between individual service providers and clients. These interactions tend to be situation-specific and immediately responsive, like the interactions that go on in effective families or classrooms. They tend to be performed by relatively autonomous professionals who exercise a fair amount of discretion in responding to needs.[13]

It is no wonder that low worker-to-family/child ratios are valued by the former foster children in the Casey Family Program. From his experience building the United Parcel Service, the program's founder, Jim Casey, recognized that a more personalized service delivered by a stable, committed workforce would provide the stability and continuity needed for the children to overcome life traumas and thrive.[14]

Personalized services are costly, in terms of the effort needed to maintain the placement as well as the individualized nature of the response to the myriad needs of the child. It is costly to provide continuous, specialized training support to the foster parents and to provide for localized decision-making by the small staff teams serving these children. To be sure, even the most optimally effective long-term foster care environment is not suitable for every child, nor even for the same child over his or her developmental life span. Each year, 8 to 10 percent of the youths in the Casey Family Program have stays in other, more restrictive institutions, such as psychiatric hospitals, alcohol or drug treatment programs, and residential treatment centers. The length of time for treatment varies and is almost always followed by community-based aftercare in the same foster home or a different one within the program. In order to respond to the child's emerging needs over time, it is important that all remedial services are flexible, have permeable boundaries, and are within a developed continuum of care system.

Public Policy and Financing

Implementing these emerging case arrangements with the public child welfare system will require certain changes in public policy and public financing.

First, fiscal support for long-term foster care needs to cover the full range of child development and habilitative requirements of the child as they emerge. Closely monitored health and mental health services, child day care, and other specialized services in which the child welfare agency is given the lead in aggressive follow-up and treatment in the preschool years, are essential to early, ongoing diagnosis and interaction. Using EPSDT as the funding mechanism (as well as the pediatric protocol for assessment and treatment for children in care), routine health treatment can be in place for every child. Similarly, interagency agreements with child mental health systems must be mandated and funded through Medicaid for all children whose parents were drug-involved.

Second, federal and state regulations that require differential payment rates between relative and nonrelative providers should be eliminated. Not only is this unequal treatment for equivalent work, but some might argue that the tensions associated with safeguarding the child's interest are more complex to manage and negotiate in a relative placement. This justifies more—not less— support for relative placements.

Third, individualized and small-group, team-oriented training for foster care providers, alone and with social workers, is a fundamental feature of successful long-term care. Grants for training social work staff as well as foster care providers need to be revived as a major part of the federal role in child welfare. We must realize, as successful corporations do, that professional training is an ongoing obligation of the aggressive employer that can be directly related to quality performance and worker/foster parent accountability for child well-being.

Fourth, lower worker caseloads are equally important. Studies of the success of family preservation indicate that giving workers the time necessary to do an adequate job, as well as other supports, can be directly tied to positive client outcomes.

Fifth, respite, peer support groups for foster families, and regularly scheduled family and marital therapy for difficulties that may arise within the foster family are critical means to assure that the substitute care arrangements are and remain sound and well-functioning.

Nearly all of the items noted above are federally reimbursable under Title IV-E and enhanced Title IV-B funds, assuming permissive federal policies. With local dollars, political will, and the time of skilled people, a public child welfare agency can knit together a combination of its own or purchased services and supports that move toward accessible, appropriate long-term foster care. Those resources that are underdeveloped or too frequently unavailable (e.g., child mental health or drug treatment) require venture capital for development and widespread application. We must realize that the required long-term investments are difficult to pull together, especially in the fiscal climate and discouraging prospects confronting the child welfare administrator today.

Moving forward, past the sense of immobility and despair that confronts the field today, may require a public and private collaboration of a manageable scale in a large urban setting. A pilot effort with private local and federal funds initiated in a neighborhood or district of a major city can tell us much about costs and benefits of enhanced efforts and can effect change as well.

Over the long term, carefully planned and well-documented research studies on the efficacy of long-term care as a treatment resource for drug-exposed children will help sharpen and clarify what we are beginning to learn through empirical research in too few settings. Federal, state, and private sponsorship of such an effort will help increase our base of knowledge in order to better address a growing need.

Notes

1. Kathryn Barnard, Neal Halfon, and Ann Streissguth, "Impacts of Parents' Dysfunctional Behaviors on the Development of Children in Out-of-Home Care: Panel Presentation in Preparing for the Future," The Casey Family Program Symposium on Children and Youth in Long-Term Out-of-Home Care, edited by Jennifer Cargal and Virginia Senegal (Seattle, WA: The Casey Family Program, 1991), 111; Barry Zuckerman, "Drug-Exposed Infants: Understanding the Medical Risk," in *The Future of Children* 1, no.1, edited by Richard E. Berman (Los Altos, CA: Center for the Future of Children, 1991), 34.

2. Barnard, Halfon, and Streissguth, 99.

3. Zuckerman, 34.

4. *Maternal Drug Abuse and Drug-Exposed Children: Understanding the Problem* (Washington, DC: U.S. Department of Health and Human Services, 1992), 46.

5. Barnard, Halfon, and Streissguth, 99.

6. *Ibid.*, 100-101; Mary E. Pharis and Victoria S. Levin, "A Person to Talk to Who Really Cared: High-Risk Mothers' Evaluations of Services in an Intensive Intervention Research Program," *Child Welfare* 70, no. 3 (May/June 1991): 314.

7. Barnard, Halfon, and Streissguth, 100-101; Pharis and Levin.

8. Kathleen Kufeldt and James Allison, "Fostering Children—Fostering Families," *International Journal of Foster Cases* 2, no. 1 (Spring 1990): 10.

9. Marion I. Lowe, "The Challenge of Partnership: A National Foster Care Charter in the U.K.," *Child Welfare* 70, no. 2 (March/April 1991): 153-154.

10. County Welfare Directors Association of California, Chief Probation Officers Association of California, and California Mental Health Directors, *Ten Reasons to Invest in the Families of Children* (Sacramento, CA: Author, 1990).

11. Fred H. Wulczyn and Robert M. Goerge, "Foster Care in New York and Illinois: The Challenge of Rapid Change," *Social Service Review* 66 (1992): 278–294.

12. Jim Whittaker, "The Leadership Challenge in Family-Based Services: Policy Practice and Research," *Families in Society* 72, no. 5 (1991): 2, 4, 95, 296.

13. Cited by Lisbeth Schorr in "Successful Programs and the Bureaucratic Dilemma: Current Deliberations," speech reprinted by The National Center for Children in Poverty, 1991.

14. David Fanshel, Stephen J. Finch, and John Grundy, *Foster Children in a Life Course Perspective* (New York: Columbia University Press, 1990).

Kinship Care

Ivory L. Johnson

Until recently, children removed from their parents' care for abuse, neglect, or exploitation were almost always placed in nonrelative family foster care, typically with foster parents who would have been approved and licensed by the state to provide temporary or long-term substitute care. Many of these children had relatives who were willing to provide them with short- or long-term care, but who were unable to do so due to financial hardship, inadequate or absent services or supports, or agency barriers. Willing relatives were often denied AFDC because they were not licensed foster parents and were unable to meet certain licensing standards such as the number of bedrooms required for household size.

Since 1985, the number of court-adjudicated children placed with relatives, now popularly known as *kinship care*, has skyrocketed. States such as New York, Illinois, and California report that kinship placements constitute one-third or more of their foster care caseloads. New York City, for example, reports that, as of June 1990, 22,000 children were in relative placements—over half of the city's total foster care population.[1]

The significant increase in kinship care placements has generated intense discussion about their benefits and potential pitfalls. Ideally, they can provide the best opportunity for a child to maintain a sense of family identity, self-esteem, social status, and continuity of family relationships. If, however, kin-

221

ship placements are instituted without the necessary agency planning, program development, and appropriate legislative and regulatory policies, they can be another system of abuse and neglect for vulnerable children. In fact, many child advocates believe that the levels of services and safeguards for kinship caregivers are inadequate when compared to those provided for nonrelative caregivers.

The use of kinship care has expanded so rapidly that child welfare agencies have been forced to make policy, program, and practice decisions without the benefit of a substantive knowledge base or best-practice experience. There is an emerging consensus that child welfare agencies must develop a practice philosophy that affirms relative placement as a first priority when a child must be removed from parental care and custody. This practice must be based on sound agency policies and programs that affirm the value of family for rearing children and view kinship care as an extension of the biological family. Agencies must provide the necessary training and supports to assure that kinship care is a viable and appropriate option.

Current Issues

Three factors are contributing to the surge in kinship placements. First, the child welfare system is severely strained, especially regarding foster family placement resources. As the number of nonrelative family foster homes began to decrease while the number of children requiring placement began to rise rapidly, and family foster providers became less willing to care for young children who have been exposed prenatally to chemicals, the child welfare system had to seek out relatives as placement resources. Second, a consensus is growing that children fare better in their own families, and that extended family members should be given priority for placement when biological parents are unable or unwilling to parent. Many child welfare professionals believe that placement with extended family is less traumatic than placement with strangers and that the child welfare system should not unnecessarily disrupt family, community, and cultural ties. Third, court rulings have encouraged placement with relatives. In 1979, the U.S. Supreme Court ruled that relatives who act as foster parents are entitled to the same levels of federal foster care reimbursement as nonrelative foster parents.[2] A decade later, a Ninth Circuit Court ruled that foster children have a constitutional right to associate with relatives, which the state may not impermissibly burden by failing to use relatives as foster parents.[3]

Additionally, many professionals in child welfare believe that abusive and neglectful parents are themselves the products of maltreating parents. This concept, often referred to as the intergenerational cycle of abuse, suggests that kinship families will also engage in patterns of abuse. Studies of intergenerational patterns of family behavior do support the hypothesis that certain dynamics, such as physical and sexual abuse, can move from one generation to the next. The surge in kinship placements, however, is being driven primarily by the significant increase in drug abuse among mothers: the most common reason for placement is parental condition or absence, with fewer children coming into care because of "protective issues."[4] At the same time, grandparents and other "older" relatives are usually not drug users. However, they are often struggling with poverty, social violence, racism, and the general decline in community supports and infrastructure—all of which detract from the family's ability to protect and nurture its children.

Our unspoken concern with relative placement is based on the common belief that such low-income families are less capable, less educated, and therefore less suited for the task of rearing their relatives' children. And yet, many of the concerns about the ability of kinship caregivers to meet the medical, educational, and emotional needs of children are issues for unrelated caregivers as well.

Agency caseworkers often view a relative placement as something less than a "real" placement because the child is still with the family. As a result, the family tends to receive fewer social worker contracts, fewer services, and less support. On a more subtle level, racial differences between the caseworker and the family often create cognitive distances, which in turn prevent the placement agency from providing full support. It is easier for a Caucasian social worker to relate to a Caucasian foster parent than to an African American family from a different socioeconomic background.

A common concern is whether standards are "lowered" for kinship caregivers, that is, are agencies overlooking certain safeguards required of nonrelative caregivers in order to facilitate a kinship placement? The elements critical to the evaluation of kinship families as a placement also need to be identified. We must look beyond the family's low socioeconomic status, poor speech patterns, and limited formal education and begin to assess the relative's attachment and commitment to the child. Most important is the relative's ability to nurture and protect. Other obstacles such as poor housing and parenting skills and the inability to utilize appropriate community resources can be removed if the agency is willing to commit the necessary staff and resources.

Making kinship placement a viable option requires differential case planning and an awareness of the importance of racial differences. In addition, those setting the standards for assessing kinship caregivers must take regional environmental differences into consideration. Families living in large urban communities will confront a different set of problems than will those in small newer communities. For example, poor housing and overcrowding may be more common in eastern and southern urban areas than in western rural states where urban "decay" is not a major issue. Managing educational systems and health care is also likely to be more difficult in older urban communities.

Much of the current debate over relative placement is focused on a few main areas of concern. First, should relative caregivers be paid the AFDC rate or the foster care rate? Given that foster care payments are generally much higher than AFDC grants, some believe that low-income families will voluntarily place their child with relatives as a way of increasing total family income. Some states are already reporting fraud in some cases. Two studies of relative caregivers in New York City, however, suggest that caregivers are not in it for money but are committed to providing care for their kin.[5]

Second, the question of permanency is cited by some as a major pitfall in kinship placement. It is suggested that if the higher foster care rate is paid, families will become dependent on the increased household income and will be reluctant to work toward reunification and the concomitant return to AFDC grant levels. This notion presumes that the biological parent lives with the relative caregiver and is a beneficiary of the increased income. This is an assumption that has yet to be proven. Finally, the relatives' ability to protect the child is a source of debate. Again, the assumption is that the relative, because of the close emotional ties with the parent, will not adhere to the agency policy or case plan regarding parental contact and conduct.[6]

The New York study, "Kinship Foster Care: The Double-Edged Dilemma," undercuts many of these concerns.[7] For example, of the 100 New York City family cases reviewed, 78 percent of the biological mothers did not live in the relative caregiver's home. The argument that relatives are often too old to care for young children also was not supported by the study. The mean age of the caregivers in the study was 45.9; no caregiver was older than 68. On the other hand, in one-third of the cases, judges had issued orders of protection, indicating their concern for the safety of the children and their caregivers.[8]

Clearly, when the state intervenes in family life, there should be compelling reasons for breaking parental ties. When these ties are broken, every effort should be made to preserve the children's connection to their family of origins, their community, and their heritage. The appropriate use of kinship placement is most likely to provide the sense of continuity of family life and belonging that is vital to healthy growth and development.

The Meaning of Family

A lack of understanding of family as defined by non-Western culture has created most of the current debate over what role, if any, kinship care should have in child welfare. The extended family structure has been viewed as a variant family form because its structure is different from what has traditionally been considered the ideal structure of the nuclear family. The nuclear family has been described as "particularly well-adapted to the needs of the American economy for a fluid and mobile labor market."[9] For the African American family, however, the kinship care arrangement is a practice rooted in the African and American experience. The African American extended family was and is a source of economic interdependency and survival in this country. A 1973 study by William C. Hayes showed that, compared to Caucasian families, African American families interacted with extended kin and perceived them as more significant. African American families also received help from their extended kin with child care and they tend to get this type of assistance more often than Caucasians.[10]

Native American culture has long been a culture of interdependence based on sharing and cooperation. Special spiritual significance was accorded to children in need. Oral traditions passed down taught these people that the care of their brothers' and sisters' children was their responsibility should the parents be unable to provide care.

Most Native American languages contain no words that translate into "foster care," yet the extended family and clan system in traditional Indian culture provided a wealth of substitute care resources for children when death or disability claimed their parents. The responsibility to assume care of relatives' children was both implied and expressly stated in the oral traditions and spiritual teachings of most tribes.

These traditions and orientation toward family are supported by practitioners of the ecological approach in child welfare practice. John Laird defines the ecological approach as follows:

> Ecologically oriented child welfare practice attends to, nurtures, and supports the biological family. Furthermore, when it is necessary to substitute for the biological family, the practice dictates that every effort be made to preserve and protect important kinship ties. Intervening in families must be done with great care to avoid actions that could weaken the natural family system, sap its vitality and strength, or force it to make difficult and costly adjustments.[11]

Extended family has been defined as "a multigenerational, interdependent kinship system which is welded together by a sense of obligation to relatives; is organized around a 'family-based' household; is generally guided by a 'dominant family figure'; extended family network; and has a built-in mutual aid system for the welfare of its members and the maintenance of the family as a whole."[12]

Implications for Policy and Practice

Until recently, if relatives wished to receive foster care payments, most agencies treated them the same as nonrelative foster parents, requiring them to submit to a standard family foster care process such as home evaluation, licensing, and inservice training. Those who opted to receive AFDC, instead, were often "forgotten" by the system. The children were left to drift in their care.

To view kinship care as simply a form of family foster care ignores the unique dynamics and varied definitions of family within a multicultural context and places the kinship caregivers in the traditional foster parent role conflict of parent versus professional team member. Additionally, there are the conflicts of divided loyalties between child, parent, kinship caregiver, and the family. Therefore, the question must be asked, "Is it reasonable to expect or require kinship caregivers to have the same roles and responsibilities as foster parents and to achieve appropriate case planning goals through the same process as with nonrelated foster parents?"

In kinship care, an established pattern of relationships uniquely affects the planning, casework process, protection, and permanency planning outcome for each family situation. These family relationships and accompanying dynamics must be considered in the casework process. Staff members must be sensitive and skilled regarding the contextual fabric of family dynamics and responsive to the strengths and needs of the child, parent, and caregiver within the family. It is for these reasons that kinship care must be viewed as distinct and separate from family foster care.

Agencies must develop clear policies regarding expectations, roles, and safety standards for kinship caregivers. Staff members must receive adequate training in cultural responsiveness and sensitivity to the populations served. They must be skilled in family assessment to be able to understand the implications of chemical abuse and dependency on one's ability to provide adequate parenting and protection. The dynamics of chemical abuse and dependency must be part of the core training for kinship caregivers and staff members. Finally, without unnecessary intrusion into the family system, agencies must support and assist relative caregivers in their role as substitute parents.

If the placement of a child with relatives is to be successful, intensive agency supervision and support services must be provided. Kinship caregivers are subject to some of the same social and economic conditions of the parents from whom the child was removed. They may need housing assistance, day care services, financial assistance, or family counseling to help them in their role as caregiver. These service needs, however, should not deter agencies from seeking out children and placing them with relatives.

Although it is true that families can be quite resourceful when basic survival needs are at stake, and that they may look to the foster care system as a source of additional income, the real policy question is whether or not the system provides adequate supports for families in which the state has intervened. This question of foster care payments versus AFDC for kinship caregivers may force the system to confront the more basic issue of AFDC grant levels and supportive services for vulnerable families. The current system appears to punish parents who need governmental assistance in meeting their parental responsibilities, yet is quite willing to spend thousands of dollars to maintain children outside of their kinship circle. States and local jurisdictions struggling to use kinship placement must balance its utility as a family preservation strategy against their responsibility to adequately protect and plan for children entrusted to their care. How should such a balance be achieved?

Kinship care should be viewed in its ecological context—as an extension of family—and should therefore be afforded the same agency supports and services that are provided to biological parents. At the same time, there should be appropriate levels of casework involvement to ensure that safety measures, case planning, and decision-making are in the child's best interest.

Notes

1. Bernard S. Meyers and Mary Jane K. Link, "Kinship Foster Care: The Double-Edged Dilemma," study prepared for the New York Task Force on Permanency Planning for Children, Rochester, New York, October 1990.

2. Miller v. Youakim, 440 U.S. 125 (1979).

3. Lipscomb v. Simmons (Ct. App. 9th Cir. 1989).

4. Toshio Tatara, "Child Substitute Care Population Trends FY 82 through FY 91—A Summary," *VCIS Research Notes*, no. 6 (August 1992).

5. Meyers and Link; Jesse L. Thornton, "An Investigation into the Nature of the Kinship Foster Home," DSW dissertation, Yeshiva University, New York, 1987.

6. Thornton.

7. Meyers and Link.

8. *Ibid*, 30.

9. Marvin B. Sussman, "The Isolated Nuclear Family: Fact or Fiction," in *Sourcebook in Marriage and the Family*, ed. Marvin B. Sussman (Boston: Houghton-Mifflin Company, 1974), 25–30.

10. William C. Hayes and Charles H. Mindel, "Extended Kinship Relations in Black and White Families," *Journal of Marriage and the Family* 35, no. 1 (February 1973): 51–57.

10. Joan Laird, "An Ecological Approach to Child Welfare," in *Social Work Practice: People and Environments*, ed. Carel Germain (New York: Columbia University Press, 1979), 175–209.

11. Elmer P. Martin and Joanne Mitchell Martin, *The Black Extended Family* (Chicago: The University of Chicago Press, 1978).

17

LEGAL GUARDIANSHIP

Carol W. Williams

Since the passage of the Adoption Assistance and Child Welfare Act of 1980 (P.L. 96–272), the child welfare field's quest to stabilize children's lives has focused primarily on family reunification and adoption. Ten years of experience implementing P.L. 96-272 have made it clear, however, that there are children who are unable to return home and also unable to secure adoption. Many of these children are being cared for in family networks or long-term family foster care arrangements. Although they may be receiving high-quality care, they lack legally sanctioned permanency.

It is time to consider a different permanency option—legal guardianship of the person—for those children who will grow up in a long-term care arrangement other than adoption. Guardianship would provide legal sanction for relationships in which children receive good care (such as kinship care), make those relationships as autonomous as possible, and protect the children from inappropriate placement disruption.

A *legal guardian* is a person appointed by the court who has control over a minor's person and property. Legal guardianship of dependent or needy children represents a new application of an old legal concept. In the past, legal guardianship was used primarily to protect the interests of wealthy children; rarely has it been used to protect the person of and secure permanence for needy children.

229

Kinship and Guardianship

Several trends speak to the need for adding guardianship to the array of permanency options. In particular, in recent years, placement of children in relative family foster care has increased dramatically in some states.[1] Case law decisions and service strategies have documented the lack of service to children placed with relatives and have led to the development of specialized services to assure placement appropriateness, stability, and protection.[2] In the absence of appropriate nonrelative foster homes, the escalating entry of young, medically fragile children into care—including the children of drug abusers—will require increased mobilization of kinship networks.

Many of the children of drug addicts come from families of African American and Latino descent, families that—historically and today—function in the context of extended family networks. Although the parents have major problems, relatives (grandparents, aunts, uncles, etc.) are often available to become substitute parents for the children. In fact, many of these children already live in informal arrangements that never come to the attention of public social service agencies. Given the pervasiveness of substance abuse, this pattern of informal intrafamilial arrangements is increasing among families of other backgrounds as well.[3]

Guardianship is particularly complementary to the social and cultural reality of many children of color. Building on the responsiveness of extended family networks, the concept of legal guardianship of the person offers the potential to stabilize the lives of these children by appointing the available grandparents, aunts, uncles, or other relatives as permanent guardians, not just informal caregivers. The potential can be realized if appropriate legal and social safeguards and supports are built into guardianship policy and procedures.

How It Works

Guardianship as a legal institution was known in Roman law. Developed as a method of substituting for absent parents, guardianship is based on the law of infancy, which recognizes minors as individuals who cannot make decisions or manage their own affairs due to their age and immaturity. Like adoption, guardianship is a legal and social mechanism that compensates for the natural limitations of children by giving adults personal responsibility for major decisions affecting the lives of the children in their care.

Unlike adoption, the appointment of a legal guardian by the court transfers to the guardian some, but not all, of the biological parents' responsibilities and rights. The guardian is not responsible for the support or education of the child except as provided for from the resources of the minor's estate or socially provided income. The guardian and ward (the child) are not entitled to inherit from each other. The guardian is under the supervision of the court, and any change in the child's living arrangements must be approved by the court. Because guardianship does not require termination of parental rights, parents retain residual rights and responsibilities, including the rights to reasonable visitation, to consent to adoption, and to determine a child's religious affiliation. The parents, when living, remain responsible for financial support of the child. Guardianship, however, may be established when parental ties have been terminated by relinquishment or judicial action. In this situation, the parents can no longer claim these residual rights and responsibilities, and the guardian assumes the right to consent to adoption.[4]

Despite the existence of a statutory base that authorizes the judicial appointment of a guardian for the person of a minor child, guardianship is rarely used as a resource for dependent children.

Children usually are found to be in need of a court-appointed guardian for one of two reasons: the absence of the biological or adoptive parents or the inability or unwillingness of the parents to fulfill their childrearing responsibilities.

Parental Absence

Parental absence leading to the court appointment of a guardian may take several forms.

1. Children without living parents who are cared for in their family networks but who are without testamentary nomination of guardians:

    Ms. A., the mother of three children, died of a drug overdose. The father of the children had abandoned them and did not support them. The mother's oldest sister informally assumed full responsibility for the children, but the relationship had no legal protection.

2. Children whose ties to their parents have been surrendered or judicially terminated and who have not been placed for adoption:

Frank, age 16, was abandoned by his biological mother at age five. He was found wandering in an amusement park on New Year's Eve. He was placed in out-of-home care and parental ties were involuntarily terminated when a family applied to adopt him. Frank was placed in adoption, but the adoption disrupted. Frank was returned to out-of-home care, where he remains.

3. Children whose adoptions have been annulled and whose custody has been returned to the public agency:

John was adopted as a nine-year-old. He had serious emotional problems. The family sought treatment and worked with John. By the time he was 14 years of age, however, he was running away and was a threat to the safety of his parents. Frustrated, the parents had the adoption revoked and refused further contact with John, who is currently in residential care.

Legally, these children belong to no one. At best, they are in the custody of an agency or an interested party. Where the agency assumes guardianship, it is administrative in nature and lacks the personal commitment of an individual who has a personal relationship with the child. Such a person would understand the child's situation intimately and could act on that knowledge on the child's behalf.

Incapable or Unwilling Parents

The incapacity or unwillingness of parents to care for their child may also set the stage for legal guardianship.

1. Children who are placed informally (without agency assistance) on a long-term basis by their parents in the homes of friends, relatives, and sometimes strangers:

Six-year-old Dwanna Smith has been living with the Jones family since she was five months old. She was placed with Mrs. Jones by her mother. Ms. Smith was 16 when Dwanna was born; at the time, she was in intense conflict with her own parents.

The Jones family and the mother have an amicable relationship. They see Ms. Smith as a troubled young woman who needs help. The Jones family indicated a high level of commitment to Dwanna, but are reluctant to pursue adoption. They feel that adoption would require them to take Dwanna away from her mother and that they have a relationship and an "understanding" with the mother. They do not want to be placed in an adversarial relationship with the mother and feel that asking her to surrender the child or having legal action taken to terminate parental rights would jeopardize the relationship and the placement of the child.

Legally, the mother could demand return of the child at any time. Dwanna's relationship with the Jones is unprotected.

2.   Children who are in placement and whose parents, although they visit regularly, are unable to provide 24-hour care:

Mark, age five, has been in a foster home since he was 18 months old, after having suffered physical abuse at the hands of his mother's boyfriend. Mark suffered brain damage and now has developmental difficulties that require a high level of specialized care and continual medical supervision. Currently, the mother maintains her own household and is caring for Mark's five older siblings. The care of these children is a heavy burden on her. She visits Mark and takes him home for the weekend regularly. Mark is receiving good care, and has meaningful relationships with his mother and his siblings.

It is anticipated that Mark will remain in care because of his special needs and the demands on his mother. The foster mother has agreed to keep Mark, but does not want to adopt him because of his special needs and his mother's active involvement. Because his mother maintains a significant relationship with him, there is a reluctance to terminate parental rights.

Benefits for Children

For children such as these, legal guardianship has both legal and psychosocial significance. The legal appointment of a guardian gives the guardian-ward relationship sociolegal sanction. It also establishes the permanence of the relationship, since a judicial decision is required to terminate the relationship as long as the child is a minor. The legal sanction creates an expectation of continuity that may be absent in less formal arrangements.

The legal sanction also clarifies who is the major authority in the child's life and the extent of the powers that the authority figure can exercise. Many children find themselves in relationships with caregivers who are neither their parents nor their legal guardians and have no legal authority over them. The legal term for this kind of relationship is *in loco parentis*. The caregivers may act "in the place of the parents," but they have no continuing legal obligation toward the child. The assumption of parental rights and responsibilities is not genuine or binding, but is simply the result of the situation in which the child and parent-substitute find themselves at that point in time.[5] This relationship is tenuous and lacks the legal standing that would formalize it and lend it greater stability. The caregiver's status of in loco parentis changes with any change in the physical custody of the child.[6]

Some children also find themselves in situations in which authority over them is divided between the caregiver and the state, through a delegated public agency. In such situations, it is not clear which rights and responsibilities are exercised by the caregiver and which are exercised by the designated agency.

The psychosocial significance of guardianship stems from the problems inherent in tenuous child-caregiver relationships, which are magnified by ambiguous authority (as is often the case in foster care). Relationships that are without legal sanction can be disrupted at any time. This places children in a dilemma that affects their psychosocial development. On the one hand, children may make a significant attachment to parental figures and the relationship may be disrupted, leading to short-term trauma from loss and possible long-term trauma (often reflected in the inability to attach and relate to others).[7] On the other hand, they may not attach to their caregivers or may attach in a superficial manner in order to protect themselves from anticipated separation. Their developmental progress may also be limited in that maturation is fostered by a nurturing and stable relationship. Legally sanctioned, socially safeguarded guardianship protects the relationship from casual disruption, and can facilitate appropriate attachment between the child and the parent-substitute.

Another significant aspect of guardianship is the clarity of authority it provides. When children are unclear about who is responsible for decision-making in matters that affect them, or when they perceive that the caregivers are sharing responsibility with some other person or entity, they may be less able to channel normal childhood impulsiveness into socially sanctioned behaviors. The ability to achieve this is reduced when parental authority is diffused.

Finally, decision-making that flows from authority in children's lives ought to reflect a clear understanding of each child as a unique individual with particular strengths, limitations, interests, needs, and aspirations. This basis for decision-making is facilitated when the person appointed as guardian is an individual who is known to or has a personal relationship with the child. With this in mind, guardians may serve as advocates for children by assuring that decisions reflect the children's best interests.[8]

Suitability of Guardians

Guardianship has as its goal the establishment of a substitute parent-child relationship that is continuous and that facilitates the child's healthy development. The assumption is that this relationship is secure enough that it can operate without periodic court oversight. The authority for the child is vested in the guardians. To achieve this goal, two findings are essential. First, it must be determined that guardianship is the plan of choice for the child. This would require that the child's parents are absent or unable or unwilling to fulfill their childrearing responsibilities, and that adoption is either inappropriate for, or unavailable to, the child. The second major determination to be made is that the individuals who are assuming guardianship are capable of meeting the needs of the child on a long-term basis.[9]

To be appropriate, guardians must be able to effectively parent children who are not their own. This requires an ability to help children accept both their biological and social identities.[10] These tasks require warmth, flexibility, emotional maturity, and the ability to accept the biological parents. Only when these criteria are met does guardianship achieve its protective function. In the absence of these characteristics, children may be subject to abuse, neglect, exploitation, and poor socialization.

The judicial appointment of a guardian carries with it the implication that society has approved that person and has assured that he or she is an appropriate long-term parental substitute. With a placement in which biological parents may continue to be involved, the guardian must be able to assume parental responsibility and manage a redefined relationship with both parents. This requires the establishment and implementation of legal and social safeguards in the appointment of guardians.

To protect the legal integrity of guardianship, the appointment of a guardian should take place in a court that has jurisdiction over child custody matters and thus the expertise to make such decisions.[11] The guardian should be accountable to the court for the care of the child. Provision should be made for time-limited judicial supervision, and clear criteria and time frames should be established for the termination of court oversight. Guardianship policy should articulate specific grounds for the termination of the guardian-ward relationship to minimize the likelihood of easy disruption.

To protect the social integrity and the quality of guardian-ward relationships, no guardianship of the person should be approved without a psychosocial study that determines the need for guardianship and the suitability of the proposed guardian for the child in question. The assessment of the need for guardianship should be based on the child's lack of access to biological or adoptive parents and the existence of a significant bond between the child and the proposed guardian. Determination of the suitability of the proposed guardian should involve an examination of the quality of the existing relationship, the commitment of the proposed guardian to the child, and the potential for a sustained relationship during the child's minority years.

The Need for Supports

Although designed to be a self-sustaining relationship, two additional social supports may be necessary in selected situations to ensure stability of the guardianship. The guardian and ward may need access to social services and socially provided income. Children whose parents use drugs heavily often have had very troubled beginnings. Perhaps medically fragile at birth, they may have experienced deprivation and trauma even before being placed in care. These children and their caregivers may need supportive services such as counseling, special education, and mental health services. Children in legal guardianship may have periodic crises that can be resolved or minimized with access to social services. These services should be available based on the need to strengthen and prevent the disruption of the guardian-ward relationship and thereby assure its permanence for the child.[12]

Many of the children who are candidates for guardianship come from low-income families whose primary financial support is AFDC. These children have no resources for their own support and, quite often, their potential guardians—relatives and foster parents—have only a limited ability to provide for their total support. In some jurisdictions, the appointment of a guardian makes a child ineligible for AFDC-BH, and thus creates a disincentive to permanence through guardianship. Needy children protected by guardianship should have access to socially provided income as do children in family foster care and subsidized adoptive situations.

Guardianship of the person has the potential to stabilize the lives of children whose families of origin cannot be preserved, but who have significant relationships with relatives who are willing to assume responsibility for their care. Guardianship may also be a resource for those children who find themselves in long-term out-of-home care because they are without biological parents, adoptive parents, or relatives. For both groups of children, guardianship can bring clarity and authority to the relationship between caregiver and child, as well as a sense of permanence. Achieving permanence through guardianship, however, will require a strengthening of legal and social safeguards in guardianship policy.

With the acceptance of guardianship as a permanency option, the opportunity for long-term care arrangements for children living with relatives and children needing long-term permanent care will be increased, and fewer children will suffer the damaging effects of unplanned long-term foster care.

Notes

1. County Welfare Directors Association of California, Chief Probation Officers Association of California, and California Mental Health Directors, *Ten Reasons to Invest in the Families of Children* (Sacramento, CA: Author, 1990).

2. Marcia R. Lowry, "Derring-Do in the 1980s: Child Welfare Impact Litigation after the Warren Years," in *Protecting Children from Abuse and Neglect,* ed. Douglas J. Besharov (Springfield, IL: Charles C Thomas, 1988), 265–294.

3. Robert Hill, *Informal Adoption among Black Families* (New York: National Ur-

ban League, 1977); Robert Hill, *The Strengths of Black Families* (New York: National Urban League, 1992).

4. U.S. Department of Health, Education, and Welfare, Social Security Administration, *Legislative Guides for the Termination of Parental Rights and Responsibilities and the Adoption of Children* (Washington, DC: Children's Bureau (Publication no. 194), 1961); Irving Weisman, "Guardianship: A Way of Fulfilling Public Responsibility for Children," (Washington, DC: Children's Bureau (Publication no. 330), 1949); Esther Appelberg, "The Significance of Personal Guardianships for Children in Casework," *Child Welfare* 49 (1970): 6–14; Carol W. Williams, "Legal Guardianship: A Minimally Used Resource for California Dependent Children: 1848–1980," D.S.W. dissertation (University of Southern California, 1980); Bogart R. Leshore, "Demystifying Legal Guardianship: An Unexplored Option for Dependent Children," *Journal of Family Law* (University of Louisville, School of Law) 2/3, no. 3 (1984): 391–400.

5. Henry Campbell Black, *Black's Law Dictionary* (4th ed., rev) (St. Paul, MN: West Publishing, 1968), 896.

6. A. Delafield Smith, *The Right to Life* (Chapel Hill, NC: University of North Carolina Press, 1955).

7. Barbara A. Rutter, *A Way of Caring: The Parents' Guide to Foster Family Care* (Washington, DC: Child Welfare, 1978).

8. Lela B. Costin and Charles A. Rapp, *Child Welfare Policies and Practices (3rd ed.)* (New York: McGraw-Hill, 1984).

9. Ibid.

10. H. David Kirk, *Shared Fate* (New York: Free Press, 1964).

11. Williams.

12. Ibid.

18

THE QUALITY—NOT THE CATEGORY—OF CARE

Marilyn B. Benoit

D. W. Winnicott, M.D., introduced the concept of the "holding environment" in describing the milieu in which children are raised. He believed that the nature of that environment either facilitated or impeded the total development of the dependent child.[1] A child's first holding environment is the physical universe of the mother's womb. Post partuition, the emotional milieu in which the child develops takes on significant importance, more so than the physical space in which the child is raised.

This paper discusses the physical, emotional, and developmental needs of children and identifies the elements that are critical to meeting those needs. These needs should be the primary criteria for evaluating care arrangements for dependent children. The foremost question for decision makers is not "Does this arrangement fit our policy priorities?" but rather, "Does this arrangement provide an adequate 'holding environment' for this particular child?"

The Child's Physical World

Before discussing the emotional needs of children, we must first acknowledged that their need for adequate physical care is paramount. According to

239

Greenspan, "This includes proper medical care, nutrition, protection from abuse and neglect, and adequate nurturing."[2] It is indeed a sad fact that many fetuses endure gestation in a hostile, toxic womb environment secondary to maternal drug/alcohol abuse, physical abuse of the mother, and poor nutritional/health status of the mother.[3] The neonatal intensive care units are populated with many such babies. The boarder baby phenomenon of the late 1980s and the early 1990s is a result of physical abandonment of babies by mothers addicted to drugs—usually crack—who demonstrate such an attachment deficit that they literally do not stay around to administer physical care to their newborn children.

Good physical care of children, however, goes beyond simply feeding and clothing them. Their needs—to be held securely, comforted, talked to, interacted with, and allowed to rest—when met, contribute to their ability to establish a sense of trust. Erikson, in *Childhood and Society*, discusses how children first develop a sense of trust in their own body functioning as a prelude to developing an ability to trust the world upon which they are so dependent.[4] The mother plays an important role in minimizing any distress imposed on children by monitoring their behavior and by "reading" subtle, nonverbal cues that provide information to the "tuned-in mother" about children's physical needs. A "good-enough" mother and a biologically and temperamentally well-endowed child generally have little or no problem negotiating this period of preverbal communication, and the child will be adequately responded to and cared for. In the case of a temperamentally difficult child or a child who is neurodevelopmentally delayed or deviant, however, the demands on the parent to "read" the child's signals are greater.

In those cases, it takes a particularly invested and involved parent to be appropriately responsive to the child. Children who are exposed to intrauterine toxins are at greater risk for being born small for gestational age or with neonatal complications.[5] If they develop the neurodevelopmental disorders for which they are at increased risk, these children tend to be more difficult to "read" and hence have a harder time having their needs met adequately and appropriately. Their parenting needs are more complex. These children are the very ones who are most likely to be born to impaired parents, who, in turn, are ill-prepared to deal with the difficulties and demands of special-needs children.

The Child's Emotional World

The primary emotional need of children is to have a positive attachment to their mother. This, of course, develops as mothers tend to the physical needs of their children in an interested manner, demonstrating and confirming the mother's delight. During this early period of the child's life, the mother, in spite of the child's demands upon her, experiences a sense of falling in love with her baby and entering into an almost exclusive world of the mother-infant dyad.[6] Erikson describes the process that ensues as one in which the primary experience of the child is one of "taking in."[7] Infants take in not only physical nutrients, but also their mother's adoration, as well as sights, sounds, touch textures, smells, warmth, and cold. This taking in through all the senses—with the mother functioning as a protective barrier, balancing the child's experiences so that they are neither too sparse nor too overwhelming—helps children to begin to organize their world in a manageable and predictable way. It provides an emotional holding environment that children can trust. Here, then, is the second building block of trust, the first being that children have come to trust that their body's biological functioning is predictable.

It is during the first six months of life that the seeds of trust are sown. This trust is necessary to allow children to submit to dependent relationships in which their nurturance takes priority. As Winnicott states, "Dependence is real. That babies and children cannot manage on their own is so obvious that the simple facts of dependence are easily lost. It can be said that the story of the growing child is a story of absolute dependence moving steadily through lessening degrees of dependence and groping towards independence."[8] The shift from dependence to healthy independence parallels growing internalization of trust—from trusting significant others to take care of them to trusting that they can take care of themselves.

After the establishment of basic trust, other aspects of the child's emotional world proceed to develop. Greenspan identifies six: mood and self-esteem; sexuality, pleasure, and excitement; anger and aggression; such seemingly negative emotions as separation anxiety, fears, sadness, and competition; the capacity to concentrate, process information, and learn; and peer and group relationships.[9] This author would add frustration tolerance and delayed gratification as explicit entities, although they are implicit in Greenspan's listing.

Young children develop a positive sense of self-esteem from their parents. It is the gleam in parents' eyes, the delight they express in their interactions with their children, the message that they impart that their children are valued people simply for being who they are. These are the early building blocks of self-esteem. Self-esteem is further enhanced when parents help their children to regulate themselves. This regulation pertains to control of anger, aggression, body functions, eating, sleeping, and playing. A child who feels an inner sense of adequate self-regulation is a child who can better adapt to an increasingly frustrating world. It is the parents' duty to monitor their children's development and, without being overcontrolling, overdemanding, or overchallenging, to present them with appropriate opportunities to expand their world and gain mastery of it. It is the gradual and incremental mastery that children accomplish that significantly contributes to an internal sense of competence and translates into positive self-esteem, especially when recognized and acknowledged by the most important persons in their lives—their parents.

As children get older and have to move into the world of peers and school (with new authority figures called "teachers"), their early experiences with trust versus mistrust continue to have a significant impact on the way in which they adapt to the demands of more complex and demanding environments.[10] Those children who have been denied the earlier foundation of trust born of consistent nurturing in a stable, protective environment are at tremendously greater risk of failure in their school-age years. At school age, children are expected to conform to society's expectations of normative behavior. They are supposed to be "socialized."

The socialization process is one that involves putting the brakes on impulses and learning what is socially acceptable behavior. Parents have the delicate job of assisting their children with control by setting firm, consistent limits on behavior while allowing them some opportunity to develop and internalize their own controls. Some sophisticated psychological capacities are expected to be in place by school age. The expectations are that one possesses the ability to invest in learning, enjoy playing with peers, control one's aggression, calm oneself, not be impulsive, wait one's turn, negotiate compromises, and obey authority. All children continue to need help with meeting those expectations. During this early school-age period, children move from the world of primary relationships within the nuclear family to a world of secondary relationships.[11] It is important to note that, if these secondary relationships are positive, they have the potential to have a mitigating effect on earlier emotional deprivation. In the words of Parens, "secondary relationships can be strongly enriching, and may in fact play a vital salutary part, especially where primary relationships are impoverished."[12]

Environmental Failure

Because children live in a dynamic emotional system—ideally with two parents—their emotional holding environment is subject to the effects of many variables. Any variable that has a negative impact upon any person within that system called the family will have some effect on the growing child. Surely, no family is without problems of some sort. It is when problems are of such immensity that they result in obvious trauma, emotional or physical, to the child that developmental failure of some sort results. Winnicott uses the broad term "environmental failure" to refer to problems in the child's holding environment.

The current epidemic of substance abuse has resulted in environmental failure in many families. This has occurred especially in families of the lower socioeconomic class where poverty, as a single variable in and of itself, has already created a compromised environment. Poverty, now compounded by substance abuse, results in even higher rates of abandonment by parents, violence, crime and parental incarceration, serious and chronic medical illness, infant mortality and infant morbidity, and school dropout and teenage pregnancy. In such an environment, children's basic needs are simply not met. They lose their caregivers, they lack consistency in their lives, they cannot develop a sense of predictability and trust, they feel unprotected, and they come to realize that dependency—to which they are entitled—is not safe.

Because the very environment upon which they depend is a hostile one, and young children are indeed helpless, many of these children become victims of physical, sexual, and emotional abuse. Many then develop a learned helplessness and are at greater risk for emotional and behavioral problems.

When the ability to attach to another dependable human being and develop a trusting relationship is severely compromised, other areas of emotional development suffer as a result. Frustration tolerance can emerge only when a child has the inner belief that the degree of frustration will be tolerable, not overwhelming. Anger can be regulated only when there has been good modeling by the parents, rather than a childhood filled with physical abuse or family violence.

Implications for Social Policy

The essentials for children then, are good physical and medical care; positive, enduring relationships with reliable and consistent adults; socialization; and education. Where there is an environmental failure on the scale found in the poverty-stricken, drug-ridden, violent urban ghettos of America, children become the silent, disenfranchised victims. The recent report by the National Commission on Children outlines the sorry plight of America's children.[13] Twenty percent of all children live in poverty, which has long been identified as the single most critical variable that puts people at risk for adverse medical and social effects.[14] With numbers like this, the situation must be viewed as a major public social/health problem. Any problem of such magnitude and complexity requires government involvement at the local, state, and federal levels. Attempting to solve it will require money from the public coffers.

Any good residential program costs money. Money invested in providing a good-enough holding environment for our high-risk children should be considered well spent, because frontloading spending on our children is really cost-shifting. To quote Bays, "The short-term costs may be high, but the long-term costs will be much higher if we do not act."[15] To nurture, stabilize, socialize, and educate our high-risk children is to enrich our society and ultimately decrease the spending on our juvenile detention centers and, in the long term, on our adult jail populations.

Although no immediate solutions are available, the children who need services are already here on the public doorsteps. Society, regardless of its moral position on drug abuse, teenage pregnancy, and welfare families, has an ethical and moral obligation to take care of these children. Taking the needs of children into consideration, those in the public domain who approve and fund programs that provide for these children can require that any such program use those essentials as a guide in determining whether placement alternatives are appropriate. Such an approach will eliminate the need to come up with a single workable model and will allow the type of flexibility that permits several alternatives.

Similarly, there ought not to be a knee-jerk reaction against the concept of orphanage-type care, if such arrangements have built into them the capability of providing the essentials that children need. In other words, rather than being emotionally reactive to suggested alternatives, politicians, social scientists, and policymakers will be thoughtful and objective, weighing the pros and cons of all alternatives, while remaining attentive to children's basic needs. It is important to state that perfection is not the goal. In child psychiatry, we use the statement that "good enough is good enough." That applies to mothering, to parenting, and to families. What that means is that there will have to be an acceptance of flaws in any alternatives, problems will come up and, indeed, several can be anticipated. But that should not be cause for paralysis. Children are growing up in destructive settings while we continue the seemingly endless debate on "doing the right thing." In the words of the National Commission on Children's report, let's move beyond rhetoric and provide these "at-risk" children with some of their basic needs so that they can be afforded the best possible chances to develop and avail themselves of the many opportunities that exist in America to become productive members of this society.

Recommendations

Several alternatives can be considered for placement outside of the primary family when need is established. The question of short-term versus long-term placement ought to be decided on the basis of a medical, psychiatric/psychological, and social assessment of the parents and the reasons for their difficulties in parenting. Every possible effort should be made to provide alcohol/ drug rehabilitation opportunities for substance-abusing parents and ultimately, to help them to resume their parenting roles. A realistic plan, based on such an assessment and the parent's ability to use appropriate and available intervention services, should guide decisions concerning length of out-of-home placement of drug-affected children.

When short-term placement is deemed appropriate, placement with family or traditional foster families should be considered. All potential placement families should be evaluated and trained to meet preset criteria. The guide should be, "Can they provide a good-enough holding environment for the child?"

One of the most critical elements of such placements, aside from safety, would be sustaining some continuity of relationship with a significant person in the child's life. For short-term placements where the parent is involved with a treatment program, this can be accomplished by allowing consistent and predictable visiting by the parent. This will minimize the sense of disruption and instability that is inevitable when social agencies have to intervene to protect children. Unfortunately, some parents simply would not comply with treatment and rehabilitation, and some of their children do not have access to any kinship care. These are the children who end up in the current foster care system. As it is now, the foster care system creates the iatrogenic problem of "bouncing" which, as a single variable, produces its own negative emotional effect on children. "Bouncing" is so counter to children's basic need for a significant and enduring primary relationship leading to stability, consistency, predictability, and, ultimately, a sense of mastery and competence that we must immediately decide how we can best avoid or, at least minimize, its negative effects. Because an enduring, good-enough relationship with a significant adult is by far the most essential need of children, it would make sense that, failing the presence of such a person within their families, providing a social service person who can assume such a role and provide continuity of a relationship, in spite of foster care bouncing, would be the immediate next best solution. From a clinical point of view, such a sustaining relationship would provide some measure of protection against the many negative psychosocial forces in the lives of foster children.

For long-term placement, foster families are less desirable. Long-term placement should establish a sense of permanence, a sense of belonging, a sense of security. To provide the already stated critical elements that children need, permanent kinship care would be the best alternative. In such a setting, the children will best experience a sense of belonging (by reason of kinship) and permanence rather than a feeling of expendability. Adoption by nonrelative families wherever possible would be the next best alternative. Failing those two, residential placement should be considered. Such institutional placements of children has often been met with disfavor. The quality, rather than the category of care, is really what needs objective and critical analysis. Again, using the "good-enough holding environment" as a guide, it is indeed possible to design and implement long-term residential care that is able to create a sense of stability in children's lives by providing them with lasting, significant, and predictable nurturing relationships in an environment that assures their well-being and safety and that offers a feasible and preferable alternative to the current long-term foster care placement.

Notes

1. Donald W. Winnicott, *Babies and Their Mothers* (New York: Addison Wesley Publishing Co., Inc., 1970).

2. Stanley Greenspan and Nancy T. Greenspan, *The Essential Partnership: How Parents and Children Can Meet the Emotional Challenges of Infancy and Childhood* (New York: Viking Penguin, Inc., 1989), 2.

3. Louis G. Keith, Scott MacGregor, Stanley Freidel, Marvin Rosner, Ira J. Chasnoff, and John J. Sciarra, "Substance Abuse in Pregnant Women: Recent Experience at the Perinatal Center for Chemical Dependence of Northwestern Memorial Hospital," *Obstetrics and Gynecology* 73 (1989): 715–20; Barry S. Zuckerman, Hortensia Amaro, and William Beardslee, "Mental Health of Adolescent Mothers: The Implications of Depression and Drug Use," *Developmental and Behavioral Pediatrics* 8 (1987): 111–116; Mark G. Neerhof, Scott N. MacGregor, Sandy S. Retsky, and Terence P. Sullivan, "Cocaine Abuse During Pregnancy: Peripartum Prevalence and Perinatal Outcome," *American Journal of Obstetrics and Gynecology* 161 (1989): 633–38; Daniel R. Neuspiel and Sara C. Hamel, "Cocaine and Infant Behavior," *Journal of Developmental Behavioral Pediatrics* 12 (1991): 55–64.

4. Erik H. Erikson, *Childhood and Society* (New York: W.W. Norton and Co., Inc., 1950), 72.

5. Neerhof et al., 633–38; Sandra McCalla, Howard L. Minkoff, Joseph Feldman, Isaac Delke, Martin Salwin, Gloria Valencia, and Leonard Glass, "The Biologic and Social Consequences of Perinatal Cocaine Use in an Inner-City Population: Results of an Anonymous Cross-Sectional Study," *American Journal of Obstetrics and Gynecology* 164 (1991): 625–30.

6. Stanley Greenspan and Nancy T. Greenspan, *The Essential Partnership: How Parents and Children Can Meet the Emotional Challenges of Infancy and Childhood* (New York: Viking Penguin, Inc., 1989), 3.

7. Erikson, 72.

8. Winnicott, 83.

9. Greenspan and Greenspan, x.

10. Erikson, 250.

11. Henry Parens, *Aggression in Our Children—Coping with It Constructively* (Northvale, NJ: Jason Aronson, Inc., 1987).

12. *Ibid.*, 172.

13. "Beyond Rhetoric: A New American Agenda for Children and Families," final report of the National Commission on Children (Washington, DC: Government Office, 1991).

14. Michael Rutter, "The City and the Child," *American Journal of Orthopsychiatry* 51 (1981): 610–625.

15. Jan Bays, "Substance Abuse and Child Abuse: Impact of Addiction on the Child," *Pediatric Clinics of North America* 37 (1990): 901.

Epilogue

Douglas J. Besharov

The most heartrending victims of the current epidemic of drug use are the children. What to do about children and families in the grip of so powerful a destructive force as drug addiction is one of the most difficult policy issues today.

Can the recommendations in this book be adopted? Making it easier to terminate parental rights, for example, is certain to be controversial; it may come about only with the active support of the disadvantaged communities most affected. Similarly, the restructuring of foster care placements into long-term supportive environments will require a level of administrative commitment and capability that has too often been absent in foster care agencies.

The main obstacles to adopting these and other reforms, however, are budgetary and conceptual in nature. Ironically, it is the latter obstacle that probably poses the greater challenge.

Fiscal Limitations

The severe financial difficulties that confront most state and local governments have a direct impact on the quality and scope of child welfare services. In recent years, over 30 states have experienced such substantial budget deficits that they have had to cut or freeze child welfare spending. Twenty and 30 percent cuts in services are all too common. These are the realities within which child welfare services must be planned and provided. They should shape our understanding of what contemporary child welfare services can—and cannot—accomplish.

It would be wrong to kid ourselves about long-term services being somehow less expensive than short-term services. Yet, they are not as expensive or as out of reach as some may fear. The key is in the structure and orientation of the services.

Cases involving parental drug addiction are characterized by patterns of repeated reports on the same families—over the course of many years and often across generations. Thus, in a horribly distorted sense, we do have long-term services. We open a case on a family and we close it and we open another one on the same family and we close it again, year after year, generation after generation.

Hence, agencies often end up providing services to drug-involved families for many years, but there is an additional cost. More time is spent investigating the repeated reports than is spent trying to help the family with its problems. And, of course, there is neither the continuity of service nor the continued momentum of sustained therapeutic involvement needed to achieve personal change.

This is not to suggest that keeping such cases open would result in vast savings. It seems clear, however, that real efficiencies could be achieved—as well as more effective services provided to clients—if we recognized that many drug-using parents will be reported again and again and again. Thus, a long-term orientation toward services could save investigative and administrative resources that would be better used for treatment services.

Other efficiencies are also possible. Considerable savings could be achieved by reducing the number of inappropriate reports of suspected child abuse and neglect.[1] Improved professional and public education about what should and what should not be reported and improved screening at intake hotlines are needed.

Of course, a real expansion of long-term services will require additional funds. Even this is possible, however. The Family Preservation and Support Act of 1993 provides additional federal aid to state child welfare programs and increases the flexibility of reimbursement rules. Some of this new money could be used to build long-term service capabilities. Thus, even in the current fiscal atmosphere, calling for an increase in the amount of long-term services available to the clients of child welfare agencies is not as quixotic as it might seem.

Nevertheless, providing long-term services can be prohibitively expensive unless agencies adopt new strategies for the provision of services. The core of a long-term service strategy should be a modified version of a home-visitor service, an idea that C. Henry Kempe personally nurtured for many years and that was endorsed by the Federal Advisory Board on Child Abuse and Neglect.[2] In addition, an attempt should be made to recruit entry-level staff who have more in common with the families they are seeking to help, that is, who share similar social and economic backgrounds with their clients.

Thinking Long-Term

A bigger barrier to developing long-term services, though, is conceptual and perhaps ideological in nature. As a field and as a society, we do not like to think long-term. Three examples will illustrate.

First, it is difficult to build support for a strategy that does not promise immediately dramatic results. A long-term strategy just isn't sexy. In fact, it requires agencies to lower their programmatic sights from cure to stabilization. That's simply not an inspiring goal—it is hard to generate excitement for a program that, instead of promising to cure drug-related child abuse, seeks merely to manage it.

Second, working with drug-addicted parents and their children is not for the faint of heart. Often the parents—and sometimes the children as well—do not welcome intervention, however well-meaning. Instead, such clients may be unpleasant and even outright hostile to caseworkers and other helping professionals. Even when families do want help, they can be frustratingly unable to keep appointments, let alone to follow through with treatment plans. Behavioral change, in other words, comes slowly, if at all.

Third, a long-term perspective on client needs raises many controversial and discomforting issues. Family planning and contraception come immediately to mind. One need not agree with me about contraception to recognize how the issue is much more likely to arise during a long-term service relationship than in a brief one. That is the point. Making a real commitment to these families means trying to address their real and multiple needs, whether for education, job training, employment, or contraception.

If we are to meet the needs of the children of drug-addicted parents, we cannot avoid these issues.

Notes

1. Douglas J. Besharov, *Recognizing Child Abuse: A Guide for the Concerned* (New York: Free Press, 1990).

2. U.S. Advisory Board on Child Abuse and Neglect, *Creating Caring Communities: Blueprint for an Effective Federal Policy on Child Abuse and Neglect* (Washington, DC: September 15, 1991).

SELECTED READINGS

American Public Welfare Association, Voluntary Cooperative Information System, no. 6, 1993.

Anglin, M.D., and Y. Hser. "Treatment of Drug Abuse." In *Drugs and Crime*, edited by M. Tonry and J.Q. Wilson. Chicago: University of Chicago Press, 1990.

Anglin, M.D., G.R. Speckart, M.W. Booth, and T.M. Ryan. "Consequences and Costs of Shutting Off Methadone." *Addictive Behaviors* 14 (1989): 307–326.

Appelberg, Esther. "The Significance of Personal Guardianships for Children in Casework." *Child Welfare* 49 (1970): 6–14.

Apsler, R., and W.M. Harding. *Cost-Effectiveness Analysis of Drug Abuse Treatment: Current Status and Recommendations for Future Research. NIDA Drug Abuse Services Research Series, no. 1*. Rockville, MD: National Institute on Drug Abuse, in press.

Ards, S. "Estimating Local Child Abuse." *Evaluation Review* 13 (October 1989): 484–515.

Bachman, J.G., L.D. Johnston, and P. O'Malley. "Explaining the Recent Decline in Cocaine Use among Young Adults: Further Evidence That Perceived Risks and Disapproval Lead to Reduced Drug Use." *Journal of Health and Social Behavior* 31 (June 1990): 173–184.

253

Ball, J.C., W.R. Lange, C.P. Myers, and S.R. Friedman. "Reducing the Risk of AIDS through Methadone Maintenance Treatment." *Journal of Health and Social Behavior* 29 (1988): 214–226.

Bane, M.J., and P.A. Jargowsky. *Urban Poverty Areas: Basic Questions Concerning Prevalence, Growth and Dynamics.* Prepared for the Committee on National Urban Policy, National Academy of Sciences, February 1988.

Barth, R.P. "Adoption of Drug-Exposed Children: Developmental Outcomes and Parental Satisfaction." *Children and Youth Services Review* 13 (1991): 323–342.

Barth, R.P. "Educational Implications of Prenatally Drug-Exposed Children." *Social Work in Education* 13 (1991): 130–136.

Barth, R.P. "Shared Family Care: Child Protection without Parent-Child Separation." In *Families Living with Drugs and HIV: Intervention and Treatment Strategies*, edited by R. Barth, J. Pietrzak, and M. Ramler. New York: Guilford, 1993.

Barth, R.P. "Sweden's Contact Family Program: Informal Help for Vulnerable Families." *Public Welfare* 49 (1991): 36–42, 46.

Barth, R.P., and M.B. Berry. "Implications of Research on the Welfare of Children under Permanency Planning." In *Child Welfare Research Review*, edited by R.P. Barth, J. D. Berrick, and Neil Gilbert. New York: Columbia University Press, 1994.

Bays, J. "Substance Abuse and Child Abuse: Impact of Addiction on the Child." *Pediatric Clinics of North America* 37 (1990): 881–904.

Black, Henry Campbell. *Black's Law Dictionary* (4th ed., rev.). St. Paul, MN: West Publishing, 1968.

Besharov, D.J. "The Children of Crack: Will We Protect Them?" *Public Welfare* 51 (Fall 1989): 7–11.

Brown, B., J. Hickey, A. Chung, R. Craig, and J. Jaffe. "Waiting for Treatment: Behaviors of Cocaine Users on a Waiting List." In *Problems of Drug Dependence, 1988: Proceedings of the 50th Annual Scientific Meeting, The Committee on Problems of Drug Dependence, Inc.*, edited by L.S. Harris. Rockville, MD: National Institute on Drug Abuse, 1988, 351.

California Senate Office of Research. *California's Drug-Exposed Babies: Undiscovered, Unreported, Underserved.* Sacramento, CA, 1990.

Carver, J.A. "Drugs and Crime: Controlling Use and Reducing Risk through Testing." *National Institute of Justice Reports* (September/October 1986).

Chasnoff, I.J. "Perinatal Effects of Cocaine." *Contemporary Ob-Gyn* 29, no. 5 (May 1987): 163–179.

Chasnoff, I.J., C.E. Hunt, R. Kletter, and D. Kaplan. "Prenatal Cocaine Exposure is Associated with Respiratory Pattern Abnormalities." *American Journal of Diseases of Children* 143 (1987): 583.

Chavkin, W. "Drug Addiction and Pregnancy: Policy Crossroads." *American Journal of Public Health* 4 (1991): 483.

Clayton, R., and H. Voss. "Young Men and Drugs in Manhattan: A Causal Analysis." *Research Monograph 39*. Rockville, MD: National Institute on Drug Abuse, 1981.

Cohen, S., E. Lichtenstein, J.O. Prochaska, J.S. Rossi, E.R. Gritz, C.R. Carr, C.T. Orleans, V.J. Schoenbach, L. Biener, D. Abrams, C. DiClemente, S. Curry, G.A. Marlatt, K.M. Cummings, S.L. Emont, G. Giovino, and D. Ossip-Klein. "Debunking Myths about Self-Quitting: Evidence from 10 Prospective Studies of Persons Who Attempt to Quit Smoking by Themselves." *American Psychologist* 44 (1989): 1355–1365.

Costin, Lela B., and Charles A. Rapp. "Child Guardianship." In *Child Welfare Policies and Practices* (3d ed.). New York: McGraw Hill, 1984.

County Welfare Directors Association of California, Chief Probation Officers Association of California, and California Mental Health Directors, *Ten Reasons to Invest in the Families of Children* (Sacramento, CA: Author, 1990).Courtwright, D. *Dark Paradise: Opiate Addiction in America before 1940*. Cambridge, MA: Harvard University Press, 1982.

Cushman, P. "Methadone Maintenance: Long-Term Follow-Up of Detoxified Patients." In *Recent Developments in Chemotherapy of Narcotic Addiction*, edited by B. Kissin, J.H. Lowinson, and R.B. Millman. *Annals of the New York Academy of Science*, 311 (1978): 165–171.

Daro, D., and K. McCurdy. *Current Trends in Child Abuse Reporting and Fatalities: The Results of the 1991 Annual Fifty State Survey*. Chicago: National Committee for Prevention of Child Abuse, 1992.

Dinkins, D. *Testimony before the Subcommittee on Children, Family, Drugs, and Alcoholism*. Washington, DC: U.S. Government Printing Office, February 5, 1990.

District of Columbia Pretrial Services Agency. *Drug Test Statistics*. (Monthly bulletin).

Dole, V.P., J.W. Robinson, J. Orraga, E. Towns, P. Searacy, and E. Caine. "Methadone

Treatment of Randomly Selected Criminal Addicts." *The New England Journal of Medicine* 280 (1969): 1372–1375.

Elmer-DeWitt, P. "A Plague Without Boundaries." *Time*, 6 November 1989, 95-7.

Erikson, E.H. *Childhood and Society*. New York: W.W. Norton and Co., Inc., 1950.

Fanshel, D. "Parental Failure and Consequences for Children: The Drug-Using Mother Whose Children Are in Foster Care." *American Journal of Public Health* 65 (1975): 604–612.

Feig, L. "Drug-Exposed Infants and Children: Service Needs and Policy Questions." Office of Social Services Policy, Division of Children and Youth Policy, U.S. Department of Health and Human Services. Washington, DC: U.S. Government Printing Office, 1990.

Garbarino, J., and A. Crouter. "Defining the Community Context of Parent-Child Relations: The Correlates of Child Maltreatment." *Child Development* 49 (September 1978): 604–616.

Garbarino, J., and D. Sherman. "High-Risk Neighborhoods and High-Risk Families: The Human Ecology of Child Maltreatment." *Child Development* 51 (1980): 188–198.

Garbarino, J. "The Human Ecology of Child Maltreatment: A Conceptual Model for Research." *Journal of Marriage and the Family* 39 (November 1977): 721–735.

Glassberg, Eurydice. *Guardian Law and the Poor Child. Social Work Process* Monograph Series 18, no. 1. Philadelphia, PA: University of Pennsylvania, 1973.

Gerstein, D.R., and H.J. Harwood, eds. *Treating Drug Problems: Volume I*. Washington, DC: National Academy Press, 1990.

Gomby, D.S., and P.H. Shiono. "Estimating the Number of Substance-Exposed Infants." In *The Future of Children: Drug-Exposed Infants*, edited by Richard E. Behrman. Los Altos, CA: The Center for the Future of Children, The David and Lucile Packard Foundation, 1991.

Greenspan, S., and N.T. Greenspan. *The Essential Partnership: How Parents and Children Can Meet the Emotional Challenges of Infancy and Childhood*. New York: Viking Penguin, Inc., 1989.

Gunne, L., and L. Gronbladh. "The Swedish Methadone Maintenance Program. In *The Social and Medical Aspects of Drug Abuse*, edited by G. Serban, 205-213. Jamaica, NY: Spectrum Publications, 1984.

Hall, S.M. "Methadone Treatment: A Review of the Research Findings." In *Research on the Treatment of Narcotic Addiction: State of the Art*, edited by J.R. Cooper, F. Altman, B.S. Brown, and D. Czechowicz, 575-632. Rockville, MD: National Institute on Drug Abuse, 1983.

Hayes, W.C., and C.H. Mindel. "Extended Kinship Relations in Black and White Families." *Journal of Marriage and the Family* 35, no. 1 (February 1973): 51-57.

Hser, Y., M.D. Anglin, and C. Chou. "Evaluation of Drug Abuse Treatment: A Repeated Measures Design Assessing Methadone Maintenance." *Evaluation Review* 12 (1988): 547-570.

Hubbard, R.L., M.E. Marsden, J.V. Rachal, H.J. Harwood, E.R. Cavanaugh, and H.M. Ginzburg. *Drug Abuse Treatment: A National Study of Effectiveness*. Chapel Hill, NC: The University of North Carolina Press, 1989.

Institute of Medicine. *Broadening the Base of Treatment for Alcohol Problems*. Washington, DC: National Academy Press, 1990.

Johnson, W., and J. L'Esperance. "Predicting the Recurrence of Child Abuse." *Social Work Research and Abstracts* 20 (1984): 21-31.

Kamerman, S. B., and A. Kahn. "Social Services for Children, Youth, and Families in the United States." *Children and Youth Services Review* 1/2 (1990): 1-184.

Keith, L.G., S. MacGregor, S. Freidel, M. Rosner, Ira J. Chasnoff, and J.J. Sciarra. "Substance Abuse in Pregnant Women: Recent Experience at the Perinatal Center for Chemical Dependence of Northwestern Memorial Hospital." *Obstetrics and Gynecology* 73 (1989): 715-20.

Kirk, H. David. *Shared Fate*. New York: Free Press, 1964.

Kusserow, R. "Crack Babies." *Inspector General* (June 1990): 1.

Laird, Joan. "An Ecological Approach to Child Welfare." In *Social Work Practice: People and Environments*, edited by C. Germain, 175-209. New York: Columbia University Press, 1979.

Leshore, Bogart R. "Demystifying Legal Guardianship: An Unexplored Option for Dependent Children." *Journal of Family Law* (University of Louisville, School of Law) 2/3, no. 3 (1984): 391-400.

Lipscomb v. Simmons (Ct. App. 9th Cir. 1989).

MacGregor, S.N., L.G. Keith, I.J. Chasnoff, M.A. Rosner, G.M. Chisum, P. Shaw, and

J.P. Minogue. "Cocaine Use during Pregnancy: Adverse Perinatal Outcome." *American Journal of Obstetrics and Gynecology* 157 (1987): 686.

Magjaryi, T. "Prevention of Alcohol and Drug Problems among Women of Childbearing Age: Challenges for the 1990s." Paper presented at the OSAP Conference, Healthy Women, Healthy Infants: Emerging Solutions in the Face of Alcohol and Drug Problems. Miami, FL, 1990.

Martin, E.P., and J. Mitchell Martin. *The Black Extended Family*. Chicago: The University of Chicago Press, 1978.

Martin, S. L., C. T. Ramey, and S. Ramey. "The Prevention of Intellectual Impairment in Children of Impoverished Families: Findings of a Randomized Trial of Educational Day Care." *American Journal of Public Health* 80 (1990): 844–847.

McCalla, S., H.L. Minkoff, J. Feldman, I. Delke, M. Salwin, G. Valencia, and L. Glass. "The Biologic and Social Consequences of Perinatal Cocaine Use in an Inner-City Population: Results of an Anonymous Cross-Sectional Study." *American Journal of Obstetrics and Gynecology* 164 (1991): 625–30.

McGlothlin, W.H., and M.D. Anglin. "Shutting Off Methadone: Costs and Benefits." *Archives of General Psychiatry* 38 (1981): 885–892.

Meyers, B. S., and M.K. Link. "Kinship Foster Care: The Double-Edged Dilemma." Study prepared for the New York Task Force on Permanency Planning for Children, New York City Department of Human Resources, Child Welfare Administration, October 1990.

Miller v. Youakim, 440 U.S. 125 (1979).

Morgan, L. J., and P. Marckworth, eds. *Intensive Family Preservation Services: Resource Book*. Cleveland, OH: Case Western Reserve University, 1991.

National Black Child Development Institute. *The Status of African American Children: Twentieth Anniversary Report 1970-1990*. Washington, DC: National Black Child Development Institute, 1990.

National Black Child Development Institute. *Who Will Care When Parents Can't?* Washington, DC: National Black Child Development Institute, 1990.

National Commission on Child Welfare and Family Preservation. *A Commitment to Change*. Washington, DC: American Public Welfare Association, 1991.

National Commission on Foster Care. *A Blueprint for Fostering Infants, Children, and Youth*. Washington, DC: Child Welfare League of America, 1991.

National Committee for Prevention of Child Abuse. *Current Trends in Child Abuse Reporting and Fatalities Continue: The Results of the 1989 Annual 50 State Survey.* Chicago: National Committee for Prevention of Child Abuse, 1990.

National Institute of Justice. "Drug Use Forecasting, 1992 Annual Report, Drugs and Crime in America's Cities." *National Institute of Justice Research in Brief.* Washington, DC: U.S. Department of Justice, October 1993.

National Institute of Justice. "Drug Use Forecasting, First and Second Quarters, 1992." *National Institute of Justice Research in Brief.* Washington, DC: U.S. Department of Justice, May 1993.

National Institute on Drug Abuse. *An Assessment of the Incidence and Prevalence of Drug Abuse in the United States: Report on the Technical Review Meeting.* Rockville, MD: National Institute on Drug Abuse, 1991.

National Institute on Drug Abuse. *Smoking, Drinking, and Illicit Drug Use among American Secondary School Students, College Students, and Young Adults, 1975-1992, Volume 1, Secondary Students.* Rockville, MD: National Institute on Drug Abuse, 1993.

Neerhof, M.G., S.N. MacGregor, S.S. Retsky, and T.P. Sullivan. "Cocaine Abuse During Pregnancy: Peripartum Prevalence and Perinatal Outcome." *American Journal of Obstetrics and Gynecology* 161 (1989): 633-38.

Neuspiel, D.R., and S.C. Hamel. "Cocaine and Infant Behavior." *Journal of Developmental Behavioral Pediatrics* 12 (1991): 55–64.

Northwest Indian Child Welfare Institute, a model curriculum for Indian child welfare practice.

Nurco, D.N., I.H. Cisin, and M.B. Balter. "Addict Careers. III. Trends across Time." *International Journal of the Addictions* 16 (1981): 1357–1372.

O'Malley, P., J.G. Bachman, and L.D. Johnston. "Period, Age, and Cohort Effects of Substance Use among Young Americans: A Decade of Change." *American Journal of Public Health* 78 (1988): 682–688.

Olds, D.L. "Home Visitation for Pregnant Women and Parents of Young Children." *American Journal of Diseases of Children* 146 (1992): 704–708.

Olds, D.L., and H. Kitzman. "Can Home Visitation Improve the Health of Women and Children at Environmental Risk?" *Pediatrics* 86 (1990): 108–116.

Parens, H. *Aggression in Our Children—Coping with It Constructively.* Northvale, NJ: Jason Aronson, Inc., 1987.

Portis, K. "Intake and Diagnosis of Drug-Dependent, Pregnant Women." Workshop presented at the NIDA National Conference on Drug Abuse Research and Practice, An Alliance for the 21st Century. Washington, DC, 1991.

"Pre-Placement Prevention Services: Emergency Response and Family Survey of Selected Characteristics for Cases Closed during April 1985." Sacramento, CA: State Department of Social Services, 1986.

"Pre-Placement Prevention Services: Emergency Response and Family Survey of Selected Characteristics for Cases Closed during January 1989." Sacramento, CA: State Department of Social Services, 1990.

Reuter, P., R. MacCoun, and P. Murphy. *Money from Crime: A Study of the Economics of Drug Dealing in Washington, DC.* Santa Monica, CA: RAND, 1990.

Ricketts, E.R., and I.V. Sawhill. "Defining and Measuring the Underclass." *Journal of Policy Analysis and Management* 7 (Winter 1988): 316–35.

Ricketts, E.R., and R. Mincy. "Growth of the Underclass: 1970–1980." *The Journal of Human Resources* 25, no. 1 (Winter 1990): 137–145.

Riordan, E.E., M. Mezritz, F. Slobetz, and H.D. Kleber. "Successful Detoxification from Methadone Maintenance: Follow-Up Study of 38 Patients." *Journal of the American Medical Association* 235 (1976): 2604–2607.

Roberts, D. "Child Welfare Services for Drug-Exposed and HIV-Affected Newborns and Their Families." In *Families Living with Drugs and HIV: Intervention and Treatment Strategies*, edited by R.P. Barth, J. Pietrzak, and M. Ramler. New York: Guilford Press, 1993.

Rogalski, C.J. "Factor Structure of the Addiction Severity Index in an Inpatient Detoxification Sample." *International Journal of the Addictions* 22 (1987): 981–992.

Rutter, Michael. "The City and the Child." *American Journal of Orthopsychiatry* 51 (1981): 610–25.

Sells, S.B., ed. *Effectiveness of Drug Abuse Treatment.* (Vols. 1 and 2). Cambridge, MA: Ballinger, 1974.

Shikles, J.L. *Preliminary Findings: A Survey of Methadone Maintenance Programs.* Washington, DC: Statements of the U.S. General Accounting Office before the House Select Committee on Narcotics Abuse and Control, House of Representatives, August, 1989.

Simpson, D.D., and S.B. Sells. "Effectiveness of Treatment for Drug Abuse: An Overview of the DARP Research Program." *Advances in Alcohol and Substance Abuse* 2 (1983): 7–29.

Simpson, D.D., L.J. Savage, and M.R. Lloyd. "Follow-Up Evaluation of Treatment of Drug Abuse during 1969 to 1972." *Archives of General Psychiatry* 36 (1979): 772–780.

Smart, R. "Reflections on the Epidemiology of Heroin and Narcotic Addictions from the Perspective of Treatment Data." In *The Epidemiology of Heroin and Other Narcotics*, edited by J.D. Rittenhouse, 177–182. NIDA Research Monograph 16, Washington, DC: Government Printing Office, 1977.

Smith, A. Delafield. *The Right to Life*. Chapel Hill, NC: University of North Carolina Press, 1955.

St. Claire, N. "The Child's Developmental Path: Working with the Family." In *Families Living with Drugs and HIV: Intervention and Treatment Strategies*, edited by R.P. Barth, J. Pietrzak, and M. Ramler. New York: Guilford Press, 1993.

Substance Abuse and Mental Health Services Administration, Office of Applied Studies. *National Household Survey on Drug Abuse: Main Findings, 1991*. Rockville, MD: SAMHSA, May 1993.

Substance Abuse and Mental Health Services Administration, Office of Applied Studies. *Preliminary Estimates from the 1992 National Household Survey on Drug Abuse: Selected Excerpts, Advance Report, no. 3*. Rockville, MD: CSAP National Clearinghouse for Alcohol and Drug Information, June 1993.

Sussman, M.B. "The Isolated Nuclear Family: Fact or Fiction." In *Sourcebook in Marriage and the Family*, edited by M.B. Sussman, 25–30. Boston: Houghton-Mifflin Company, 1974.

Tatara, Toshio. "Child Substitute Care Population Trends FY 82 through FY 91—A Summary." *VCIS Research Notes*, no. 6 (August 1992): 1–5.

Tatara, Toshio. *Characteristics of Children in Substitute and Adoptive Care: A Statistical Summary of the VCIS National Child Welfare Data Base*. Washington, DC: American Public Welfare Association, 1993.

Tatara, Toshio. *Child Substitute Care Flow Data for FY 90 and Child Substitute Care Population Trends since FY 86 (Revised Estimates)*. Washington, DC: American Public Welfare Association, 1991.

Tatara, Toshio. *Memorandum to Mr. Larry Guerrero and Dr. K.A. Jahannathan*. Washington, DC: American Public Welfare Association, October 16, 1989.

The Infant Health and Development Program. "Enhancing the Outcomes of Low-Birth-Weight, Premature Infants: A Multisite, Randomized Trial." *Journal of the American Medical Association* 22 (1990): 3035–3042.

Thiel, K. S., M. Weil, B. Ferleger, W. Russell, C. Jo, and A. Kwinn. *California's Adolescent Family Life Program: Evaluating the Impact of Case Management Services for Pregnant and Parenting Adolescents.* Los Angeles, CA: University of Southern California, School of Social Welfare, 1990.

Thompson, M. "Drug-Exposed Infants and Their Families: A Coordinated Services Approach." In *Families Living with Drugs and HIV: Intervention and Treatment Strategies*, edited by Richard P. Barth, Jeanne Pietrzak, and M. Ramler. New York: Guilford, 1993.

Thompson, M. "Healthy Infant Program: An Alternate Approach to Families of Drug-Exposed Infants." *Henry Ford Hospital Medical Journal* 38 (1990): 140-141.

Thornton, Jesse Lemuel. "An Investigation into the Nature of Kinship Foster Home." DSW dissertation, Yeshiva University, 1987.

Tillman, Robert. "The Size of the 'Criminal Population': The Prevalence and Incidence of Arrests." *Criminology* 25 (Fall 1987): 561–579.

Tyler, M. "State Survey on Placement Prevention and Family Reunification Programs." Oakdale, IA: The National Resource Center on Family Based Services, 1990.

U.S Bureau of the Census. "Poverty in the United States: 1988 and 1989." *Current Population Reports*, Series P-60, no. 171. Washington, DC: U.S. Government Printing Office, June 1991, 19.

U.S. Department of Health and Human Services. *Drug-Exposed Infants and Children: Service Needs and Policy Questions.* Paper prepared by L. Feig. Washington, DC: U.S. Government Printing Office, 1990.

U.S. Department of Health and Human Services. *Maternal Drug Abuse and Drug Exposed Children: Understanding the Problem.* Washington, DC: U.S. Government Printing Office, DHHS Publication No. (ADM) 92–1949, 1992.

U.S. Department of Health and Human Services. *National Household Survey on Drug Abuse, 1988 Population Estimates.* Washington, DC, Publication No. (ADM) 89–1636.

U.S. Department of Health and Human Services. Preliminary Results released by Donna Shalala, Secretary of the U.S. Department of Health and Human Services. Press release, January 31, 1994.

U.S. Department of Health, Education, and Welfare, Social Security Administration. *Legislative Guides for the Termination of Parental Rights and Responsibilities and the Adoption of Children.* Washington, DC: Children's Bureau (Publication no. 194.), 1961.

U.S. General Accounting Office. *Drug Exposed Infants: A Generation at Risk.* Washington, DC: U.S. Government Printing Office (GAO/HRD-90-128), June 1990.

U.S. House of Representative Committee on Ways and Means. *Overview of Entitlement Programs (1990 Green Book).* Washington, DC: U.S. Government Printing Office, 1990.

U.S. House of Representatives Select Committee on Children, Youth, and Families. *No Place to Call Home: Discarded Children in America.* Washington, DC: U.S. Government Printing Office, January 12, 1989.

U.S. House of Representatives Subcommittee on Human Resources of the Committee on Ways and Means. *The Enemy Within: Crack-Cocaine and America's Families.* Washington, DC: U.S. Government Printing Office, June 12, 1990.

Vaillant, G.E. "A 20-Year Follow-Up of New York Narcotic Addicts." *Archives of General Psychiatry* 29 (1973): 237–241.

"Voluntary Family Maintenance Program for Substance-Exposed Infants." San Mateo County, California, 1990.

Walker, C., P. Zangrillo, and J. Smith. *Parental Substance Abuse and African American Children in the Child Welfare System.* Washington, DC: National Black Child Development Institute, 1991.

Weisman, Irving. *Guardianship: A Way of Fulfilling Public Responsibility for Children.* Washington, DC: Children's Bureau (Publication no. 330), 1949.

Williams, Carol W. "Legal Guardianship: A Minimally Used Resource for California Dependent Children: 1848-1980." D.S.W. dissertation, University of Southern California, 1980.

Wineck, C. "Maturing out of Narcotic Addiction." *U.N. Bulletin on Narcotics* 14 (1962): 1–7.

Winnicott, D.W. *Babies and Their Mothers.* New York: Addison Wesley Publishing Co., Inc., 1970.

Wish, E. "U.S. Drug Policy in the 1990s: Insights from New Data on Arrestees." *International Journal on Addictions* 25, no. 3A (1990-91): 377–409.

Wulczyn, Fred H. "The Changing Face of Foster Care in New York State." New York State Department of Social Services Division of Family and Children Services, February 1990.

Zuckerman, B.S., H. Amaro, and W. Beardslee. "Mental Health of Adolescent Mothers: The Implications of Depression and Drug Use." *Developmental and Behavioral Pediatrics* 8 (1987): 111–116.

Zuckerman, B., and K. Bresnahan. "Developmental and Behavioral Consequences of Prenatal Drug and Alcohol Exposure." *Pediatric Clinics of North America* 38 (1991): 1387–1406.

Zuckerman, B. "Developmental Considerations for Drug- and AIDS-Affected Infants." In *Families Living with Drugs and HIV: Intervention and Treatment Strategies*, edited by R.P. Barth, J. Pietrzak, and M. Ramler. New York: Guilford Press, 1993.

Zuckerman, B. "Heavy Drug Users as Parents: Meeting the Challenge." Paper presented at "Protecting the Children of Heavy Drug Users" conference, Williamsburg, VA, July 18–12, 1991.

Zuravin, S.J. "The Ecology of Child Abuse and Neglect: Review of the Literature and Presentation of Data." *Violence and Victims* 4, no. 2 (1989): 101–120.

ABOUT THE AUTHORS

Robert Apsler is an assistant professor of psychology in the Department of Psychiatry at Harvard Medical School, and senior research associate at the Bigel Institute for Health Policy of the Heller School at Brandeis University. He is also president of Social Science Research and Evaluation, Inc. and partner at Social Science Research Enterprises. Dr. Apsler has served as principal investigator for many studies on alcohol and substance abuse and has published numerous articles on drug abuse.

Sheila Ards is an assistant professor at the Hubert Humphrey Institute of Public Affairs at the University of Minnesota. She serves on the steering committee for the Children, Youth, and Family Consortium at the University of Minnesota; chairs the Committee on the Status of Blacks in the Profession of the American Political Science Association; and is treasurer of the National Conference of Black Political Scientists. Her previous experience includes positions as an assistant professor at the University of Maryland School of Public Affairs and a research scholar at the Urban Institute.

Karen Baehler is a Ph.D. candidate in social welfare at the University of Maryland School of Public Affairs. She has served as a program associate for the Joyce Foundation, a program manager for the Roosevelt Center for American Policy Studies, a consultant for the Pew Charitable Trusts, and a research associate for the American Enterprise Institute. She has conducted research and written on such topics as child welfare, poverty, and economic development policy. She is the co-author of *Information, Competition and Place: Connecting Theory and Practice in U.S. Rural Development.*

Richard P. Barth is the Hutto Patterson Professor at the School of Social Welfare, University of California at Berkeley. He is the co-director of the Family Welfare Research Group and co-principal investigator of Berkeley's National Child Welfare Research Center. He is also principal investigator of the National Abandoned Infants Assistance Resource Center. Professor Barth has authored several books about child abuse, child welfare, and adoption and is an editor and author of *Families Living with Drugs and HIV.*

Marilyn B. Benoit, a child and adolescent psychiatrist, is the medical/executive director of the Devereux Children's Center of Washington, D.C., and is a national policy advocate for children and adolescents. Dr. Benoit has served on the American Bar Association's Center on Children and the Law Advisory Committee for the development of the first *Benchbook for Judges,* for use in aiding judges with disposition issues regarding children in family law cases. She has been a member of the Head Start Advisory Research Implementation Panel and has been appointed to the National Advisory Council of Physicians against Violence. Dr. Benoit is also a clinical associate professor in the Department of Psychiatry at the Georgetown University Medical Center.

Douglas J. Besharov is a resident scholar at the American Enterprise Institute for Public Policy Research and a visiting professor at the University of Maryland School of Public Affairs. Mr. Besharov was the first director of the U.S. National Center on Child Abuse and Neglect. He began his career as an assistant corporation counsel for the City of New York, where he supervised a staff of 37 lawyers assigned to juvenile delinquency, ungovernability, child protection, nonsupport, and spouse abuse cases in the New York Family Court. Mr. Besharov has taught family law and policy at the Georgetown University Law Center since 1985 and has written numerous books and articles on child abuse and neglect, welfare reform, and teen sexual behavior, among other issues. His most recent book is *Recognizing Child Abuse: A Guide for the Concerned.* Kristina W. Hanson is his assistant.

Edwin J. Delattre is a professor of education, dean of the School of Education, and professor of philosophy in the College of Liberal Arts at Boston University. He is an adjunct scholar at the American Enterprise Institute for Public Policy Research in Washington, D.C., and president emeritus of St. John's College in Annapolis, Maryland, and Santa Fe, New Mexico. Dr. Delattre was director of the National Humanities Faculty and professor of philosophy at the University of Toledo. He has published numerous articles on ethics in American life, illegal narcotics, organized crime, and urban gangs. He is the author of *Education and the Public Trust* and *Character and Cops: Ethics in Policing.*

Ramona L. Foley is the director of Family Preservation and Child Welfare Services in the South Carolina Department of Social Services. She also teaches in the graduate program of the College of Social Work at the University of South Carolina. Ms. Foley has more than 27 years of experience in public social services, and is president of the National Association of Foster Care Managers. She has also served as president of the National Association of Public Child Welfare Administrators. Ms. Foley has been a trainer and speaker throughout the United states and England on issues related to child welfare and social services.

Wade F. Horn is the director of the National Fatherhood Initiative and an adjunct fellow with the Hudson Institute. He is the former commissioner of the Administration for Children, Youth, and Families and chief of the Children's Bureau in the U.S. Department of Health and Human Services, and served as a presidential appointee to the National Commission on Children. Previously, Dr. Horn was the director of outpatient psychological services and vice chairman of the Department of Pediatric Psychology at the Children's Hospital National Medical Center in Washington, D.C.; an associate professor of psychiatry and behavioral sciences at the George Washington University School of Medicine; and an assistant professor in the Department of Psychology at Michigan State University.

Judy Howard is professor of pediatrics at UCLA. Since 1982, she has been chair of the UCLA Child Abuse Policy Committee and, for 10 years, was medical director of the UCLA Suspected Child Abuse and Neglect (SCAN) team. For the past 17 years, Dr. Howard has worked extensively with developmentally high-risk children and their families through provision of comprehensive early intervention services. In addition, she has been principal investigator on a variety of service, training, and research projects related to substance-abusing families. In connection with these grant projects, Dr. Howard has taken a leadership role in programs promoting comprehensive services for pregnant addicts, their offspring, and other family members within Los Angeles County and throughout California.

Ivory Johnson is deputy director of the Department of Social Services in San Diego County. She is responsible for the administration of the Children's Services Bureau, which provides child protection, adoption, and foster care services as well as other child welfare services. Ms. Johnson was director of the Division of Child Protective Services in the Delaware Department of Social Services for Children, Youth, and Families. She has over 20 years experience in public child welfare services, training, and social administration.

Beverly Jones is director of the Arkansas Department of Human Services, Division of Children and Families. She is the former assistant director of Child Welfare Services, Anne Arundel County Department of Social Services in Annapolis, Maryland. From 1987 to 1989, she was senior field consultant for child welfare with the Child Welfare League of America. Previously, she served as program manager for Child Protective Services with the Baltimore Social Services Administration and worked with the Baltimore City Department of Social Services as a social work assistant, intake supervisor, training specialist, and district supervisor for child abuse.

Ruth Massinga is the chief executive of the Casey Family Program, a long-term foster care agency providing family support in 13 states to more than 1,000 children. From 1983 to 1989, she was secretary of the Maryland Department of Human Resources. Ms. Massinga began her career as a caseworker in New York City at Harlem Hospital, Community Services Society, and the New York City Department of Public Welfare. She has been acting director of Blundon Group Homes in Baton Rouge, Louisiana; Director of Family Development Center of the San Francisco Services Agency; and an instructor in social work at Southern University and Louisiana State University.

Ronald B. Mincy is a program officer at The Ford Foundation. He was the principal investigator for the Urban Institute's projects that tested alternative explanations for the underclass and developed a demonstration project to increase academic achievement and reduce premature fatherhood among adolescent males in underclass areas. Previously, Dr. Mincy worked as an analyst for the Department of Labor studying minimum wage noncompliance and as a consultant with the Minimum Wage Study Commission. He has taught economics at Purdue University, Bentley College, and the University of Delaware.

Peter Reuter is a professor of social policy at the University of Maryland's School of Public Affairs. He was previously a senior economist in the Washington office of the RAND Corporation, where he was also co-director of the Drug Policy Research Center. Before joining RAND, he was a guest scholar at the Brookings Institution. Since 1983, he has worked primarily on drug policy issues and has published a number of papers and studies on drug enforcement. He has authored numerous publications on drug enforcement. Patricia Ebener is a behavioral scientist at the RAND Corporation. Dan McCaffrey is an associate statistician in the social policy department at the RAND Corporation.

Barbara J. Sabol is the former administrator/commissioner of the New York City Human Resources Administration. She was a member of Mayor Dinkins' cabinet and served *ex officio* as a member of the Board of Directors of the New York City Health and Hospitals Corporation. Previously, Ms. Sabol served as executive deputy commissioner of the New York State Department of Social Services. From 1983 to 1987, she served in Kansas Governor John Carlin's Cabinet as Secretary of the Department of Health and Environment. During the Carter Administration, she administered the Title XX program in the U.S. Department of Health and Human Services and directed the 10 regional offices of the Office of Human Development Services.

Richard Schottenfeld is an associate professor of psychiatry at the Yale University School of Medicine. He is director of the Substance Abuse Treatment Unit at the Connecticut Mental Health Center and chief executive officer of the APT Foundation in New Haven, Connecticut. Dr. Schottenfeld is principal investigator on a research demonstration project funded by the National Institute on Drug Abuse evaluating the effectiveness of different service delivery models for drug-abusing women and on a NCCAN-funded grant providing interventions for high-risk children of drug-dependent parents. Richard

Viscarello is associate chairman of Obstetrics and Gynecology at Stamford Hospital in Connecticut. Judy Grossman is a former project director at the Mothers' Project at Yale University. Lorraine V. Klerman is professor and chairperson at the Department of Maternal and Child Health, School of Public Health, University of Alabama at Birmingham. Steven F. Nagler is an assistant clinical professor at the Child Study Center at Yale University. Jean A. Adnopoz is an associate clinical professor at the Child Study Center at Yale University.

Michael Wald, Jackson Eli Reynolds professor of law at Stanford University, is currently on leave serving as deputy general counsel at the U.S. Department of Health and Human Services. At Stanford, he taught courses on public policy toward children and conducted research focused on the treatment of children in the legal system. Professor Wald has served as a juvenile court judge in California and has been actively involved in developing legislation regarding children in many states. He has been a member of the Board of Directors of the National Committee for the Prevention of Child Abuse, and a member of the National Academy of Science's Committee on Child Development Research and Public Policy.

Clarice Dibble Walker is the commissioner of the D.C. Commission on Social Services and associate professor at the Howard University School of Social Work, where she was previously chairperson of direct services. She began her career as a psychiatric social worker at Montreal General Hospital and was a psychiatric social worker in the Department of Psychiatry at the University of Chicago Hospital; director of health, psychological, and social services for the United Planning Organization in Washington, D.C; and director of social services (and later executive director) of Capital Head Start in Washington, D.C. Ms. Walker has contributed to numerous publications on minority children and the child welfare system. She is currently president of the board of directors of the National Black Child Development Institute.

Carol Williams is an associate commissioner of the Children's Bureau, Administration for Children, Youth, and Families. She was previously a senior research analyst at the Center for the Study of Social Policy in Washington, D.C. From 1984 to 1990, Ms. Williams was an assistant professor at the School of Social Work and director of the National Child Welfare Leadership Center at the University of North Carolina at Chapel Hill. She began her career as a probation officer and child welfare worker in Los Angeles County and was assistant professor at the School of Social Welfare at the University of California, Los Angeles. She has contributed to numerous publications on child welfare issues.

Barry Zuckerman is professor and chairman of the Department of Pediatrics at the Boston University School of Medicine and the Boston City Hospital. His research involves investigations of the effects and interrelationship of maternal depression, drug and alcohol use, and teenage pregnancy and parenting and their impact on children's growth, development, and behavior. He has developed a number of programs that have served as national models, including the Child Development Project, which places early childhood educators in hospitals and community health settings in order to provide parent support and early identification and intervention for young children and their parents. He has also developed the Women and Infants Program, which places addiction counselors in pediatric primary care clinics.